# ENGLISH WORKSHOP

THIRD COURSE

**HOLT, RINEHART** AND **WINSTON**

*Harcourt Brace & Company*

**Austin** • New York • Orlando • Chicago • Atlanta
San Francisco • Boston • Dallas • Toronto • London

# TABLE OF CONTENTS

# PREWRITING: FINDING IDEAS FOR WRITING

Writing actually begins when you think up ideas, not when you pick up your pencil. Your experiences, observations, feelings, and opinions are rich sources of topics and ideas. The following prewriting techniques can help you find and explore ideas.

## WRITER'S JOURNAL

Use a *writer's journal* to record experiences, observations, feelings, opinions, ideas, and questions. Your journal might be a notebook, a blank book, or a special folder. Write in it daily, and date your entries.

- Use your imagination; write down dreams, daydreams, parts of songs, and stories.
- Collect poems, articles, quotations, and cartoons. When you include something, tell why you like it or what it reminds you of.
- Don't worry about spelling, grammar, or neatness. Just keep track of your ideas.

## FREEWRITING

When you *freewrite*, you write whatever comes to mind. You don't worry about what you are saying or how you are saying it. Freewriting can help you to relax about writing. It can also give you some ideas for later writing.

- Use a timer, and write for three to five minutes.
- Begin with a word or topic that is important to you. Write whatever the word or topic makes you think of. Don't worry about grammar, spelling, or punctuation. Just write!
- If you get stuck, copy the same word or phrase until you think of something else.

## EXERCISE 1   Using Prewriting Techniques

Plan a paragraph about something that you have learned through experience. It might be a fact, a skill, or a new way of thinking. To find and develop your ideas, write a page for your writer's journal. Combine two prewriting techniques by freewriting in your journal for three to five minutes.

# PREWRITING: BRAINSTORMING AND CLUSTERING

## BRAINSTORMING

When you *brainstorm*, you free your mind to come up with ideas in response to a word. You can brainstorm alone, with a partner, or in a group.

- Write a word or subject on a sheet of paper. Then list every idea about the word or subject that comes into your mind. If you are brainstorming with a partner or group, one person should record all the ideas.
- Do not stop to judge the ideas. You can do that later.
- Keep going until you have no more ideas.

## CLUSTERING

*Clustering* is also called webbing or making connections. When you cluster, you use a series of circles and connecting lines. This process helps you break a large subject into its smaller parts.

- Write your subject in the center of a sheet of paper. Circle it.
- Around the subject, write all the related ideas that occur to you. Circle the ideas, and draw lines to connect them to the original subject.
- Let your mind wander. Add new ideas to the original subject and to its related ideas. Keep writing, circling, and connecting until your paper is filled.

## EXERCISE 2  Brainstorming and Clustering

With a partner, choose one of the subjects below. Work together to brainstorm a list of related ideas or subjects. Then, working alone, choose one of the ideas, and use it as the subject of a cluster. When your cluster diagram is finished, meet with your partner to compare and contrast your clusters.

| | | |
|---|---|---|
| dangerous jobs | sports heroes | comedy |
| government | hobbies | modern life |

## PREWRITING: ASKING QUESTIONS

### ASKING THE *5W-HOW?* QUESTIONS

One way to collect information about a subject is by asking the *5W-How? questions: Who? What? Where? When? Why?* and *How?* Not every question applies to every subject. Sometimes you won't need all of the questions. You may also use some of the questions more than once. Here is an example of the way you might use the questions to gather information about the woman known as Typhoid Mary.

- *Who?*     Who was Typhoid Mary?
- *What?*     What did she do to spread typhoid?
- *Where?*     Where did she live and work?
- *When?*     When did this happen?
- *Why?*     Why did she spread the disease? Why wasn't she cured?
- *How?*     How was she finally stopped from spreading typhoid?

### ASKING "WHAT IF?" QUESTIONS

Asking **"What if?" questions** can help you generate a variety of ideas for creative writing. You explore what might follow if something occurred.

- *What if some historical moment had been different?* (What if President Kennedy had not been assassinated? What if the wheel hadn't been invented?)
- *What if something amazing happened to a common person?* (What if a street musician won a million-dollar lottery? What if a teenager suddenly became middle-aged?)
- *What if a character had special powers or abilities?* (What if I woke up with the ability to read people's minds? What if a young girl could instantly transport herself to other places?)*

### EXERCISE 3   Using the *5W-How?* Questions

You are writing a report about one of the subjects below. On your own paper, make a list of the *5W-How?* questions that you can use to explore the subject.

| | | |
|---|---|---|
| the Carnegie Hero Fund | trampolines | mummies |
| the Vietnam Veterans Memorial | Seattle | Hawaii |

## EXERCISE 4    Using "What if?" Questions

Working with a partner, choose two of the following items. Then work together to write five "What if?" questions for each of the two items. Write your questions on the lines below.

1. a rocket ship
2. an inflatable boat
3. a small gold charm
4. tap water

5. rain
6. elections
7. the latest fashions
8. telephones

*Item 1* _____

_____

_____

_____

_____

_____

_____

*Item 2* _____

_____

_____

_____

_____

_____

_____

# PREWRITING: ARRANGING IDEAS

After you have gathered ideas, you need to spend some time arranging, or ordering, them. There are four common ways to order ideas.

| ARRANGING IDEAS | | |
|---|---|---|
| Type of Order | Definition | Examples |
| Chronological | Narration: order that presents events as they happen in time | Story, narrative poem, explanation of a process, drama, history, biography |
| Spatial | Description: order that describes objects according to location | Descriptions (near to far, outside to inside, left to right, top to bottom) |
| Importance | Evaluation: order that gives details from least to most important or the reverse | Persuasion, description, explanations, evaluation |
| Logical | Classification: order that relates items and groups | Definitions, classifications |

## EXERCISE 5   Arranging Ideas

On your own paper, identify the method of organization that would be best for each of the following writing situations. Be prepared to explain your choice of order.

1. You are writing a report on Guatemala and are describing the Mayan city of Tikal.
2. You want to give three reasons why your school should get a new gymnasium.
3. You want to discuss the differences between high school basketball and professional basketball.
4. You want to explain how to make a pizza.

# WRITING A FIRST DRAFT

At some point, you have to stop gathering information and start writing a first draft. People take different approaches to drafting. Some write quickly, while others work more slowly and carefully. Some people work from rough notes, while others use a detailed outline. As you write your first draft, you might try these suggestions.

- Use your prewriting plans as a guide.
- Write freely, and focus on expressing your ideas clearly.
- You may discover new ideas as you write. Include these new ideas in your draft.
- Don't worry about catching or correcting errors in grammar, usage, or mechanics while you are drafting. You will be able to focus on these aspects later.

Here is a first draft of a paragraph about the silk industry. Notice how the writer has inserted questions and notes. They will remind the writer to return to prewriting to gather more information before the final draft. Also, notice that the writing still needs more polishing. The polishing comes later.

Silk is a natural fiber that is spun by the silkworm [Latin name?] as it spins it ~~coccoon~~ cocoon. Each silkworm cocoon is actually one single fiber. [how long?] To harvest the silk, the cocoons are first washed and heated. Then they are unwound and several [how many].fibers are spun together to make a single thread. Then the thread is dyed. This process was discovered by the Chinese about 2600 B.C. ~~and~~ For years, they kept the secret inside China. ~~In fact a law prevented anyone from telling~~

## EXERCISE 6   Writing a First Draft

Using what you've learned about arranging ideas in chronological order, draft a narrative about how to do some simple process. For example, you might explain how to cover and decorate a textbook, or how to make your locker look truly unique. Just be sure it's a process you know how to do. Write your first draft on your own paper. Include specific details that will help readers identify the steps you followed and the order in which you performed them. When you have finished, share your first draft with other students.

# EVALUATING AND REVISING

## EVALUATING

Evaluating is the first step in improving a draft. To *evaluate* is to look for the strengths and weaknesses of your paper. A good way to identify strengths and weaknesses is to use a checklist or set of standards. Below are four examples of standards for good writing.

- The writing is interesting and holds a reader's attention.
- The main ideas are clear and supported with details.
- There are no unrelated ideas, and any unfamiliar terms are explained.
- The details are arranged in a sensible order, and the connections among them are clear.

Professional writers evaluate their own work, but they also ask for other opinions. They get valuable feedback from their peers, or equals. You can ask your peers, or classmates, to help you evaluate your work. Here are some tips that can help you evaluate your own writing or that of a peer.

| Self-Evaluation | Peer Evaluation |
|---|---|
| 1. Set your draft aside for a while to give yourself a fresh eye the next time you read it. | 1. Provide encouragement by telling your classmate what parts are particularly good. |
| 2. Read your draft several times: once for content, once for organization, and once for style. | 2. Make specific suggestions for improvement. |
| 3. Read your draft aloud, and listen to yourself. You may notice things that you missed during a silent reading. | 3. Focus on content and organization. Errors in mechanics, including spelling, can be caught during proofreading. |
| | 4. Be sensitive to the writer's feelings. Ask helpful questions. |

## EXERCISE 7   Practicing Peer Evaluation

Practice your peer-evaluation skills by evaluating the paragraph below with a partner. Use the standards for good writing listed at the top of the previous page. Write your evaluation on your own paper, beginning with a comment about what's good about the paragraph. Then write suggestions that would help a writer improve the paragraph.

1   One of the most famous lighthouse keepers of all times was a

2   young woman, Ida Lewis. The Lewis family moved to Lime Rock

3   lighthouse in 1857. Mr. Lewis was supposed to keep the lamps lit all

4   night. Soon after they arrived, he had a stroke, and his daughter Ida

5   took over the work. She was the oldest of four children. Three

6   soldiers were in a boat and Ida rescued one of them. Then she saved

7   three men and a sheep. Her sister was sick, and Ida became sick. In

8   1869, during a blizzard, she saved two men from drowning. A

9   newspaper learned about this rescue and the earlier ones. Ida Lewis

10   became famous, but she remained a lighthouse keeper. In fact, the

11   governor made her job official.

**For Better or For Worse®**                               **by Lynn Johnston**

For Better or For Worse copyright 1986 Lynn Johnston Prod. Reprinted with permission of Universal Press Syndicate. All rights reserved.

## REVISING

When you *revise,* you make changes in your draft to correct weaknesses found when evaluating. Use the following techniques to make changes when you revise.

| REVISION TECHNIQUES | |
|---|---|
| **Technique** | **Example** |
| 1. **Add.** Add new information: words, phrases, sentences, even paragraphs. | Navajo weavers use dyes made <br> *berries, roots,* and *flowers taken from* <br> of plants. |
| 2. **Cut.** Take out unrelated or repeated ideas, words, or details. | Navajo rugs are quite beautiful⊙ <br> ~~and nice to look at.~~ |
| 3. **Replace.** Replace weak or awkward words with more precise, vivid language. | Chokecherries are used to make <br> *soft red* <br> preserves with a ~~nice~~ color. |
| 4. **Reorder.** Move information for variety and clarity. | Cream, brown, and black are some of the natural colors of the wool used in Navajo rugs ~~and~~ ~~also~~ gray. |

## EXERCISE 8    Evaluating and Revising a Piece of Writing

Read the narrative you wrote for Exercise 6. Then use the standards on page 7 to evaluate your first draft. Next, revise your draft, using the techniques described above. Make your changes by hand, directly on your paper. Finally, rewrite the narrative on your own paper, and incorporate the revisions.

# PROOFREADING AND PUBLISHING

## PROOFREADING

When you *proofread,* you read carefully for mistakes in grammar, spelling, capitalization, and punctuation. It's easier to spot such mistakes if you put your writing away for a while before looking at it. Peer proofreading is also useful. Exchange papers with a partner, and look for errors in each other's papers. Use the following guidelines when you proofread.

| Guidelines for Proofreading |
|---|
| • Is every sentence a complete sentence instead of a fragment or a run-on? |
| • Does every sentence begin with a capital letter? Are all proper nouns capitalized? |
| • Does every sentence end with an appropriate punctuation mark? Are other punctuation marks used correctly? |
| • Do the verbs agree in number with their subjects? |
| • Are the verb forms and tenses used correctly? |
| • Are the subject and object forms of personal pronouns used correctly? |
| • Does every pronoun agree with its antecedent in gender and in number? Are the pronoun references clear? |
| • Are all the words spelled correctly? |

| Symbols for Revising and Proofreading | | |
|---|---|---|
| ≡ | South america | Capitalize a letter. |
| ℓ | to to school | Take out a word, letter, or punctuation mark. |
| ∽ | twon *of* | Change the order of words or letters. |
| ∧ | the city Dallas | Insert a word, letter, or punctuation mark. |
| # | saltmarsh | Insert a space. |

## EXERCISE 9   Proofreading a Paragraph

Proofread the paragraph below. Use proofreading symbols to mark the ten errors in the paragraph.

[1] The japanese architect Tange Kenzo hasan international

reputation. [2] Kenzo's creations in his his own coutry include the

town hall in Kawaga the Atami Gardens Hotel, and a cathedral in

Tokyo. [3] Later, he branched out overseas and he developed a

reputation in Europe and the Middle east. [4] However, Kenzo did

not not stop working in his own country. [5] he also desinged

important civic buildings for both Tokyo and Yokohama..

## PUBLISHING

The final step of writing is *publishing* your work, or sharing it with readers. There are a number of ways you can publish.

- Invite friends and classmates to read what you have written.
- Submit your work to a school or community newspaper. Your opinion on a local issue could become a letter to the editor.
- Enter a writing contest. Your teacher or counselor can probably give you information about such contests. Many contests award prizes.
- Find out which magazines publish student stories, poems, essays, and articles. Most magazines have special guidelines for the submission of work. A copy of the magazine or a guide to writers' markets will explain these guidelines. Look in the reference section of your library.
- Keep a portfolio of your best work. Provide a special folder, notebook, or envelope for the final copies.

---

| **Guidelines for Manuscript Form** |
|---|

1. Use only one side of a sheet of paper.
2. Write in blue or black ink, type your paper, or use a word processor. If you type, double-space the lines.
3. Leave one-inch margins at the top, sides, and bottom of each page.
4. Indent the first line of each paragraph.
5. Follow your teacher's instructions for placing your name, the date, and the title of the paper.
6. Keep your pages neat and clean. Use correction fluid if needed, but be sure that it is barely noticeable to the reader.

## EXERCISE 10    Finding Ideas for Publishing

Read the following descriptions of types of writing. On the lines after each description, list one or two publishing ideas for the piece.

1. a science fiction story _____

   _____

2. an essay on the effects of television advertising aimed at young

   children _____

   _____

3. a review of a free open-air concert held in your city last weekend _____

   _____

4. an article about how to keep a photographic journal _____

   _____

## EXERCISE 11    Preparing a Final Copy

Proofread and correct the draft that you revised for Exercise 8 on page 9. Then prepare a clean, final copy of the paper, using the manuscript guidelines above. Meet with a group of classmates, and take turns reading your work aloud. Finally, discuss ways that each of you might publish your writing.

# MAIN IDEAS AND TOPIC SENTENCES

Most paragraphs have one *main idea*. This main idea, which tells what the paragraph is about, is usually expressed in a single sentence called the *topic sentence*. A topic sentence can help you keep your focus as you write or read a paragraph. A topic sentence can also suggest how you should order details in a paragraph.

A topic sentence can appear anywhere in a paragraph, but it often appears as the first or second sentence. In the following paragraph, the topic sentence comes at the beginning. It tells the reader what to expect in the rest of the paragraph.

> Grains of pollen are very tiny and come in a variety of shapes. One grain of pollen can be as minuscule as 1/5000 inch or as big as 1/125 inch, which is still extremely small. Some grains of pollen are shaped like footballs. Others are round. Pine pollen appears to have a tiny ear on each side of the grain.

Not all paragraphs have topic sentences, however. For example, a paragraph that relates a sequence of events or actions may not have a topic sentence or even a single main idea. The following paragraph has no topic sentence, but it does relate a sequence of events.

> The girl trudged across the rocky terrain. The wind sneaked through the edges of her fur-lined hood and mittens. By the time she found a campsite, it was nearly dark. She gathered firewood and set up a grill. While the fish she had just caught was cooking, she built a lean-to. After hiking all day, she was almost too tired to worry about the shelter, but it looked as if the storm would arrive before morning.

## EXERCISE 1   Identifying Main Ideas and Topic Sentences

On your own paper, write the main idea of each paragraph in your own words. If the paragraph has a topic sentence, underline it.

1. Seagaia is Japan's attempt to recreate a tropical paradise. Seagaia is an indoor beach that can accommodate as many as ten thousand people. In this controlled environment, rain never spoils the family vacation. The roof can be closed when it's raining and opened when the sun is shining. The ocean that washes the 280-foot-long shoreline is perfectly clean, salt-free, and temperature-controlled. A computer ensures that surfers get perfect waves to

ride several times a day. But this perfect beach provides more than water. Artificial breezes ruffle the leaves of plastic palm trees. And a mechanically produced chorus of birds serenades the contented Japanese beachgoers.

2. Before he was appointed to the U.S. Supreme Court, Thurgood Marshall worked effectively as the chief attorney for the National Association for the Advancement of Colored People (NAACP). He travelled throughout the country, fighting within the legal system. And he overcame many social and legal obstacles to improve social opportunities for African Americans. His main accomplishment was in the area of school desegregation, where he was the lead attorney in the *Brown vs. Board of Education of Topeka* case, in which the U.S. Supreme Court finally prohibited racially segregated schools.

3. Even though drive-in theaters may not be as popular today as they were in the 1950s, they are still around. At the height of their popularity, more than 4,000 drive-in theaters dotted the American landscape. However, attendance at drive-ins dropped drastically during the 1970s and 1980s. This change probably resulted from the growing popularity of television and the introduction of home videos. Many drive-in owners were forced to close their theaters. By 1993, only 870 theaters remained in operation. Most of these theaters are able to make a profit, however, by opening on Friday and Saturday evenings only and by showing wholesome movies that appeal to parents who want an inexpensive evening out with their children.

4. Carlos looked up and saw the beach ahead. Without much effort, he leaped out of the water. Two seconds later, he crossed the line. He heard the spectators cheering as he squirmed into his bike shorts and T-shirt and fastened his helmet. Carlos completed the ride around the lake in record-breaking time. After quickly changing clothes, Carlos stretched his legs to prepare for the long run ahead. He had a three-minute lead over his nearest competitor when he dashed to the road to begin the final leg of the triathlon.

# UNITY

A paragraph has *unity* when all the sentences work together to express or support one main idea. Sentences can work as a unit in one of three ways.

**(1) All Sentences Relate to the Main Idea Stated in the Topic Sentence.** In the following paragraph, the topic sentence tells the main idea. Each of the supporting sentences provides details related to that idea.

> Idioms are colorful expressions that add interest and, occasionally, a touch of humor to our everyday language. *Chewing the fat, biting someone's head off,* and *raining cats and dogs* are examples of idioms that create lively and somewhat humorous mental images. Such expressions are more interesting than simple, direct statements. *Taking the plunge,* for example, seems much more daring and adventurous than *trying to do something.*

**(2) All Sentences Relate to an Implied Main Idea.** The following paragraph doesn't have a topic sentence. Each sentence, however, helps support an implied main idea: Producing electrical power causes problems.

> Hydroelectric plants do not pollute the air or water, but the dams destroy wildlife habitats. Nuclear energy plants do not produce smog, but there is no proven safe way to store nuclear waste. Burning wood or coal produces smoke and depletes natural resources. It seems that if we are to have electrical power, we must make some hard decisions.

**(3) All Sentences Relate to a Sequence of Events.** The following paragraph does not have a clearly stated main idea. But each detail is part of a sequence that begins when the character faces an emergency situation.

> Thick smoke seeped under the door of the room. Neka began to cough. Realizing what was happening, she went to the door. It felt warm to her touch. Then she went over to the window and looked down twenty stories. Fire apparatus and emergency vehicles filled the street below. Neka tried to recall what she had read about surviving a fire in a high-rise building. After a few moments, she went into the bathroom. She soaked a towel in water and stuffed it under the door. Then she soaked a face cloth and held it to her mouth and nose.

## EXERCISE 2    Identifying Sentences That Destroy Unity

In each paragraph below, find the sentence that doesn't support the main idea of the paragraph. Draw a line through that sentence.

1. Paintings that appear on the walls of buildings are called murals. Many artists, however, prefer to paint on canvas. Murals often tell a story. The subjects of these stories vary according to the inspiration and intention of the artist. Murals are often in clear view of all passersby and can be appreciated by a vast audience. Because these paintings reach so many people, some Hispanic and African American artists, among others, have used this art form to protest social conditions.

2. Lugging her two heavy suitcases, Dee got off the train. She stood for a moment on the platform and looked around. The escalator that would take her to the main concourse was straight ahead. The train station had recently been renovated. At the top of the escalator, Dee spotted Uncle Carter. She waved. He waved back and moved toward her, taking the bags from her hands. After giving her a quick hug and a peck on the cheek, he said, "Follow me, Dee. We're going home."

3. A traffic light should be installed at the intersection of Central Street and Liberty Square Road. Although the $150,000 cost will mean an increase in property taxes, the light is necessary for three reasons. The town spends more money for things that are less vital. First, the light will keep traffic flowing smoothly at that busy intersection. Second, a light will allow pedestrians to cross safely. The third and most important reason for installing the light is that it will help prevent accidents.

4. Lamont knelt in the on-deck circle, waiting, worrying, hoping that Rodríguez would not strike out. "Ball four!" the umpire called. Rodríguez walked to first base. Lamont stood up slowly and took a couple of practice swings. "I think I'm going to be sick," he thought as he walked to the batter's box. "Relax. Stay cool," he muttered to himself softly. "So what if you don't get a hit? Lots of players don't get a hit their first time at bat." But Lamont couldn't relax. He was anything but cool. Sweat ran down his face and neck. Everyone was watching—his parents, his three brothers, his grandfather, thirty-one thousand spectators. The stadium held thirty-five thousand people. "Please let me get a hit," he whispered softly.

# COHERENCE

A paragraph in which all the ideas are sensibly arranged and clearly connected has *coherence*. You can create coherent paragraphs if you pay attention to two things: (1) the order in which you arrange your ideas, and (2) the connections you make between ideas.

## ORDER OF IDEAS

Arrange, or order, your ideas in the paragraph in a way that makes sense to the reader. Often, the subject you're writing about will suggest the most sensible order of ideas.

**Chronological Order.** When you write about a series of actions or events, it makes sense to arrange them according to the order in which they happened.

**Spatial Order.** Writers sometimes order details according to how they are spaced—nearest to farthest, left to right, or any other reasonable arrangement.

**Order of Importance.** Sometimes one detail or piece of information is more important than another. Then the writer may arrange ideas by order of importance, perhaps starting or ending with the most important information.

**Logical Order.** It may make sense to group or arrange ideas together to show how they are related. For example, a writer might use logical order in a paper about the differences between football and soccer.

## EXERCISE 3    Choosing an Order of Ideas

On your own paper, identify which order of ideas would make the most sense for each topic below: *chronological order, spatial order, order of importance,* or *logical order*. For some topics, more than one order might work.

1. kinds of healthful snack foods
2. making a barometer with a glass jar
3. the view from your bedroom window
4. deciding who to vote for in school elections
5. three characteristics of a great action video game

## CONNECTIONS BETWEEN IDEAS

Besides ordering ideas in a paragraph in a sensible way, you need to show how the ideas are connected. You can show connections by (1) making *direct references* to something else in the paragraph or (2) using words that make a *transition*, or bridge, from one idea to another.

**Direct References.** Direct references link ideas by (1) referring to a noun or pronoun used earlier, (2) repeating a word, or (3) using a word or phrase that means the same thing as one used earlier.

**Transitional Words and Phrases.** Transitional words and phrases connect ideas and show *how* the ideas are connected. They include conjunctions and prepositions that show chronological or spatial order.

| | |
|---|---|
| **Comparing Ideas** | also, and, another, moreover, similarly, too |
| **Contrasting Ideas** | although, but, however, in spite of, instead, nevertheless, on the other hand, still, yet |
| **Showing Cause and Effect** | as a result, because, consequently, for, since, so, so that, therefore |
| **Showing Time** | after, at last, at once, before, eventually, finally, first, meanwhile, next, then, thereafter, when |
| **Showing Place** | above, along, around, before, behind, down, here, in, inside, into, next to, over, there, under, up |
| **Showing Importance** | first, last, mainly, more important, then, to begin with |

## EXERCISE 4   Identifying Direct References and Transitions

On your own paper, make two lists of the connections in the paragraph below: one list of direct references and one list of transitions.

The otter glided effortlessly down the icy river, looking for food. All at once, he dove into the water. When the otter came up again, he held a squirming sunfish in his mouth. The otter flung the fish on a patch of ice and quickly hoisted himself up next to the flopping creature. With his nose, he began playing with the fish. As he pushed it slowly along the ice, it slid and skidded over the slippery surface. Eventually, the otter tired of the game and ate his unlucky prey.

# USING DESCRIPTION

One strategy writers use to develop a paragraph is description. You use *description* to tell what something is like or what it looks like. You look at the individual features of whatever you are describing. In a description, you'll use sensory details to support your main idea. *Sensory details* are pieces of information that a writer observes through any of the five senses—sight, hearing, touch, taste, and smell. And you'll often use spatial order to organize those details. Notice how the following paragraph uses sensory details and spatial order to describe an old library building.

It has been thirty-five years since my first visit to the West End Library, but I remember it as if it happened yesterday. When I close my eyes, I am once again walking up those wide, concrete steps, holding tightly to the wrought-iron handrails. French lilacs grew tall and bushy on one side of the stairway, perfuming the air in early spring. A willow tree grew on the other side. At the top of the stairs was a flagstone landing. Light gray marble benches curved around either side of the landing. They flanked the huge oak double doors that led to the inside of the building. Those benches stayed cool all the time, making me shiver whenever I sat on them, even on hot summer days. The entrance doors opened out, and I had to step up over a high marble threshold to get inside. Once inside, the first thing I noticed was the darkness, and the second thing was the librarian's desk. The huge desk was located about twenty feet from the front door in the center of the room. Piles of books always sat on top of the desk, beside it, in front of it, and behind it. Even now, I can hear Mrs. Morrison whispering, "Watch where you step, Joanie. These books cost money, you know!"

## EXERCISE 5  Using Description as a Strategy

Choose one of the subjects below. On your own paper, list the features that will help describe the subject you have chosen. Try to focus on sensory details. After you run out of ideas, arrange the details in spatial order.

1. the strangest place you've ever seen
2. your classroom first thing in the morning, before the teacher arrives
3. a crowd of people watching a parade or other public event
4. a well-known actor during a performance
5. your favorite shoes

# USING EVALUATION

When you use *evaluation*, you attempt to determine the value of a subject. You make a judgment about it. For example, you are evaluating when you say that all high school students should do volunteer work in the community.

Once you tell your readers your evaluation, or statement of opinion, you also need to give them some reasons to support it. One way to organize your reasons is by order of importance. You might begin with your most important reason. Or you might begin with your least important reason and conclude with your most important.

| | |
|---|---|
| EVALUATION | There are many good reasons why the entertainment committee should select the Back Roads to play at |
| REASON | our class fund-raiser dance. First, the Back Roads is the most popular local band around. A large crowd means we will sell a lot of tickets and make a lot of |
| REASON | money. In addition, the band is fun to listen to. They play original music and the most popular dance music. |
| REASON | Finally, the Back Roads will play for free. All the band members are Crawford High School graduates and are willing to donate their time. |

## EXERCISE 6   Using Evaluation as a Strategy

Choose two of the three subjects below, and evaluate them. On your own paper, write at least one sentence stating your evaluation of, or opinion about, each subject. Then list two or three reasons to support each judgment.

EX   1. Music Videos
Evaluation: Music videos should be phased out.
Reasons: (1) Viewers don't have to use their own imagination while listening to the words and music of a song. (2) Music videos often have nothing to do with the songs.

1. a book you've recently read (Would you recommend it to someone else? Why or why not?)
2. after-school jobs (Should the number of hours that high school students work be limited?)
3. sports safety equipment, such as bicycle helmets (Should individuals have the right to decide whether or not to wear protective gear, or should wearing protective gear be the law?)

# USING NARRATION

What happened when you moved to a new town? How did you meet your best friend? What caused you to quit the baseball team? When you answer these questions, you use *narration*.

Narration looks at changes over a period of time. Since narration looks at events and actions in time, you will usually use chronological order to arrange ideas and information. You can use narration to tell a story or relate an incident (what happened at last night's baseball game), to explain a process (how to build a campfire), or to explain causes and effects (the effects of water pollution).

**Telling a Story.** One way to develop a narrative paragraph is to tell a story—to tell what happened. The story may be true, or it may be imaginary (fiction). In the following paragraph, the writer tells a story to explain how the car got dented.

> Kelsey had never driven in the snow before and did not realize how slippery the roads could become. Everyone on the highway was driving quite slowly, but Kelsey felt she could have walked faster than the big yellow snowplow in front of her. As soon as she pulled left to pass, in the rear view mirror she saw a giant truck coming up fast. It couldn't seem to slow down, and it bumped her car. Kelsey tried to stay on the slippery road, but the car spun around two times and then slid into the median strip. Fortunately, there were no trees or overpasses in her path, and she was not hurt.

**Explaining a Process.** Another way to develop a narrative paragraph is to explain a process—to tell how something works or how to do something. In explaining a process, the writer uses narration to look at a subject as it changes over time. In the following paragraph, the writer explains how to prepare falafel.

> Combine chickpeas, eggs, bread crumbs, herbs, spices, and oil in a large bowl. Use a wooden spoon or your hands to mix the ingredients until the eggs have been totally incorporated and the mixture sticks together. Then moisten your hands with cold water. Break off a small piece of the mixture—about two tablespoons—and hold it in the palm of one hand. Place the other hand over the mixture, and roll it until it forms a patty. Then you fry the patties.

21

**Explaining Cause and Effect.**   To explain what caused something or what the effects of something are, you have to look at the way things have changed over the course of time. The following paragraph looks at the effects of cutting and peeling onions.

CAUSE
EFFECT

EFFECT

EFFECT

    A woman sliced an onion in half with a sharp kitchen knife. Immediately, molecules from the cut onion were released into the air. The onion molecules drifted up into the woman's face and came in contact with the watery fluid in her eyes. The onion's molecules combined with the salty water in the woman's eyes and changed into sulfuric acid. At that moment, the woman's eyes started stinging, and tears began to trickle down her face.

## EXERCISE 7   Identifying Narrative Paragraphs

In a magazine, newspaper, or book, find a paragraph that uses the strategy of narration. On your own paper, identify the source (the name of the magazine, newspaper, or book). Below the source, identify the topic of the paragraph, and list the supporting details. Then tell whether narration is being used to tell a story, to explain a process, or to explain causes and effects.

## EXERCISE 8   Using Narration as a Strategy

Following the instructions for using narration, develop the items below. Write your lists on your own paper.

1. Select one of the subjects below, and list at least three actions that took place.
   a. the time I got on the wrong bus after a concert (Make up the actions.)
   b. how the Underground Railroad operated (Check in an encyclopedia or a history book.)
2. Select one of the subjects below, and list at least four steps in the process.
   a. how to make popcorn (If you don't know how, ask someone.)
   b. how to wash clothes (If you don't know how to do laundry, this is a good time to learn.)
3. Select one of the subjects below, and list at least three causes or effects.
   a. arriving home two hours after your curfew (Identify the causes.)
   b. the bombing of Pearl Harbor on December 7, 1941 (List the effects. You may need to check some newspapers or magazines or to talk to someone who is an expert in this area.)

# USING CLASSIFICATION

What are the major differences between schools in Japan and schools in the United States? To answer this question, you need to look at one subject as it relates to other subjects in a group. You need to *classify*. When you use **classification** to develop a paragraph, you may divide a subject into its parts (the parts of a guitar), define it (what is freedom?), or compare and contrast it (road bikes and mountain bikes).

**Dividing.** You may need to look at the parts of a subject in order to explain it. For example, to explain the structure of the government of the United States, you may have to divide it into its executive, legislative, and judicial branches. The following paragraph uses the strategy of dividing to explain the separate layers of growth in a rain forest.

> The Amazon rain forest has three distinct layers of growth. The top layer, known as the *canopy*, is exposed to bright sunlight. The trees and plants that make up the lush green canopy grow up to a height of 130 feet. The middle layer of the forest, which grows to about 80 feet, is known as the *understory*. The plants and vines in this layer of growth compete with each other for the scant rays of sunshine that manage to penetrate the thick canopy above. The *forest floor* is the bottom layer of the forest. It is seldom, if ever, touched by direct sunlight. Hardly anything grows on the forest floor.

**Defining.** To define a subject, first identify the large class or group it belongs to. Then tell what makes the subject different from other members of that group. In the following paragraph, the first sentence defines *honey*. The other sentences give examples to explain what honey is and to tell how it is different from other sugary substances.

> Honey is a sticky, sugary substance. Produced by honey-making bees, it is twenty-five percent sweeter than sugar. Honey also contains forty percent more calories than sugar. The flavor and aroma of honey come from the flower nectar used to produce it. Honeybees will gather nectar from any and all of the flowers in their nectar-gathering area. But the honey's essential flavor comes from the flower that supplies the majority of the nectar. For example, nectar that is gathered in an area near an orange grove will most likely produce a honey that tastes like citrus blossoms.

**Comparing and Contrasting.**   Comparing and contrasting are closely related to dividing and defining. For example, the paragraph about the rain forest divides the subject of the rain forest into three layers and looks at the differences (contrasts) among those layers. You can look at subjects by comparing them (telling how they are alike), contrasting them (telling how they are different), or by both comparing and contrasting them. The following paragraph contrasts board games and video games.

> Many board games require a minimum of two players. Video games, on the other hand, can be played alone and most often are. Because board games are played by at least two people, they promote lively and sometimes humorous discussion. People playing video games often don't speak to anyone for long stretches of time. The electronic bleeping and humming of the computer may be the only noises that break the silence. Board games require strategy and patience as players decide how to proceed. But video games require quick reflexes and excellent hand-eye coordination.

## EXERCISE 9    Using Classification as a Strategy

Follow the directions below that tell which classification strategy to use to develop each main idea below. Work in a group with two other classmates. Choose one member of your group as the recorder, and then work together to list ideas. After you finish your lists, discuss the strategies. Which one was the most difficult to use? the easiest? How did the strategies help you stay focused on your subject?

| Main Idea | Classification Strategy |
|---|---|
| 1. Whatever your ability, there is a type of athletic activity that will suit you. | Look at the subject of athletics by dividing it into types; then list details for each type to support this main idea. |
| 2. White blood cells help in the healing process. | Look at the subject of white blood cells by defining it. Identify the larger group to which these cells belong, and then list some features that make them different from other blood cells. |
| 3. If you like one movie an actor starred in, will you also like another movie in which the actor stars? | Compare and contrast two movies starring the same actor by listing likenesses and differences. |

# PLANNING A COMPOSITION

Writing a composition, like writing a single paragraph, requires planning. Before you begin to write, you need to complete these steps.

- Choose a topic, and decide on your main idea.
- Gather information related to your topic and main idea.
- Organize the information in a way that will make sense to readers.

You can organize your ideas by making an early plan or a formal outline.

## THE EARLY PLAN

To create an *early plan*, or rough outline, sort your ideas or facts into groups, and then arrange the groups in order.

GROUPING.    After you have gathered details on your topic, group the details that have something in common. Write a heading for each group to show how the details in that group are related. (Details that don't fit into any group may be useful later. For now, put them in a separate list.)

ORDERING.    Next, order the details within each group, and order the groups themselves. There are several ways to order, or arrange, ideas.

| |
|---|
| *Chronological* (time) *order* presents events in the order that they happen in time. |
| *Spatial order* presents details according to where they are located. |
| *Order of importance* presents details from most important to least important, or vice versa. |
| *Classification* presents your topic in logical order by defining it, or by comparing and contrasting it with something else. |

## THE FORMAL OUTLINE

A *formal outline* is a highly structured, clearly labeled writing plan. It divides a subject into main headings and subheadings that are labeled with letters and numbers. There are two kinds of formal outlines. A *topic outline* states ideas in words or brief phrases. A *sentence outline* states ideas in complete sentences. A sample topic outline appears at the top of the next page.

Title:  Neighbors Helping Neighbors
Main Idea Statement:  Although natural disasters such as hurricanes and floods cause widespread destruction, they also tend to bring out the best in people.

I.   Hurricane Rita

   A.   Description of storms
   B.   Devastation and destruction
   C.   Areas affected
   D.   Examples of how people helped each other

II.  Flooding of New Orleans

   A.   Events leading up to the flood
   B.   Areas affected
   C.   Immediate effects of the flood
   D.   What people did to help each other
      1.   Volunteering at clinics and hospitals
      2.   Organizing relief programs

## EXERCISE 1   Creating an Early Plan

Below are some notes for a composition about the ways in which a major invention helped to modernize America. Work with a partner to organize the notes into two separate groups. On your own paper, write a heading for each group to show what the notes in that group have in common. Finally, arrange the notes within each group in a sensible order.

*airmail—faster communication*

*the airplane revolutionized warfare*

*1945—airplanes used to track hurricanes*

*airplanes are useful in agriculture to distribute pesticides, weed-killers, and fertilizers*

*1919—first use of airplanes to drop water to fight wildfires*

*1932—Amelia Earhart, first woman to fly solo across the Atlantic Ocean*

*1903—Orville and Wilbur Wright— first successful flight of an airplane*

*1927—Charles Lindbergh, Spirit of St. Louis, first nonstop flight from New York to Paris*

*1918—World War I, interest in air travel grows*

## EXERCISE 2   Creating a Formal Outline

Using the early plan you made for Exercise 1, create a formal outline on your own paper. You can use a topic or a sentence outline. Add a title and a main idea statement.

# WRITING INTRODUCTIONS

A composition begins with an *introduction.* The introduction has three important functions.

1. **CATCHING THE READERS' INTEREST.**   The introduction should make readers want to continue reading. It should arouse readers' interest or curiosity.

2. **SETTING THE TONE.**   The introduction should also set the composition's *tone*—its general feeling. For example, the tone might be serious and formal or humorous and lighthearted.

3. **PRESENTING THE THESIS.**   Most importantly, the introduction should tell readers what the composition will be about. In other words, it should present a *thesis statement*—a sentence or two that announces the composition's main idea. Often, but not always, the thesis statement comes at the end of the introduction.

 NOTE   The body of a composition contains paragraphs that support the main idea expressed in your thesis. In supporting the main idea, these paragraphs should all work together to achieve **unity** and **coherence.** For more about these two elements, see pages 15–18.

## TECHNIQUES FOR WRITING INTRODUCTIONS

Writers use a variety of techniques to grab their readers' attention in the introduction. Here are five.

- **Begin with an example or an anecdote.**   An example or an anecdote (a short, interesting, or humorous incident) draws readers in with concrete, vivid details. These details not only spark the readers' interest but also can include important aspects of the topic.

> "Stop the car!" she shouted. The taxi driver was so startled that she stopped right there on the roadway. The woman leapt from the car and ran to the side of the road. The driver looked to see what the trouble was, but there was no emergency. The woman was a newspaper photographer looking for that perfect photo opportunity.

- **Begin by stating a startling fact or by adopting an unusual position on a topic.**   A curious reader will keep reading. A surprising fact or an unexpected opinion can startle readers and arouse their curiosity.

> Imagine a place where the temperature rises above freezing only two months of the year. Imagine a place cut off from the rest of the world by frozen rivers and seas. Who could tolerate the isolation and harsh conditions of this Arctic land? The Inuit people of Canada's Northwest Territories can. They have survived in this remote area of the world for centuries.

- **Use an appropriate quotation.**  Writers can use someone else's words in an introduction if these words are interesting and make an important point. Quotations from experts, authors, or someone mentioned in the composition can add interest to the topic.

> "Brains, not brawn," my father always said to me. Sometimes brawn is necessary, but most of the time my father's words are good advice. It certainly would have helped me to have heeded this advice when I met the class bully.

- **Give some background information.**  Providing background details can help readers understand the thesis, help them recall what they already know about a topic, or simply build interest.

> Throughout their history, Mexicans have always valued the humble egg. Ancient Mayans believed that babies who were fed eggs during a special ceremony would acquire wisdom. Eggs later came to symbolize wealth and prosperity and were used to show religious devotion. Today, modern Mexicans value eggs as food and prepare them in a variety of delicious ways.

- **Begin with a simple statement of your thesis.**  A writer often states the thesis plainly, without fuss or fanfare. This technique immediately focuses readers' attention on the composition's main idea.

> The typical American family rarely, if ever, has the time to eat dinner together. Dad works two jobs and gets a bite to eat on the road. Mom barely gets in the door and has to rush off to a committee meeting at the town hall. The children can't stick around for a lengthy family dinner because of soccer practice, gymnastics practice, the basketball game, or a study group.

## EXERCISE 3   Identifying Types of Introductions

On the line after each of the following paragraphs, write the technique used in the attention-getting introduction.

1.   You sit down at your computer, carefully placing your fingers on the keyboard. You take a deep breath, flex your fingers, and begin. The sounds of rock-and-roll music fill your room. It is only your fifth lesson, but you are playing the piano like Elton John. Well, that might be a slight exaggeration, but, thanks to the latest in computer technology, you are making progress.

2.    Great-Granddad called me over and said, "Let me tell you about the most tremendous experience of my life." He pulled me up on his lap and told me the story of his meeting President John F. Kennedy.

3.    The surge of creative achievement by African Americans in the 1920s was known as the Harlem Renaissance. This cultural movement was marked by the celebrated poetry of such writers as Langston Hughes, Countee Cullen, and Claude McKay.

4.    Did you know that the average lead pencil can draw a line that is thirty-five miles long? The estimated number of English words that a pencil can write is fifty thousand. I try to remember this fact when I sit down to write a composition.

**EXERCISE 4    Writing an Introduction to a Composition**

Work with a partner to draft an introduction to a composition based on the formal outline you created for Exercise 2. Use one of the techniques for writing introductions discussed in this lesson. Write your introduction on your own paper.

# Calvin and Hobbes                           by Bill Watterson

Calvin & Hobbes copyright 1986 Watterson. Reprinted with permission of Universal Press Syndicate. All rights reserved.

# WRITING CONCLUSIONS

The *conclusion* is the last part of a composition. The conclusion should leave readers feeling satisfied that the composition is complete. To achieve this sense of completion, a conclusion must reinforce the main idea while bringing the composition to a definite close.

## TECHNIQUES FOR WRITING CONCLUSIONS

Here are six ways to write conclusions.

- **Restate the main idea.** The most direct way to end your composition is to restate the thesis *in different words*. Try to find a newer, stronger wording. The following conclusion restates in different words the idea that professional photographers are always on the lookout for the perfect photograph.

> The picture taken by the photographer in the middle of the road won first prize in a national photography contest. Was that opportunity worth stopping traffic for? Most professional photographers would answer yes. And most would agree that they would do just about anything for a perfect photo.

- **Summarize your major points.** Emphasize the major points of your composition by summarizing them in the conclusion.

> The most important piece of advice to hikers, then, is to be prepared. Make sure you have warm clothing and enough food and water to last at least twenty-four hours should you get stranded. Travel with others, and always tell someone where you are headed and when you will return. These precautions can help ensure a safe and happy adventure.

- **Close with a final idea or example.** You can reinforce, or pull together, your main points by using a final example. Below, the writer of an essay about the time demands on families leaves readers with one last thought.

> It is unlikely that American families will slow down. Finding the time to have even one meal together a week might seem impossible. But the Martínez family of Ash Creek has made the time. "Sunday evening, no matter what is going on, we eat together," says Mr. Martínez. "We use that time to catch up on everything that is happening in our busy lives. It's an important time for all of us—a small family reunion once a week."

- **Make a final comment on the topic.** Give a sense of completeness to your composition by ending with one final comment on your topic. You can provide a thoughtful observation, give a personal reaction, or project a vision of the future. In the following conclusion, the writer tells her thoughts on current immigration policies in the United States.

> The United States, which once welcomed millions of immigrants with open arms, now has an immigration policy that limits the number of legal immigrants. There are many who believe that the United States should continue to extend an unlimited welcome to anyone yearning to be free.

- **Call on your readers to take action.** If you are writing a persuasive essay, use your conclusion to urge readers to do something or to accept a belief. This approach, called the *direct appeal,* also works for other kinds of compositions, such as this one on athletics and competition.

> There will always be people who are ready to make an Olympic event out of tying one's shoes. Indeed, it often seems that just about everything in our society is competition based. However, as we've seen, the essence of sport is not competition but cooperation. In business, in our families, and especially in sports, it pays to remember that we humans are all on the same team.

- **Refer to your introduction.** A writer may make a direct reference to something in the introduction. For example, the following conclusion refers to the introduction on page 28.

> The variety and appeal of these egg dishes prove one thing for sure: Mexicans still value the humble egg.

## EXERCISE 5   Writing a Conclusion

Read the introduction and body of the composition on the following page. On your own paper, write a conclusion, using one of the techniques on this page or the previous page. Then get together with a small group of classmates, and discuss your conclusions. Why did you choose one particular technique over another? Which conclusion works best with the composition?

## Remember This

You are introduced to a new student in your school. The two of you like each other immediately, so you decide to exchange phone numbers. Just as you are about to recite the familiar numbers, your mind goes blank. You can't remember your own phone number! Your memory has shut down. Luckily, it's only a few seconds before your memory kicks back in. With an embarrassed chuckle, you quickly rattle off your number.

There is no need to be embarrassed. People are always forgetting things. To explain why we sometimes forget even the simplest things, we first have to understand why we remember things. We have to understand how the memory works. Memory is the mind's ability to recall information acquired at an earlier time. There are two main kinds of memory: short-term memory and long-term memory.

Short-term memory is the place where you put information on a temporary basis. For example, when someone gives you directions to the nearest post office, you remember the directions just long enough to find the post office. Only a certain amount of information can be put into short-term memory—directions to the post office, for example. The information in short-term memory is available to you immediately, but once used, it is usually dumped out or transferred to long-term memory.

Long-term memory is where you store all the information you have acquired in your life. It's like a giant attic. Long-term memory helps you recall the events leading up to the Civil War (from last year's social studies class) or what your cabin at summer camp looked like when you were in the first grade. Long-term memory provides you with the ability to learn a skill, such as ice-skating, or to remember when your books are due at the library.

Why, then, do people sometimes forget their telephone numbers? Why do they occasionally forget that their library books are due? Researchers have several explanations for forgetfulness. One is that new memories can interfere with old ones. For example, you have recently memorized your mother's work phone number. This memory may temporarily interfere with the memory of your home phone number. Sometimes we forget things because they get lost in our memory. For instance, suppose that you can't remember where you left your math notebook. You do remember that you had it when you left school yesterday. If you can recall exactly where you went after school yesterday, you can probably find your missing notebook. All you need are the right clues to trigger your memory. We also forget because an experience is unpleasant or painful to remember. Finally, at other times, we forget things because we are ill or under stress.

# A PERSONAL IMPRESSION ESSAY

When you write expressively, you share your thoughts and feelings. Some expressive writing you create is just for yourself. Other expressive writing, like this personal expression essay, is meant to be shared.

A *personal impression essay* is a piece of writing that tells how you feel about a person who has been important to you in some way. As you read the essay below, keep in mind the feelings that are expressed.

My Best Friend, Josephine

Josephine is my very best friend. In fact, she is the best and fairest friend anyone ever had.

I met Josephine when I was little. She and I and a bunch of other kids in the neighborhood went out to have a gigantic snowball fight. Most of the other kids ran away when a big St. Bernard dog came trotting up the road, but my mom had bundled me up in so much clothing that I could barely move at all. I tripped, and the huge dog came and sat on me. I was cold and I could hardly breathe. I was terrified. With all the other kids laughing, I also felt humiliated. Josephine was the only one who tried to help me. I could never thank her enough (until the time I saved her life, but that's a different story). Josephine has been my best friend ever since then. Everyone in the neighborhood still makes fun of me every time we see a St. Bernard. It makes me almost cry. But Josephine never laughs. She makes me feel strong and helps me ignore them. She's the kind of friend I want to be.

Another time Josephine helped me was when George Fisher, a huge, mean kid, told me he wanted to be my friend but that I had to do his homework for him. I didn't like George, but I sure didn't want to make him mad at me. I got very depressed. Eventually, I talked it over with Josephine. She suggested that I offer to help him study but not to do his homework for him. I thought this was a good idea. When I told him, he started to look real mad, all red in the face. I felt scared, but I knew I was doing what I had to do. And Josephine was behind me. Well, George finally went away. And later on, he said I was okay, and he asked me to help him study. Josephine said she thought I had done the right thing. She said she was proud of me. I've never felt prouder than when she told me that.

Josephine is the best person to do things with and to talk to. She thinks hard about what is fair, and she tries to fix things that aren't fair. I can always count on her. Even if we live far away from each other someday, Josephine and I will always be best friends, because we can rely on each other.

## Thinking About the Model

Now that you have read the model personal impression essay, answer the questions on the lines below to help you understand how the writer created it.

1. The purpose of a personal impression essay is to tell how the writer feels about a person. How does the author of the model essay feel about his or her subject?

   _____

   _____

   _____

2. A personal impression essay explains why the writer feels as she or he does about a person. What has Josephine done that makes the author feel this way about her?

   _____

   _____

   _____

3. A personal impression essay tries to use all the senses to describe the thoughts and feelings of the writer. What sensory details does the writer use to give us his or her impression of Josephine?

   _____

   _____

   _____

4. Because a personal impression essay expresses an author's thoughts and feelings, it should have a friendly tone. To achieve this tone, a writer uses informal language, like first-person pronouns (*I, me,* and *our*) and contractions. List some examples of informal language in the essay. (For more information about informal language, see page 87.)

_____

_____

_____

_____

## ASSIGNMENT: WRITING A PERSONAL IMPRESSION ESSAY

Write a short personal impression essay describing someone who has been important in your life. In your essay, express your thoughts and feelings about the person. Tell what qualities this person has that you respect or admire. Then relate events in which the person shows these qualities.

 ## Prewriting

**Step 1:** First you will want to brainstorm a list of ideas about the subject *Important People.* On your own paper, write this subject at the top of the sheet. Then list every idea that comes to your head. You might list relatives, teachers, or friends. Don't stop to judge any of the ideas. Keep going until you run out of ideas.

**Step 2:** From your brainstorming list, choose a person who is important to you to use as the subject for your personal impression essay. This person should be someone you know well and someone about whom you will want to share your thoughts with your readers. Write this person's name on the line below.

_____

**Step 3:** Freewrite about this person on your own paper. When you freewrite, you write down whatever comes to mind. Do not stop to judge or edit your thoughts; keep writing until you run out of ideas.

**Step 4:** Review your freewriting to choose the most memorable trait about this person. Is he or she loyal? generous? emotionally strong? funny? Select a trait that is important to you and that you are willing to share with your classmates and teacher. State this trait on the line below.

_____

**Step 5:** On the lines below, list two experiences you have had with this person that show this person's most memorable trait.

1. _____

2. _____

*Step 6:*  For both of these experiences, tell in chronological order what happened. Tell how the situation began, what the person did, and what happened as a result. On your own paper, answer the following questions:

1. What did the person do?
2. Why did he or she do that?
3. What character trait is this an example of?
4. How did you feel when he or she did that?
5. Why did you feel that way?

 ## Writing

Use the following plan to help you write a first draft of your personal impression essay. Write the essay on your own paper. You may want to write on every other line to allow room for your revisions and corrections.

| **Beginning** | • Identifies the person and tells your relationship to him or her<br>• Tells briefly the memorable trait you want to share about this person |
|---|---|

| **Middle** | • Uses one paragraph to give a detailed description of each experience<br>• Tells your thoughts and feelings about these experiences |
|---|---|

| **Ending** | • Restates your choice of the memorable trait<br>• Gives a final comment, perhaps a look to the future, about this person |
|---|---|

# Evaluating and Revising

When you evaluate your writing, you judge whether you have accomplished what you set out to do. You may discover ways in which your writing might be improved. When you revise, you make changes to improve what you've written. You can use the following questions to evaluate your personal impression essay before revising it.

---

### Questions for Evaluation

1. Does the beginning identify the person who is the subject of the essay? Does it state the person's most memorable trait? If not, what information should be added?

   _____

   _____

2. Does the essay describe the writer's thoughts and feelings about this person? If not, what could be added? Where could it be added?

   _____

   _____

3. Does the essay relate two or three events that show why the writer feels this way? For each event, does it tell what the person did and why he or she did it? If not, what information is missing?

   _____

   _____

4. Does the essay use details that appeal to all of the five senses? If not, what details can be added?

   _____

   _____

5. Does the ending tell clearly why the person is important to the writer? Does it give a final comment about the person? If not, what information should be added?

   _____

   _____

---

6. Is there information included that is unnecessary and distracting? If so, what information can be cut?

_____

## Peer Evaluation

Give your rough draft to a classmate for review. Ask your classmate to follow these steps.

*Step 1:*    Read the rough draft carefully.

*Step 2:*    Complete the **Questions for Evaluation** on a separate sheet of paper.

## Self-Evaluation

Next, complete your own evaluation of your rough draft. Follow these steps.

*Step 1:*    Read the peer evaluation written by your classmate. Circle any comments that you plan to use as you revise.

*Step 2:*    Reread your draft, and write your answers to the **Questions for Evaluation** on your own paper.

Using your answers to the **Questions for Evaluation**, revise your draft. You can use the space in the margins and between the lines of your rough draft for your changes.

## Proofreading and Publishing

Use the **Guidelines for Proofreading** on page 10 to find and correct errors in your paper.

*Step 1:*    a.  Check that each word in your paper is spelled and capitalized correctly. If you have any doubt about a word, look it up in a dictionary. Correct any errors you find.
             b.  Check for proper punctuation, grammar, and usage. Then correct any errors you find.

*Step 2:*    Trade papers with a classmate, and proofread each other's paper for spelling, capitalization, punctuation, grammar, and word usage. Mark any errors you find, and return the papers. When you get your own paper back, make any additional corrections that are needed.

*Step 3:*   Make a clean copy of your revised and proofread paper.

*Step 4:*   Share your writing in one of the following ways, or think up your own way to reach an audience.

     a.   Work with the class to create a collection of personal impresssions.

     b.   Send or read aloud your personal impression to the person about whom you wrote.

---

## FOR YOUR PORTFOLIO

Write down your answers to these questions, and place them with your essay in your writing portfolio.

1. a.   What have you learned about this person by writing about him or her?

    b.   What do you admire most about this person?

    c.   What can you learn from this person's life that can help you in your own life?

2. What do you think are the strengths of this personal impression essay?

3. What have you learned about expressive writing?

# A STORY POEM

What do many poems and song lyrics have in common? Rhythm and rhyme. Poems and song lyrics may also tell stories. A *ballad* is a poem that combines rhythm, rhyme, and a story. The popular music form rap also combines rhythm, rhyme, and story. Here is a poem that follows the rap music style. It is based on "Rip Van Winkle" by Washington Irving.

### Rappin' Rip

I'll tell you all a story 'bout a lazy guy,
A good-hearted man with his head in the sky.
Rip Van Winkle was a happy kind of fellow.
He whistled and sang and was always mellow.

There was just one problem with this guy named Rip:
Any hard work he would always skip.
He played and he fished and he visited friends,
But if labor called, his energy would end.

He hiked to the mountains on a bright, sunny day
And met little people along the way.
The little people shared a good-tasting potion
And several sips later, Rip quit all motion.

Some time later Rip awoke sort of groggy,
And the air on the mountain was still and foggy.
Rip seemed confused as he walked to town,
For his beard had grown down to the ground.

Rip traveled through the town at a nervous pace,
For he didn't know a single face.
He sat on a stoop and sighed and sighed.
Folks wondered who he was as they hurried by.

He looked long and hard for his kids and his wife.

He wondered what had happened to his cozy life.

"Hey, I'm Rip Winkle," he shouted, near tears.

"Hey, Rip," someone answered, "you've been gone
    twenty years."

## Thinking About the Model

Now that you've read the story poem on pages 41–42, think about how the writer created it. Then answer the following questions.

1. People use letters to indicate a pattern of rhyme (called the **rhyme scheme**) in a poem. The first rhyming sound is called *a*; the second rhyming sound is called *b*; and so on. For example:

    The purple *hat*  a
    belongs to *Nat*. a

    The green *slacks* b
    belong to *Max*. b

    Please give *Una*  c
    the orange *sock*.  d

    Please give *Luna*  c
    the yellow *smock*. d

    Figure out the model poem's rhyme scheme. Write the appropriate letters on the lines below or at the end of each line of the poem.

    _____

    _____

    _____

    _____

2. You're probably aware that rap is written in an informal style, using conversational English, slang, and dialect. Sometimes humor is used as well. List some examples of informal words and phrases from the model poem.

    _____

    _____

3. What is the story that the model poem tells? List the main events below.

   _____

   _____

   _____

   _____

4. The words of story poems and rap songs are not written to be read silently. They are written to be sung or chanted. Read the model poem aloud, snapping your fingers to the beat. How many strong beats does the average line of this poem have?

   _____

# ASSIGNMENT: WRITING A STORY POEM

Create your own version of a favorite story, myth, fairy tale, or legend. Keep in mind language, rhythm, and rhyme as you retell a story in this new and interesting way.

 **Prewriting**

Step 1:   Think of some possible stories that you might retell as story poems. Write down at least one possibility in each category below: a true story, a myth, a fairy tale, and a legend.

a true story from history (example: the story of the Battle of Gettysburg)

_____

a myth (example: the story of Pegasus, the winged horse)

_____

a fairy tale (example: "Cinderella")

_____

a legend (example: the story of Johnny Appleseed)

_____

Step 2:   Now choose the story that you would like to retell as a story poem. Write the title on the line below. Be sure that you are very familiar with your story's content. You may even want to read the story more than once.

_____

Step 3:   List the main events from your story on the lines below.

_____

_____

_____

*Step 4:* To practice telling part of your story, first choose an event from the list you made in Step 3. List that event on the line below.

_____

*Step 5:* Now, on the lines below, write about the event you chose in Step 4. Use the rhyme scheme (*aa, bb,* etc.) and the rhythm (four beats per line) of the model poem, or use a rhyme scheme and rhythm of your choice.

_____

_____

_____

_____

_____

_____

_____

 # Writing

Now combine rhythm, rhyme, and story to begin building your story poem. Use the work you completed in the prewriting section as your guide.

- Know your story well so that you can retell it clearly.

- Focus on the story's key events and the most interesting details.

- Use an informal rap style.

- Keep your rhythm in your head as you write each line.

- Make sure you follow a consistent rhyme scheme.

**Evaluating and Revising**

You will use these **Questions for Evaluation** when you evaluate your story poem to try to improve it. These questions should help you discover the poem's strengths and weaknesses. You can also use these questions to evaluate a classmate's poem.

---

**Questions for Evaluation**

1. Does the poem make sense to readers? Is it clear? If not, what should be added or rearranged?

2. Does the poem use casual, everyday language? If not, where does the language need improvement?

3. Is the rhyme scheme consistent throughout the poem? If not, how can the problem areas be fixed?

4. Do the sentences and the rhymes sound natural? Are there any lines that can be improved? How would you change them?

5. Is the poem lively and full of interesting details? Where might more details be added?

---

**Peer Evaluation**

Exchange rough drafts with a classmate. Ask your classmate to follow these steps.

*Step 1:*    Rap is meant to be spoken to a rhythmic accompaniment such as snapping fingers, clapping hands, or a drumbeat. Read the story poem draft aloud, clapping your hands or snapping your fingers as you read it. Think about what parts of the poem might be rewritten to improve the rhythm.

*Step 2:*    Complete the **Questions for Evaluation** above. Try to give specific suggestions for revision.

**Self-Evaluation**

Next, make your own evaluation of your rough draft. Follow these steps.

*Step 1:*    Read your story poem for rhyme and content, not for grammar and mechanics. Think also about the suggestions you made about your classmate's poem. How might these ideas improve your own work?

*Step 2:*    Read your poem draft out loud. As you did with your classmate's poem, clap your hands or snap your fingers. Think about how the rhythm works and how it can be improved.

*Step 3:*    Read your classmate's evaluation. Circle any suggestions you plan to use in your revision.

*Step 4:*    Reread the **Questions for Evaluation** on page 46. On a separate sheet of paper, jot down notes about specific changes you want to make.

Revise your draft until you can answer yes to each of the **Questions for Evaluation**. If you need to, you might even return to the prewriting stage to generate new ideas.

 ## Proofreading and Publishing

*Step 1:*    Check your spelling. If you are not absolutely certain that a word is spelled correctly, check a dictionary.

*Step 2:*    Next, proofread for errors in grammar, usage, capitalization, and punctuation. Use the proofreading checklist on page 10 as a guide.

*Step 3:*    Make a clean copy of your revised and proofread poem.

*Step 4:*    Publish your poem by reading it aloud to your classmates or by performing it at a school or a local talent show. If your poem is a version of a children's tale, you may want to take your performance to a local day-care center, a kindergarten class, or to some young relatives.

## FOR YOUR PORTFOLIO

If you are keeping a portfolio, you might want to include the answers to the questions below with your poem.

1. What part of creating the story poem did you enjoy most? What did you find most difficult? Write the answers to these questions, and put the answers in your portfolio.

2. The traditional folk ballads of England and Scotland told stories, were written in rhyme, and were passed orally from generation to generation. What similarities and differences are there between rap and this earlier musical form? Write your thoughts in your portfolio.

"I Think that I shall never see, a poem as lovely as a
bee, flea, sea, ski, plea, key..."

© 1991; reprinted courtesy of Bunny Hoest and Parade Magazine.

# A PRESS RELEASE

Sometimes people or groups want to publicize their plans, events, or successes. They want newspapers, news magazines, or news programs on radio or television to tell the public about an event that the group is planning or a project that the group has completed. One way to get publicity is to send a press release about the event to the editors of news organizations. A press release contains a short news story. News editors sometimes print revised or edited versions of press releases. At other times editors publish press releases, such as the one below, without changing them.

March 14, 1995

Spanish Club
Arcadia High School
Lubbock, Texas
(806) 555-1212

HIGH SCHOOL HOLDS LATIN AMERICAN FESTIVAL

The Spanish Club of Arcadia High School will hold its fourth annual Latin American Festival on Saturday, March 23, from 10:00 A.M. to 2:00 P.M. in the high school auditorium. The public is invited to attend this daylong celebration of Latin American food, dancing, and music.

Las Peruanas, a musical group from Cuzco, Peru, will provide authentic music from Peru, Ecuador, and Bolivia. Home economics students from Arcadia High School will serve a variety of Latin American foods, including empanadas and chiles rellenos.

Ticket prices will be ten dollars in advance and twelve dollars at the door. According to Lupe Martínez, Spanish Club treasurer, proceeds from the festival will finance the Spanish Club's annual field trip to Puerto Rico.

—Chandra Basnayke

# Thinking About the Model

When you write a press release, be careful to include all the correct information in an order that makes sense. Read the model press release on the previous page. Then answer the following questions.

1. The information in a press release is usually organized in *order of importance,* from most important to least important. Where does the most important information appear in the model press release?

   _____

2. The first sentence of a press release is called the *lead*. The lead answers several of the 5W-How? questions: *Who? What? Where? When? Why?* and *How?* Read the lead of the model press release, then answer the following questions.

   *What* event is being held?

   _____

   *Who* is holding the event?

   _____

   *When* is the event being held?

   _____

   *Where* is the event being held?

   _____

3. What additional information does the press release provide?

   _____

   _____

   _____

   _____

   _____

   _____

   _____

## ASSIGNMENT: WRITING A PRESS RELEASE

You are the publicity director for your high school's production of a musical called *Uptown Soundz*. The musical, which combines rap songs and contemporary dance, was written by two students from your school. The directing, acting, lighting, costumes, makeup, and stage design are all being done by students. As publicity director, your job is to announce the play to your community. You have appeared on a local radio program to talk about the musical. Your next goal is to write a press release to send to local newspapers.

 ## Prewriting

**Step 1:** Complete the chart below to identify the source of the press release. You will put this information in the upper left-hand corner of your press release.

| | |
|---|---|
| Organization name (Make up a name for your theater company.) | |
| School name | |
| City and State | |
| Telephone Number | |

**Step 2:** Write today's date. It will go in the upper right-hand corner of your press release.

_____

**Step 3:** Press releases answer the *5W-How?* questions: *Who? What? Where? When? Why?* and *How?* The lead, or first sentence, answers three or four of these questions—the three or four that are most important. Answer the following questions for your press release.

*Who* is holding the event? _____

*What* event is being held? _____

*Where* is it being held?_____

*When* is it being held? _____

Step 4:   Use the information from Step 3 to write a lead for your press release. Remember that the lead should be a single sentence.

_____

_____

Step 5:   The *body* of a press release should present additional important information. Gather information for the body of your press release by filling out the following chart. Make up the names, or use the names of your friends or classmates.

| | |
|---|---|
| Names of musical's writers | |
| Name of musical's director | |
| Names of leading actors | |
| Times of performances | |
| Price of tickets | |
| How and Where to buy tickets | |

What the musical is about (summary of the story)

_____

_____

_____

_____

_____

# Writing

Use the information from your prewriting notes to write a draft of your press release on a separate sheet of paper. Use the press release on page 49 as a model. At the top of your paper, identify the name, address, and telephone number of your organization. Also include today's date. Leave space for the headline.

Next, write the body of your press release. It should be two to four paragraphs long. Each paragraph should be short (two or three sentences). The first paragraph should begin with your lead. Arrange the rest of the information in order of decreasing importance.

Finally, write a **headline**, or title, for your press release. Base the headline on your lead. Your headline should be a short sentence (seven words or less). It should contain a subject and a verb in the present tense. Avoid using the words *a, an, the,* *is,* and *are* in a headline. [Note: You may want to look at some sample newspaper headlines first.]

# Evaluating and Revising

You can use the following questions when you evaluate the strengths and weaknesses of your press release.

---

### Questions for Evaluation

1. Are the date and the source of the press release clear? If not, what should be added?

2. Does the headline have a subject and a verb that is in the present tense? If not, what should be added?

3. Are the words *a, an, the, is,* and *are* left out of the headline? If not, what should be cut?

4. Does the lead answer any of the *5W-How?* questions? If not, how can the lead be fixed?

5. Does the press release use words and sentences that are short and simple? If not, what needs to be cut or replaced?

6. Does the press release contain all the information that readers will need to know? If not, what needs to be added?

7. Is the information arranged in order of decreasing importance? If not, what needs to be rearranged?

---

**Peer Evaluation**

Give your rough draft to a classmate to read and evaluate. Then, on his or her own paper, your classmate should answer the **Questions for Evaluation** on the preceding page.

**Self-Evaluation**

Next, evaluate the draft yourself. Follow these steps.

*Step 1:*   Read the peer evaluation written by your classmate. Circle any comments that you plan to make use of as you revise.

*Step 2:*   Reread your draft, and answer the **Questions for Evaluation.**

Now revise your draft by using your classmate's suggestions and your answers to the **Questions for Evaluation**. You can make corrections directly on your draft; you can rewrite your draft; or you can start all over again with prewriting.

## Proofreading and Publishing

*Step 1:*   Proofread the press release for errors in spelling, grammar, usage, and mechanics. Refer to the **Proofreading Checklist** on page 10. Make a clean copy of your revised press release.

*Step 2:*   Publish your press release by creating a collection of class press releases as models for other students to use.

> **FOR YOUR PORTFOLIO**
>
> Write down your answers to these questions to accompany your press release in your portfolio.
>
> 1. What was the most important lesson that you learned from writing a press release?
>
> 2. Look in a newspaper for stories announcing upcoming events. Cut out one or two that you think are good. Include them with your press release in your portfolio.

# A PERSUASIVE LETTER

Is there a change you would like to see in your community? Maybe you'd like the Parks and Recreation Commission to offer more summer art classes, or maybe you'd like a local business to sponsor a basketball tournament. A *persuasive letter* can be an effective means of suggesting a change or arguing in favor of an idea.

16 Cedar Street
Crozet, VA 22932
April 20, 2008

Ms. Laura Rasmussen
Uptown Theater
253 Cross Street
Crozet, VA 22932

Dear Ms. Rasmussen:

After I saw The Joy Luck Club, a film about Chinese American mothers and daughters, I began to think about what it is like for people who come to the United States from another country. I asked my grandmother about people immigrating because she moved here from Poland when she was nineteen years old. She told me stories about her life I'd never heard before. Because this movie is so unforgettable, I am writing to ask you to show The Joy Luck Club once more at your theater.

I think it would be a real service to the community to show it again. The movie was popular and got good reviews. Many people who had read Amy Tan's best-seller, The Joy Luck Club, wanted to see how Hollywood had turned the novel into a movie. When it was shown in our town, there were long lines of people waiting to get in to see it, and many people I know went to see it twice. I also know some people who read the novel after they saw the movie, and now they would like a chance to see the movie again.

Another reason I think it would be good to show the movie is that we have a large population of people in our community who have recently moved to the United States from other countries, such as Russia and Vietnam. I think it would be valuable for everyone to see this film.

The main reason, however, that I would like you to show this film again is that it was the best film I've seen in several years. The story, the subject, and the characters were so interesting that I haven't forgotten them. I am sure I am not the only one in our community who would be glad to have a chance to see it once more.

Thank you for considering my idea.

Sincerely,
Monica Reilly

## Thinking About the Model

The writer of the model letter has a strong opinion. Think about how she tries to persuade the movie theater owner to show the film. Answer the following questions on the lines provided.

1. An opinion is a personal belief that one cannot necessarily prove true or false. What opinion is this writer expressing in her letter?

   _____

   _____

   _____

2. An important element of a persuasive letter is a strong opening. You might choose to open with a startling fact or an anecdote. Once you have hooked the reader's attention, you can present your opinion. How does the writer try to catch the reader's attention in the opening paragraph?

   _____

   _____

   _____

3. Once you have presented your opinion, you need to back it up with reasons or evidence. How you organize these reasons is important. You can give the most important reason first, or you may choose to give it last. What reasons does the writer give to support the idea of showing the film again? In what order are these ideas presented?

   _____

   _____

   _____

   _____

   _____

4.  Another way to support your opinion is to show that other people share it. How does the writer of the model letter show that other people liked this movie?

    _____

    _____

    _____

5.  Using an example from your personal experience can add an emotional appeal to a persuasive letter. How does the writer use a personal experience to support her viewpoint?

    _____

    _____

    _____

6.  The conclusion is important because it is the reader's final impression of your opinion. In it, you can restate your opinion. Or you can end with a *call to action*—what you want the reader to do as a result of being persuaded. You might also want to include a thank-you to the reader for considering your idea or opinion. How does the writer conclude the model letter?

    _____

    _____

    _____

## ASSIGNMENT: WRITING A PERSUASIVE LETTER

The owner of a local movie theater has decided not to replay a movie that you would like to see again. Write a letter in which you try to persuade the theater owner to change his or her mind.

 ## Prewriting

1. Think about the films you've seen that you really enjoyed. They might be recent films, as well as ones you saw when you were younger. Brainstorm a list of titles on your own paper.

2. On your list, circle the name of the film that you would most like to see again. Then, in the space below, list the things you liked about it. Try to list specific details or examples.

_____

_____

_____

_____

3. What reasons can you think of to persuade the owner of a theater to show this film again? Can you think of any ways in which you can make an emotional appeal for your viewpoint? List these reasons in the space below.

_____

_____

_____

_____

4. Try to add the force of others' opinions to your letter. Did any reviewers give the movie a "thumbs up"? Did it win an Academy Award? List any awards or expert opinions below.

_____

_____

5. Decide how to organize your letter. What will be the strongest support for your opinion? The weakest? On your own paper, list your supporting details and examples. Start with the weakest, and end with the strongest.

 **Writing**

Using your prewriting notes, draft a persuasive letter on your own paper. Here are some suggestions for writing your draft.

**Beginning**  • Begin with an introduction that will grab the reader's attention. Then state your opinion clearly.

**Middle**  • Follow your introduction with reasons and evidence to support your opinion. Because you'll get details to support your reasons, you might need a paragraph for each reason.
  • Try to include details that will make an emotional appeal to the reader.
  • Always keep in mind your purpose: You are trying to convince the reader to think or act as you suggest.

**Ending**  • Create a strong ending. You could summarize your reasons, restate your opinion, or end with a call to action.
  • Add a polite thank-you to the reader for taking the time to read your letter.

# Evaluating and Revising

Now that you've written your letter, consider how you can improve it. Use the following **Questions for Evaluation** to evaluate your persuasive letter before revising it.

---

### Questions for Evaluation

1. Does the letter have a strong opening that will catch the reader's attention? If not, what can be added or reworded?

2. Does the letter clearly state an opinion? If not, what can be added or restated?

3. Is the opinion supported with reasons and evidence? Are these reasons well organized? If not, is there a better order in which to present the information?

4. Does the letter make an appeal to the emotions of the reader? If not, can you think of an emotional appeal that could be added?

5. Does the letter include others' opinions to strengthen the argument? If not, what can be added?

6. Does the letter have an effective conclusion that summarizes the reasons, restates the opinion, or calls for action? If not, what could be added to make the ending stronger?

---

## Peer Evaluation

Exchange rough drafts with a classmate. Ask the classmate to follow these steps.

*Step 1:*    Read the rough draft carefully.

*Step 2:*    Answer the **Questions for Evaluation** on a separate piece of paper.

## Self-Evaluation

Now complete an evaluation of your own rough draft. Follow these steps.

*Step 1:*    Reread your rough draft carefully.

*Step 2:*    Think about the suggestions you made for your classmate's rough draft. Do any apply to your own draft?

*Step 3:*   On a separate piece of paper, answer the **Questions for Evaluation** for your rough draft. Be sure to include notes about specific changes you want to make.

*Step 4:*   Study your classmate's suggestions. Circle any suggestions you would like to use in your revision.

Use your answers to the **Questions for Evaluation**, together with your classmate's suggestions, to revise your draft until you are satisfied with it.

## Proofreading and Publishing

A polished letter will make a positive impression on the reader. Use these steps to prepare your final version.

*Step 1:*   Begin by checking the spelling of each word. If you are uncertain of the spelling of a word, look it up in a dictionary. Pay special attention to foreign words.

*Step 2:*   Check your letter for correct punctuation, grammar, usage, and capitalization. Make sure that any numbers or statistics you cite are accurate.

*Step 3:*   Make a clean copy of your revised and proofread letter. Use the following format for a business letter.

| The Parts of a Letter | |
| --- | --- |
| **Heading** | Begin the heading to the right of the center of the page. Include the following information.<br>• writer's street address<br>• writer's city, state and ZIP Code (A comma follows the name of the city.)<br>• date of letter (A comma separates the day of the month from the year.) |
| **Inside Address** | Begin the inside address at the left margin. Include the following information.<br>• the name and, if appropriate, the title of the person you are writing to<br>• the name of the company or organization<br>• street address of company or organization |

| Salutation | Begin the salutation, or greeting, at the left margin. Begin the first word and all nouns in the salutation with a capital letter. Follow the salutation with a colon. |
|---|---|
| Body | The body of the letter contains your message. Indent the first line of each paragraph. |
| Closing and Signature | The closing should be vertically even with the heading. Use *Yours truly*, or *Sincerely*, for the closing. Sign your name in ink in the space just below the closing. Use your legal name. |

*Step 4:*   Use one of the following suggestions to publish your letter.

A. Prepare a bulletin board displaying the letters you and your classmates have written.

B. Post your letter on the refrigerator or in another spot at home so that your family members can read it.

### FOR YOUR PORTFOLIO

Look in newspapers or magazines to see if you can find reviews of the movie you wrote about. Study how the reviewer describes the movie. How does the review differ from your letter? Clip the reviews and keep them with a copy of your letter.

B.C. by Johnny Hart. By permission of Johnny Hart and Creators Syndicate.

# SENTENCE FRAGMENTS

**8a  A *sentence fragment* is a word group that does not have all the basic parts of a complete sentence and does not express a complete thought.**

To find out whether you have written a complete sentence or a sentence fragment, you can use a simple, three-part test.

1.  Does the group of words have a subject?
2.  Does it have a verb?
3.  Does it express a complete thought?

FRAGMENT   Was a great tennis player. [The subject is missing. *Who* was a great tennis player?]

SENTENCE   **Arthur Ashe** was a great tennis player.

FRAGMENT   Arthur Ashe many awards and tennis championships. [The verb is missing. *What* did Arthur Ashe do?]

SENTENCE   Arthur Ashe **won** many awards and tennis championships.

FRAGMENT   Because Ashe wanted to help young tennis players. [This group of words has a subject and a verb, but it doesn't express a complete thought. *What happened* because Ashe wanted to help young tennis players?]

SENTENCE   Because Ashe wanted to help young tennis players, **he wrote many inspiring articles and ran tennis clinics in many cities**.

**8b  A *phrase* is a group of words that does not have a subject and a verb. *Verbals* are forms of verbs that are used as other parts of speech. A *verbal phrase* is a phrase that contains a verbal. By itself, a verbal phrase is a fragment because it doesn't express a complete thought.**

FRAGMENT   Watching your game.
SENTENCE   **I enjoyed** watching your game.

FRAGMENT   To become good soccer players.
SENTENCE   **Athletes must practice hard** to become good soccer players.

**8c  An *appositive* is a word that identifies or explains the noun or pronoun it follows. An *appositive phrase*, a phrase made up of an appositive and its modifiers, is a fragment. It does not contain the basic parts of a sentence.**

FRAGMENT   A novel about World War I.
SENTENCE   **Ernest Hemingway wrote** *A Farewell to Arms*, a novel about World War I.

> **8d** A *prepositional phrase* is a group of words consisting of a preposition, a noun or pronoun that serves as the object of the preposition, and any modifiers of that object. A prepositional phrase can't stand alone as a sentence because it doesn't express a complete thought.
>
> FRAGMENT    For their sharp wit.
> SENTENCE    **The poems of Dorothy Parker are known** for their sharp wit.

## EXERCISE 1   Writing Sentences with Phrasal Fragments

On your own paper, create sentences from the phrases and clauses below. You can either attach the fragment to a complete sentence or develop it into a complete sentence by adding a subject, a verb, or both.

EX.    1.  walking on the beach
　　　 1.  Walking on the beach, we found a beautiful shell.
　　　　　　　　　　　*or*
　　　　Julia and I were walking on the beach.

1.  under the table
2.  hoping to win first prize
3.  to ask a question
4.  the captain of the team
5.  needing a ride home
6.  instead of clouds
7.  my cousin in Des Moines
8.  to solve this math problem
9.  seems to work
10. in the middle of the night
11. watering the yard
12. to look like new
13. with most of the other team members
14. on the roof near the chimney
15. after having a hard rain
16. working after school
17. a new pencil sharpener
18. adding our scores together
19. to believe a story like that
20. our neighbor down the street
21. learn the rules
22. playing chess with us
23. because coming early
24. at the tournament
25. while walking home from school

# SUBORDINATE CLAUSE FRAGMENTS

A **clause** is a group of words that has a subject and a verb. An **independent clause** expresses a complete thought and can stand alone as a sentence.

**8e  A *subordinate clause* does not express a complete thought. It is a fragment and cannot stand by itself as a sentence.**

FRAGMENT    Because Fred was late for the meeting. [*What happened* because Fred was late for the meeting?]

SENTENCE    Because Fred was late for the meeting, **he didn't hear the treasurer's report.**

FRAGMENT    Who gave the treasurer's report. [Note that this would be a complete sentence if it ended with a question mark.]

SENTENCE    **Fred can easily get the information from Arlene,** who gave the treasurer's report.

NOTE    A series of items is another kind of fragment that's easily mistaken for a sentence.

FRAGMENT    A sandwich, an apple, four pieces of celery, and some popcorn.

SENTENCE    **I ate several things for lunch:** a sandwich, an apple, four pieces of celery, and some popcorn.

EXERCISE 2    **Identifying and Revising Subordinate Clause Fragments**

In the following paragraph, underline each fragment. Revise the paragraph on your own paper by joining the subordinate clauses with the independent clauses. [Note: There may be more than one correct way to join the clauses.]

EX.    1    Although the crew members were very busy. They always

2    had a few minutes to spend with the boy.

*Although the crew members were very busy, they always had a few minutes to spend with the boy.*

1    Roman Inthisith was a six-year-old boy. Who lives in a busy

2    neighborhood in South Philadelphia. Roman moved to the

3    neighborhood recently. Who was born in California.  His

4   mother had come to California from Laos. Because

5   Roman was new to the area. He had few playmates. However, all

6   that changed. When a large group of actors, production assistants,

7   camera operators, and carpenters came to South Philadelphia to

8   film a movie. After they chose Roman's block for the filming of

9   many scenes in the movie. Roman met many of the crew

10   members. Suddenly, this curious, friendly boy made several new

11   friends. A photographer loaned Roman a small camera. That was

12   loaded with black-and-white film. One of the carpenters gave

13   Roman a hammer. Who was building sets on the street. Because

14   the crew members liked their young companion so much. They all

15   chipped in and bought him a bicycle.

## EXERCISE 3   Using Subordinate Clauses in Sentences

On your own paper, use each of the subordinate clause fragments below as part of a complete sentence. Add whatever words are necessary to make the meaning of the sentence complete. Add capitalization and punctuation as necessary.

EX.   1.   when the telephone rang
      1.   When the telephone rang, it startled me.

1. who called
2. after the meeting ended
3. if you want to see a great movie
4. because I enjoy mystery stories
5. which answered my question
6. since I finished my report
7. that she won the race
8. whom I invited
9. as if they had forgotten
10. where we set up the tent

# RUN-ON SENTENCES

**8f    A *run-on sentence* is two or more complete sentences run together as one.**

There are two kinds of run-ons. In a ***fused sentence***, the sentences have no punctuation at all between them.

RUN-ON    Jeremiah moved here from Israel he is my best friend.
CORRECT    Jeremiah moved here from Israel. **He** is my best friend.

The second kind of run-on is called a ***comma splice***. Two sentences are linked together with only a comma to separate them.

RUN-ON    Jeremiah joined the school orchestra, he plays the violin.
CORRECT    Jeremiah joined the school orchestra. **He** plays the violin.

To revise run-on sentences, you can always make two separate sentences. But if the two thoughts are related and are equal to one another in importance, you may want to make a ***compound sentence***.

RUN-ONS    The Delaware River is in eastern Pennsylvania the Ohio River is in western Pennsylvania. [fused]

The Delaware River is in eastern Pennsylvania, the Ohio River is in western Pennsylvania. [comma splice]

You can revise a run-on sentence by using one of the following techniques.

1. Use a comma and a coordinating conjunction (such as *and, but*, or *or*).

CORRECTED    The Delaware River is in eastern Pennsylvania, **and** the Ohio River is in western Pennsylvania.

2. Use a semicolon.

CORRECTED    The Delaware River is in eastern Pennsylvania**;** the Ohio River is in western Pennsylvania.

3. Use a semicolon and a word such as *therefore, instead, meanwhile, still, also, nevertheless*, or *however*. These words are called *conjunctive adverbs*. Follow a conjunctive adverb with a comma.

CORRECTED    The Delaware River is in eastern Pennsylvania**; however,** the Ohio River is in western Pennsylvania.

## EXERCISE 4   Revising Run-on Sentences

On your own paper, revise each of the run-on sentences below. Follow the directions in parentheses. Be sure to use correct end punctuation.

EX.   1.  Jamyce has worked hard on her report, it isn't finished yet. (Use a comma and a coordinating conjunction.)

    1.  Jamyce has worked hard on her report, but it isn't finished yet.

1.  Maria Tallchief was an American Indian she became one of the world's most famous ballerinas. (Split into two sentences.)

2.  Reiko Amato designed the cover for our yearbook the design won an award presented by the Houston Art League. (Use a semicolon.)

3.  Delaware is one of the smallest states, Rhode Island is even smaller. (Use a semicolon and a conjunctive adverb.)

4.  The Andes Mountains are in South America, the Alps are in Europe. (Use a comma and a coordinating conjunction.)

5.  We wanted to attend your dress rehearsal, we had to go to a late session of soccer practice. (Use a semicolon and a conjunctive adverb.)

6.  The sound of the motorcycle woke me up, I still didn't get out of bed. (Use a coordinating conjunction.)

7.  *Fifth Chinese Daughter* by Jade Snow Wong was the book we chose for the book group I am so glad we decided to read it. (Use a comma and a coordinating conjunction.)

8.  The storm moved into the area after lunch we had already found shelter. (Use a semicolon and a conjunctive adverb.)

9.  Did you attend the concert my mom wouldn't let me go on a school night. (Split into two sentences.)

10.  I have always loved animals someday I'd like to be a veterinarian. (Use a comma and a coordinating conjunction.)

11.  Chen will march in the New Year's parade his sister will not. (Use a comma and a coordinating conjunction.)

12.  Do you enjoy hiking we're planning a trip to New Hampshire next weekend. (Split into two sentences.)

13.  We will take nuts, raisins, and a small bottle of water they won't take up much space. (Use a semicolon.)

14.  His older brother is coming home for Thanksgiving, his younger brother is, too. (Use a comma and a coordinating conjunction.)

15.  Their house has an enormous attic filled with boxes treasures from the past are inside each box. (Split into two sentences.)

# REVIEW EXERCISE

## A. Identifying Fragments and Run-on Sentences

On the line before each item below, write *frag.* for *fragment*, *r.o.* for *run-on sentence*, or *C* if the sentence is correct. Then, on your own paper, revise each fragment and run-on to form a clear, complete sentence. [Note: There may be more than one correct way to revise each item.]

EX. ___frag.___ 1. After we saw the movie.

   1. *After we saw the movie, we bought a vegetable pizza.*

_____ 1. Dr. Petrakis is my dentist, she cleaned my teeth.

_____ 2. The character played by Rita Moreno in the movie.

_____ 3. Chili usually contains beans, sometimes it contains no meat.

_____ 4. Spanish settlers brought horses to North and South America.

_____ 5. Photographs taken by my grandfather when my father was a young boy.

_____ 6. Sitting on the back porch, playing a board game.

_____ 7. The Dodgers once played baseball in Brooklyn, New York, today they play in Los Angeles.

_____ 8. The singers went to Russia on a concert tour the Russian teenagers seemed to enjoy their music.

_____ 9. Georgio missed the bus, he was late for school.

_____ 10. Who left this jacket on the playing field after the game.

## B. Revising Fragments and Run-on Sentences

In the following paragraph, identify each fragment or run-on sentence. Then, on your own paper, revise each fragment and run-on, changing the punctuation and capitalization as needed to make a clear and complete sentence. [Note: There may be more than one correct way to make each revision.]

EX. 1 Thor Heyerdahl journeyed. To Rapa Nui from Norway.

   1. *Thor Heyerdahl journeyed to Rapa Nui from Norway.*

1    For almost forty years, archaeologists have studied the island

2  of Rapa Nui. Which is part of Polynesia, in the Pacific Ocean. One

3  leading archaeologist who studied Rapa Nui. Thor Heyerdahl.

4   Heyerdahl made many excavations on Rapa Nui in the 1950s,

5   further archaeological studies continue today by archaeologists

6   from Chile and the United States. Uncovered the sites of many

7   early villages and temples. The studies of Rapa Nui by foreign

8   scientists have greatly affected the island's culture, those effects

9   have been both good and bad. Modern people of Rapa Nui great

10   cultural pride from the remains of the beautiful temples. And

11   other hints about the glorious past of Rapa Nui. Books and

12   articles about the archaeological findings on Rapa Nui. Brought

13   many tourists to the island. Helped the island's economy. But

14   there have been bad effects, too, the history of the island has been

15   written largely through the eyes of its visitors. Legends that may

16   not be true appear in many books. As facts. Over the last forty

17   years, the arts and crafts of the island have changed. To match the

18   tastes of the many tourists. Rapa Nui is a beautiful island

19   community with a rich history and culture. Which should be

20   respected, and not changed, by visitors from foreign lands.

## C.   Recreating a Message

You are a member of an archaeological team in the year 2500, and you have been digging at a site outside your school. You have uncovered some torn pieces of paper. The words on the pieces are shown below. Many contain sentence fragments. Study these pieces, and use them to reconstruct a message in complete, clear sentences. Combine fragments to form sentences, adding whatever words, punctuation marks, and capital letters you need. Write the message on your own paper.

EX.   stopped running          on the highway          tank was empty
      *Our car stopped running on the highway because the gasoline tank was
      empty.*

| | |
|---|---|
| as far as three blocks away | because we were late |
| missed the big moment | when Darcy kicked the extra point |
| score 7–0 | could hear |
| jumping up and down | started running |
| cheering of the fans | greatest games I had ever seen |

# COMBINING BY INSERTING WORDS

**8g  You can combine short sentences by inserting a key word from one sentence into another.**

You may need to eliminate some of the words in sentences that are combined. You may also need to change the form of the key word.

| Using the Same Form | |
|---|---|
| **Original** | Ogden Nash wrote many short poems. His poems are funny. |
| **Combined** | Ogden Nash wrote many short, **funny** poems. |
| **Changing the Form** | |
| **Original** | Alexandre Dumas was a famous writer. He was from France. |
| **Combined** | Alexandre Dumas was a famous **French** writer. |

When you change the form of a word, you often add an ending that makes the word an adjective or an adverb. Usually this ending is *–ed*, *–ing*, or *–ly*.

## EXERCISE 5   Combining Sentences by Inserting Words

On your own paper, combine each of the following pairs of sentences by inserting the italicized word from the second sentence into the first sentence. The directions in parentheses will tell you how to change the word form if it is necessary to do so.

EX.  1.  My friend Bianca Guerra is a painter. She has *talent*. (Add *–ed* to *talent*.)

  1.  My friend Bianca Guerra is a talented painter.

1.  Her painting is not finished. It is not *complete*. (Add *–ly* to *complete*.)
2.  The painting contains many colors. The colors are *bright*.
3.  Bianca has created a painting of a sunset. Her painting is *beautiful*.
4.  If you look closely, you can see many details. The details are *hiding*. (Change *hiding* to *hidden*.)

5. Can you see the flock of birds in the sunset? The birds are *flying*.

6. Also, notice the reflection of the sun. The sun is *setting*.

7. In the reflection, a tiny sailboat floats on the water. The boat's floating seems *smooth*. (Add *–ly* to *smooth*.)

8. The sun makes the trees cast long shadows. The sun makes the trees cast *dark* shadows.

9. All of the details make for a beautiful picture. The picture has *drama*. (Change *drama* to *dramatic*.)

10. Bianca used a photograph of a scene as a model for this picture. The scene is in *Spain*, (Change *Spain* to *Spanish*.)

## EXERCISE 6   Combining Sentences by Inserting Words

On your own paper, combine each pair of sentences below by inserting words. Add commas and change the forms of words whenever you need to. [Note: There may be more than one correct way to combine each pair.]

EX. 1. The children's museum in our town is on Walnut Street. It is in the second block.

   1. The children's museum in our town is in the second block on Walnut Street.

1. I first went to the museum when I was a child. I was young.

2. In many museums, visitors can't pick up the exhibits. The visitors can't touch the exhibits.

3. At this museum, you can touch all the exhibits. It's a wonderful museum.

4. There are hundreds of exhibits. Each exhibit provides a challenge.

5. Liquid in a tank recreates the movement of ocean waves. The waves roll.

6. On the second floor of the museum, there's an oversized telephone. It is about three feet high.

7. Very young children love this telephone. They can climb all over it.

8. They can call any number on the phone. They can hear the phone ring.

9. A favorite spot of mine is the room called "Grandma's Attic." This room has trunks of old clothes to try on.

10. There is also a box of fancy hats. Some hats are old and some hats are new.

# COMBINING BY INSERTING PHRASES

You can also combine closely related sentences by taking a phrase from one sentence and inserting it into another sentence.

**8h** **A *prepositional phrase*, a preposition with its object, can usually be inserted into another sentence with no changes. You may need to leave out some of the words in one of the sentences.**

ORIGINAL    The houses along the coast were damaged. They were damaged by the storm.

REVISED    The houses along the coast were damaged **by the storm**.

A *participial phrase* acts as an adjective, modifying a noun or pronoun. It contains a verb form that usually ends in *–ing* or *–ed*.

**8i** **Sometimes you can combine two related sentences by changing the verb from one sentence into a participle and inserting the new participial phrase into the other sentence. When you insert the participial phrase into the sentence, place it close to the noun or pronoun that it modifies. Otherwise, you may confuse your reader.**

ORIGINAL    Al saw a herd of wild deer. Al sat on the back porch.
REVISED    **Sitting on the back porch,** Al saw a herd of wild deer.

An *appositive phrase* follows a noun or pronoun and helps to explain it.

**8j** **Sometimes you can combine two related sentences by changing one of the sentences into an appositive phrase.**

ORIGINAL    Dr. LaPorte has written a symphony. He is the conductor of the school orchestra.

REVISED    Dr. LaPorte, **the conductor of the school orchestra,** has written a symphony.

## EXERCISE 7    Combining Sentences by Inserting Phrases

On your own paper, revise each of the following pairs of sentences to make one sentence. The words you need to insert are italicized, and the directions in parentheses will help you. [Note: There may be more than one correct way to combine the sentences.]

EX.    1.    The painting is upside down. The painting *hangs on the living room wall*. (Insert a participial phrase.)

    1.    The painting hanging on the living room wall is upside down.

1.    I had cantaloupe for breakfast. Cantaloupe is *my favorite fruit*. (Insert an appositive phrase.)

2. She wore the suit. The suit had *green and white stripes*. (Insert a prepositional phrase.)

3. The Nile River flows for approximately 4,145 miles. The Nile River is *the longest river in the world*. (Insert an appositive phrase.)

4. The children ran through the sprinkler. The children were *laughing loudly*. (Insert a participial phrase.)

5. Earl won a first-place trophy. Earl *competed in acrobatics*. (Insert a participial phrase.)

6. Judith plays field hockey. Judith is *my oldest sister*. (Insert an appositive phrase.)

7. We moved the desk from my room. We moved the desk *to the garage*. (Insert a prepositional phrase.)

8. Our guide explained Mayan mythology. He used charts of the Milky Way. (Insert a participial phrase.)

9. All afternoon, Lou and I lay on the beach. The beach is *at La Jolla*. (Insert a prepositional phrase.)

10. I like these books. These books were *written by Naguib Mahfouz*. (Insert a participial phrase.)

## EXERCISE 8    Combining Sentences by Inserting Phrases

On your own paper, revise each pair of sentences below by inserting a phrase to make one sentence. Use your own judgment as you combine the sentences.

EX.    1.  The bones were found in a gravel pit. The pit was in the town of Piltdown.

    1.  The bones were found in a gravel pit in the town of Piltdown.

1. We read about the case of the "Piltdown Man." It was a famous hoax.

2. Parts of a skull and a jawbone were found at Piltdown, England. They were discovered between 1908 and 1912.

3. Scientists examined the bones. Scientists decided that they were very old.

4. Some scientists believed they had found the remains of a human. They believed that the human was from prehistoric times.

5. Other scientists disagreed. Other scientists did not believe the bones were 250,000 years old.

# COMPOUND ELEMENTS

**8k  You can combine sentences that have either the same subject or the same verb by making a compound subject or a compound verb. Add a coordinating conjunction such as *and, but, or, nor,* or *yet*.**

ORIGINAL   Serbia was once part of Yugoslavia. Bosnia was once part of Yugoslavia. [different subjects with same verb]

REVISED   **Serbia and Bosnia** were once part of Yugoslavia. [compound subject with same verb]

ORIGINAL   The planet Mercury measures 3,100 miles at its equator. The planet Mercury has an average surface temperature of 177° Celsius. [different verbs with same subject]

REVISED   The planet Mercury **measures** 3,100 miles at its equator **and has** an average surface temperature of 177° Celsius. [compound verb with same subject]

**8l  You can combine two related sentences by making a *compound sentence*. A compound sentence is two or more simple sentences linked by a comma and a coordinating conjunction, a semicolon, or a semicolon and a conjunctive adverb. Before linking two thoughts to make a compound sentence, make sure that the thoughts are related to one another and are equal in importance.**

ORIGINAL   Ralph collects old coins. Gina collects postage stamps from South America.

REVISED   Ralph collects old coins, **and** Gina collects postage stamps from South America. [comma and coordinating conjunction]
Ralph collects old coins; Gina collects postage stamps from South America. [semicolon]
Ralph collects old coins; **however**, Gina collects postage stamps from South America. [semicolon and conjunctive adverb]

## EXERCISE 9   Creating Sentences with Compound Subjects and Compound Verbs

On your own paper, revise each of the following pairs of sentences to make one sentence that contains either a compound subject or a compound verb.

EX.   1.  Lemons are citrus fruits. Limes are also citrus fruits.

  1.  Lemons and limes are citrus fruits.

1.  Citrus trees grow wild in parts of Asia. Citrus trees are cultivated on farms in many other places.

2. Citrus trees keep their leaves all year round. They produce fragrant flowers.

3. In the United States, Florida produces a great supply of citrus fruits. Texas produces a great supply as well.

4. Citrus plants thrive in places where there is no frost. They prefer a slightly cool, tropical climate.

5. The kumquat is a citrus fruit with bright orange skin. Similarly, the tangerine is a citrus fruit with bright orange skin.

6. My favorite citrus fruit is grapefruit. My mother's favorite citrus fruit is grapefruit.

7. I usually cut a grapefruit in half. I scoop out the fruit with a spoon.

8. Citrus fruits supply vitamin C. They also contain minerals.

9. The citron tastes sour. The lemon also tastes sour.

10. The rind, or skin, of the citron is often processed. It is used in cakes and candies.

## EXERCISE 10   Combining Simple Sentences into Compound Sentences

On your own paper, combine each pair of sentences below to form a compound sentence. [Note: There is more than one correct way to combine each pair.]

EX. 1.   My grandfather left France in 1966. My grandmother left Spain at about the same time.

1.   My grandfather left France in 1966, and my grandmother left Spain at about the same time.

1. Granddad worked as a carpenter in New York City. Grandma was a cook in a nearby restaurant.

2. Times were tough back then. Granddad rarely had enough money to eat at the restaurant.

3. But he met my grandmother one day at the vegetable store. They talked and talked.

4. They were married a year later. Granddad's "tough times" suddenly became very full and happy.

5. For years I have heard stories about Grandma and Grandpa. I like to hear these stories.

# COMBINING THROUGH SUBORDINATION

A *complex sentence* includes one independent clause—a clause that can stand alone as a sentence. It also has one or more subordinate clauses—clauses that cannot stand alone as sentences.

**8m You can combine two sentences by turning one sentence into an *adjective clause*. To do this, insert *who, which,* or *that* in place of the subject. Then use the new subordinate clause to give information about a noun or a pronoun in the other sentence.**

ORIGINAL     Lionel Ritchie is a famous singer. He was once a member of a singing group called The Commodores.

REVISED     Lionel Ritchie is a famous singer **who was once a member of a singing group called The Commodores.**

**8n You can combine sentences by turning one sentence into an *adverb clause*. Begin the adverb clause with a subordinating conjunction such as *after, although, because, if, when,* or *where.* Choose the subordinating conjunction that shows the relationship between the ideas in the adverb clause and those in the independent clause. Then use the new subordinate clause to give information about a verb, an adjective, or another adverb in the independent clause.**

When you use an adverb clause at the beginning of a sentence, use a comma to separate it from the independent clause.

ORIGINAL     The concert was over. I went backstage and met Lionel Ritchie.

REVISED     **When the concert was over**, I went backstage and met Lionel Ritchie. [The subordinating conjunction *when* shows how the ideas are related in time.]

**8o You can combine two sentences by turning one sentence into a *noun clause* and inserting it into the other sentence just like an ordinary noun. Begin the noun clause with a word such as *that, how,* or *who.***

When you place the noun clause in the other sentence, you may have to change or remove some words.

ORIGINAL     Lionel Ritchie is friendly to his fans. This fact was made obvious to me by his warm greeting.

REVISED     **That Lionel Ritchie is friendly to his fans** was made obvious to me by his warm greeting. [The word *that* introduces the noun clause, which becomes the subject of the verb *was*.]

## EXERCISE 11    Combining Sentences into Complex Sentences

On your own paper, revise each pair of sentences below to make a complex sentence. You may need to change or take out some words to make smooth combinations. [Note: There may be more than one correct way to combine each pair of sentences.]

EX.    1.  Granville Woods was an African American inventor. He was born in Columbus, Ohio, in 1856.

    1.  Granville Woods was an African American inventor who was born in Columbus, Ohio, in 1856.

1.  Granville Woods left school at the age of ten. Then he went to work at a machine shop.

2.  He worked. At the same time, he went to night school and, later, to college.

3.  He was a genius. This fact can be proved by his inventions.

4.  He invented a system of electric signals. It helped trains communicate with stations along their routes.

5.  The signals told the crews on the moving trains about the locations of other trains. There were far fewer accidents and collisions.

6.  Woods sold the device through a company. He established the company himself.

7.  He also invented an incubator. It helped poultry farmers.

8.  Chickens laid eggs. Then the eggs were put into the warm incubator to hatch.

9.  This device led to modern machines. The modern machines can hatch fifty thousand eggs at one time.

10. Granville Woods was a great inventor. He died of a stroke in Harlem Hospital in 1910.

11. Another inventor was Christopher Latham Sholes. He developed his ideas during the late 1800s.

12. With the help of two other men, he invented the first practical typewriter. This typewriter was patented in 1868.

13. Sholes was also a newspaper editor and a state legislator. Sholes held these positions before he invented the typewriter.

14. In 1884, Ottmar Mergenthaler patented the Linotype machine. Mergenthaler was a German living in the United States.

15. The Linotype is a printing machine. This printing machine creates a complete line of type at one time.

# IMPROVING SENTENCE STYLE

Combining short sentences to link related ideas can bring variety and interest to your writing. But always avoid *stringy sentences* and *wordy sentences*.

**8p  A *stringy sentence* has too many independent clauses strung together. Since all the ideas are treated equally, the reader has trouble understanding how they are related.**

There are two ways you can fix a stringy sentence.

1.  Break the sentence into two or more sentences.
2.  Turn some of the independent clauses into subordinate clauses or phrases.

STRINGY   Marisa and Gina are the leaders of the food festival, so they called a meeting, and the purpose of the meeting was to get volunteers to help, and we were interested in helping, so we went to the meeting.

BETTER   Marisa and Gina are the leaders of the food festival, so they called a meeting. The purpose of the meeting was to get volunteers to help. We were interested in helping, so we went to the meeting.

BETTER   Marisa and Gina, who are the leaders of the food festival, called a meeting. The purpose of the meeting was to get volunteers to help. Because we were interested in helping, we went to the meeting.

**8q  A *wordy sentence* contains too many words or too many fancy words that are difficult to understand.**

Here are three tips for creating sentences that aren't too wordy.

1.  Don't use more words than you need to.
2.  Don't use fancy words where simple ones will do.
3.  Don't repeat yourself unless it's absolutely necessary.

WORDY   In the event of a storm involving a downfall of water, we shall forego our plans to participate in the competition of football.

IMPROVED   If it rains, we won't play football.

## EXERCISE 12   Revising Stringy and Wordy Sentences

The writer of this letter wants to receive information, but the stringy and wordy sentences get in the way. On your own paper, revise the letter. Make it clearer and more effective.

1   Dear Dr. Feliciano:

2   It has come to my attention from the teacher with whom I am
3   studying science at the local junior high school in my community
4   that due to an assignment that I have received and must
5   accomplish after school hours, I have a requirement to receive
6   information and facts and details. Specifically, I have been
7   assigned the task of acquiring knowledge regarding the
8   importance and necessity of such domestic animals as dogs and
9   cats receiving injections and shots to prevent the dangerous and
10   perilous and hazardous disease of rabies. Is it within the realm of
11   possibility for you to transmit to my person a pamphlet or booklet
12   in regards to the dangerous and perilous and hazardous disease
13   of rabies? Looking ahead to the possibility of the receipt of this
14   material from you fills me with gratitude and thanks.
15                             Sincerely,
16                             Alfred Robinson

Peanuts reprinted by permission of UFS, Inc.

# *VARYING SENTENCE BEGINNINGS*

**8r** **The basic structure of an English sentence is a subject followed by a verb. But following this pattern all the time makes your writing dull. To make your writing more interesting, use different methods to begin some of your sentences.**

To vary the basic structure of your sentences, you might begin with a single-word modifier, a prepositional or participial phrase, or a subordinate clause.

SINGLE-WORD MODIFIER **Frightened**, the dog ran under the bed. [adjective]

PHRASE **Feeling frightened**, the dog ran under the bed. [participial phrase]

SUBORDINATE CLAUSE **Because it was frightened**, the dog ran under the bed. [adverb clause]

## EXERCISE 13   Varying Sentence Beginnings

On the lines provided, revise each of the following sentences by using a variety of sentence beginnings. You may want to add or delete a word to make the sentence sound better. Follow the directions in parentheses.

EX. 1.  Dr. Aponte leaped to her feet in surprise. (single-word modifier)
　　1.  Surprised, Dr. Aponte leaped to her feet.

1. Wide-open spaces and rolling meadows are disappearing in many small towns. (phrase) _____

_____

2. We enjoy Cuban music, so we are thrilled with Gloria Estefan's new album. (adverb clause) _____

_____

3. We were confused, so we asked for directions. (single-word modifier)

_____

_____

4. They were tired, so they stopped for a rest. (participial phrase) _____

_____

5. There are many beautiful canals in the city of Amsterdam. (phrase)

_____

_____

6. Many people enjoy the essays of Agnes Repplier because she wrote
   with a sharp sense of humor. (adverb clause) _____

_____

7. The students were excited and rushed onto the court (single-word
   modifier) _____

_____

8. We saw a mural by Mexican artist Diego Rivera at the National Palace
   in Mexico City. (phrase) _____

_____

9. Hannah was thoughtful and sent her grandmother a postcard. (single-
   word modifier) _____

_____

10. I always laugh whenever I read a story by James Thurber. (adverb
    clause) _____

_____

11. She scored two goals, and she scored them in the first half of the game.
    (phrase) _____

_____

12. Luis drove down the street, and he waved goodbye. (phrase) _____

_____

13. We visited the Blue Grotto; we visited it before we left Capri. (adverb
    clause) _____

_____

14. The game was canceled, so we met at Jared's house. (adverb clause)

_____

_____

15. I was startled, so I dropped the platter of food. (single-word modifier)

_____

_____

# CHAPTER REVIEW

## A. Proofreading a Paragraph for Sentence Fragments and Run-on Sentences

Proofread the paragraph below for sentence fragments and run-on sentences. Then, on your own paper, revise the paragraph. Be sure to change punctuation and capitalization as needed. [Note: There may be more than one correct way to revise each error.]

EX. 1 John Dykstra developed a new camera. For creating special effects in the movies.

   1. John Dykstra developed a new camera for creating special effects in the movies.

1    John Dykstra is a special-effects expert, his work has made

2 such films as *Star Wars* very exciting. Before he entered the movie

3 business, had studied industrial design at Long Beach State

4 College. In California. He began his film career by working with

5 Douglas Trumbull, Trumbull was in charge of all the special effects

6 for *Star Wars*. Dykstra won an Academy Award for the electronic

7 special effects he created. For that film. That achievement made

8 him famous, it also brought him another exciting project. Special-

9 effects creator for a television series called *Battlestar Galactica*. In

10 2002 and 2004, Dykstra was the visual effects designer. To create the

11 visual effects for *Spider-Man* and *Spider-Man 2*.

## B. Revising a Paragraph by Combining Sentences

The following paragraph contains many short, dull, choppy sentences. On your own paper, revise the paragraph by combining sentences that contain related ideas. [Note: There may be more than one way to revise the sentences.]

EX 1. Annuals are delicate flowers. They cannot survive freezing temperatures.

   1. Annuals are delicate flowers that cannot survive freezing temperatures.

1    Most annual flowers have bright colors. Most annual flowers

2 are easy to grow. This makes them popular with gardeners. They

3 are also inexpensive. A garden of annuals is a real bargain. Each

4 seed packet costs about a dollar. Each contains about fifty seeds.

5 A person can grow a plant for about two cents. Marigolds are

6   annual flowers.  Petunias are annual flowers, too.  A small, sunny
7   spot in a yard is a good place to grow them. You could also grow
8   them in a window box in a sunny space. Follow the directions on
9   the seed packet.  Have fun with your bargain garden!

## C.  Revising a Paragraph

The paragraph below contains many of the problems you have studied in
this chapter. Revise the paragraph so that (1) stringy and wordy sentences
are corrected, (2) sentences have varied beginnings, and (3) simple sentences
are combined into compound and complex sentences. [Note: There are
many correct ways to revise and improve this paragraph.]

EX.    1.  She was a photographer. She was an artist. Who painted
           landscapes.

       1.  She was a photographer, and she was an artist who painted
           landscapes.

1        Berthe Morisot was a French painter, and she was part of the
2    movement called Impressionism, and it took place in the
3    nineteenth century.  Edgar Degas, Edouard Manet, Claude
4    Monet, and Auguste Renoir were her colleagues in the movement,
5    and they greatly respected her work, in fact she was the only
6    woman invited to join them.  In the first impressionist exhibition
7    in 1874.  Morisot experimented with color.  So did the other
8    impressionist painters.  For example, in one painting a woman
9    appears in a white robe.  Called *The Bath*.  Many other colors
10   appear within the white of the robe, and they include shades of
11   pink, green, beige, and light purple, and they blend, and they
12   make shadows and creases appear in the robe.  This arresting,
13   dramatic, incredible, masterful piece of painted art is delightful
14   and marvelous to the eye.

# FORMAL ENGLISH

Just as you can change your clothes to suit different occasions, you can also "dress up" or "dress down" your language. Depending on your audience and purpose, your language could be formal, informal, or somewhere in between.

INFORMAL   I caught some z's.        I'm hoppin' mad.
  FORMAL   I napped briefly.         I am extremely angry.

You should use *formal English* when you speak at dignified occasions, such as banquets and dedication ceremonies, or when you write serious papers and reports.

The main differences between formal and informal English are in sentence structure, word choice, and tone. Here are some features of formal English.

SENTENCE STRUCTURE   often long and difficult
      WORD CHOICE   precise; often technical or scientific
             TONE   serious and dignified

## EXERCISE 1   Revising a Paragraph to Replace Inappropriate Language

The following paragraph contains informal language. Above each italicized word or phrase, write language that is more appropriate to a formal report.

                        *great deal of damage*
EX.  [1]  The earthquake created a ~~real mess~~.

[1] The Incas *sure* knew how to build.  [2] They had no modern tools, yet they built these *incredibly neat* foundations.  [3] The foundations were made of stones, and some of these were truly *humongous*.  [4] *Like*, one was fifteen feet tall, and weighed almost a hundred tons.  [5] These *dudes* used stone hammers to shape the stones in the walls.  [6] They used no mortar, but it was *no big deal*. [7] The stones fit together so tightly that even *Mother Nature couldn't knock them down with one of her earthquakes*.  [8] It took modern

scientists years to *smoke out* their methods.  [9] Even so, one step is

still a *big fat question mark*.  [10] How the Incas got the stones to the site

is *anybody's guess.*

## EXERCISE 2    Identifying Formal English

In each sentence below, underline the word or words in parentheses that are formal English.

EX.   1.   That new group plays (groovy tunes, <u>sensational music</u>).

1.   I just read (a really rad, an excellent) book on surfing.

2.   (Chill out, Relax)! We'll meet our deadline.

3.   Alex bought (an attractive, a cool) shirt on sale.

4.   That dress is (outta sight, the lastest fashion).

5.   Unfortunately, John had a (boring party, bogus bash).

6.   The music, flags, and other (attention-getting devices, gimmicks) drew me into the store.

7.   Joshua is wearing some (bad threads, fashionable clothes) today.

8.   Charlene began to (relax, hang loose) once her homework was completed.

9.   We will (skidoo, leave) when the bell rings.

10.   (Snap out of it, Stop worrying). This bridge is safe.

# INFORMAL ENGLISH

*Informal language* is the language you hear around you every day. It is probably the language you use when you talk to your friends and family.

*Informal English* is often used in everyday conversations at home, school, work, and places of recreation. You also find informal English in personal letters, journal entries, and many newspaper and magazine articles.

The main differences between formal and informal English are in sentence structure, word choice, and tone. Here are some features of informal English.

| | |
|---|---|
| SENTENCE STRUCTURE | short and easy |
| WORD CHOICE | simple and ordinary; often includes contractions, colloquialisms, and slang |
| TONE | conversational |

*Colloquialisms* are the informal words and phrases of conversational language. Many colloquialisms are figures of speech that aren't meant to be taken literally.

EXAMPLES    I thought my parents would **have a fit,** but they didn't.
We waited until the rain **let up,** and then we left.
When I wasn't invited to the party, I considered **crashing** it.

*Slang* is made up of newly coined words or of old words used in unconventional ways. It is usually clever and colorful. It is often created by specific groups of people, such as musicians and computer engineers.

EXAMPLES    The orchestra gave an **awesome** concert last night.
This new MP3 player is **cool.**

NOTE    Colloquialisms and slang often fit well in short stories. They can help make your characters believable. However, do not use colloquialisms or slang in test answers, essays, reports, or other types of formal writing.

## EXERCISE 3    Replacing Slang and Colloquialisms with Formal English

On your own paper, rewrite each of the sentences below, using formal English. Use a dictionary to find the meaning of any slang or colloquialism that you do not understand.

EX.   1.  That friend of yours certainly is spacey.
      1.  That friend of yours certainly is eccentric.

1.  At the wedding, all they played was this schmaltzy music.
2.  We're going to be late unless you get a move on.
3.  The night before our trip, I was too keyed up to sleep.
4.  I'm psyched that I got an *A* on my term paper.
5.  This is a holiday weekend, so the cops are going to crack down on speeders.
6.  In our building the rule is to keep your junk off the stairs.
7.  The Brazilian soccer team wiped out every other team that year.
8.  Ms. Molina jumped on us for speaking English in Spanish class.
9.  Perhaps Delia needs a vacation; she has a short fuse after a long day at work.
10.  How can I type my paper if you hog the computer?
11.  Give me a ring when you're ready to leave.
12.  Demetri was an old hand at restringing a guitar.
13.  In order to win first place, Stephen must ace the other bowlers.
14.  The lights suddenly going out caused quite a flap in the lab.
15.  Would you slide those noodles this way, please?
16.  That hunk of a meteor created a tremendous crater.
17.  Mother flipped over the flowers that Carlos sent her.
18.  Bonnie shed some light on our math problem.
19.  How could I draw a blank on my own address?
20.  Kaspar is right up there with the best of the hockey goalies.
21.  I'd better hold up here before I forget something.
22.  Tonight's vegetable soup is a hodgepodge from our garden.
23.  My grandfather footed the bill for my parents' wedding.
24.  Our meeting lasted so long, we decided to send out for supper.
25.  Marjorie and Jim were in cahoots on Mom's birthday gift.

# DENOTATION AND CONNOTATION

The *denotations* of a word are its dictionary meanings. The *connotations* of a word are the meanings suggested by, or associated with, that word.

Two words can have the same denotation yet have very different connotations. For instance, the words *error* and *blunder* have the same denotation. They both mean "mistake." However, the word *blunder* sounds far more negative. It suggests lack of ability or experience. Words can also be neutral, such as the words *walk* or *car*.

Word choice can have an important effect on readers and listeners. To take advantage of this effect, be aware of the connotations that words have.

## EXERCISE 4   Responding to Connotations

For each sentence below, underline the word in parentheses that best fits the sentence. On the line after the sentence, write the reason for your choice.

EX.   1.   The evening air felt pleasant, so Miguel (*strolled*, *plodded*) downtown.
          *Strolled creates a more relaxed image than plodded.*

1. My parents (*screamed*, *cheered*) when I crossed the finish line first.

   _____

   _____

2. This antique clock is expensive because it is (*unique*, *strange*).

   _____

   _____

3. No one was surprised when the (*daring*, *reckless*) explorer was injured. _____

   _____

4. Mrs. Cohen is one of my favorite teachers; she's (*stubborn*, *firm*), but she's fair. _____

   _____

## EXERCISE 5    Analyzing the Connotations of Words

Decide which of the words below have positive connotations, which have negative ones, and which are neutral. On the line before each word, write *pos.* for *positive*, *neg.* for *negative*, or *neut.* for *neutral*.

EX.    _neg._  1. dangerous

_____  1. precious

_____  2. green

_____  3. adventuresome

_____  4. pushy

_____  5. diagonal

_____  6. cozy

_____  7. slimy

_____  8. gallant

_____  9. scorch

_____ 10. middle

_____ 11. jealous

_____ 12. magnificent

_____ 13. pastel

_____ 14. sloppy

_____ 15. fascinating

_____ 16. eastward

_____ 17. steal

_____ 18. sixteen

_____ 19. destroy

_____ 20. beautiful

_____ 21. coward

_____ 22. nosy

_____ 23. easy

_____ 24. gossip

_____ 25. brief

_____ 26. dirty

_____ 27. gentle

_____ 28. fake

_____ 29. lying

_____ 30. gleaming

_____ 31. joyful

_____ 32. elementary

_____ 33. conceited

_____ 34. ignore

_____ 35. temporary

_____ 36. cheap

_____ 37. dusty

_____ 38. snuggle

_____ 39. unprepared

_____ 40. neatly

_____ 41. concerned

_____ 42. elegant

_____ 43. last

_____ 44. faithful

_____ 45. twinkle

_____ 46. obvious

_____ 47. thirsty

_____ 48. noisy

_____ 49. distinguished

_____ 50. everlasting

## CHAPTER REVIEW

### A. Identifying Formal English

In each sentence below, underline the word or words in parentheses that are formal English.

EX. 1. Our last ride at the amusement park was really (*wild*, <u>*exciting*</u>)!

1. The statue is inside a temple, so don't (*act up*, *misbehave*).

2. Those people speak a (*lingo*, *language*) that I don't understand.

3. Our sergeant did not want to hear any (*arguments*, *lip*).

4. I've been feeling (*weak*, *run-down*) since this cough began.

5. One Russian queen had more than fifteen thousand dresses (*hanging*, *squirreled away*) in closets.

6. My (*pal*, *friend*) and I will start with the tabouli.

7. On weekends, I like to (*be*, *hang*) with my friends.

8. The jeans that I want cost thirty-five (*bucks*, *dollars*).

9. Dr. Cabral is the only (*highbrow*, *intellectual*) speaker on the program.

10. This meal is free, so let's (*chow down*, *eat it*) and enjoy it.

### B. Revising Informal English

On your own paper, rewrite each of the sentences below using formal English.

EX. 1. That guy doesn't have a clue!
   1. That man does not understand what is happening.

1. When Ali learned he had won, he was on top of the world!
2. Don't bug me about my homework, because it's done.
3. I guess you can kiss that money goodbye.
4. We haven't won a single game, so let's call it quits.
5. Gloria and Margaret raced neck and neck for the finish line.
6. Finally, we were only one light-year away from solving the chemistry equation.
7. Eliot made a mad dash for the door at the same time as Terry.
8. How many teeny-boppers are at the party tonight?
9. For some reason, Terrel is at the tail end of the line every day.
10. The teacher said the scores on our geometry test were bodacious.

## C.   Analyzing the Connotations of Words

For each sentence below, decide whether the italicized word or phrase has the correct connotation. If it does not, write a better word or phrase choice on the line before the sentence. If it does, write C.

EX. _____mohair_____   1.  One mannequin wore a beautiful, *hairy* sweater.

_____   1.  My father works the night shift, so we all try to *sneak around* the house when he's sleeping.

_____   2.  The entire apartment *reeked* of baking bread.

_____   3.  The new girl that I *confronted* in Spanish class is very pleasant.

_____   4.  Although I did not win first prize, I feel *smug* that I tried.

_____   5.  I love the Canadian flag, with its *garish* maple-leaf design.

_____   6.  Determined women are *wishing for* equal treatment in the job market.

_____   7.  After such a hot day, the *cool* night air felt wonderful.

_____   8.  Each pilgrim enters Mecca wearing a *sanitized* white robe.

_____   9.  Your room is lovely, and it is easy to clean because it's *cramped*.

_____  10.  The politician *nagged* everyone to vote for him.

## D.   Collaborating on Connotations

Using your own paper, work with two or three partners to list at least ten animals that could have positive and negative connotations when used to describe people. Then choose five animals from your list. On the same page, write five sentences. In each sentence use a different animal to describe a person. Label each sentence as positive, negative, or neutral connotations.

EX.   1.  swan
      Consuela is as graceful as a swan. (positive)

# NOUNS

| The Eight Parts of Speech | | | |
|---|---|---|---|
| noun | adjective | pronoun | conjunction |
| verb | adverb | preposition | interjection |

**10a** A *noun* is a word used to name a person, a place, a thing, or an idea.

| | |
|---|---|
| **Persons** | sister, Uncle Abdul, weaver, friends |
| **Places** | house, Malaysia, Milky Way, Detroit |
| **Things** | chopsticks, August, Skylab, table |
| **Ideas** | love, hate, cooperation, courage |

**10b** A *proper noun* is a word that names a particular person, place, thing, or idea and is always capitalized. A *common noun* is a word that names any one of a group of persons, places, things, or ideas and is not capitalized.

| Common Nouns | Proper Nouns |
|---|---|
| singer | Leontyne Price, Willie Colon |
| scientist | Leo Esaki, Marie Curie |
| country | China, Canada |
| holiday | New Year's Day, Labor Day |
| school | Dwight Morrow High School |

**10c** A *concrete noun* names an object that can be perceived by the senses. An *abstract noun* names an idea, a feeling, a quality, or a characteristic.

| | |
|---|---|
| **Concrete Nouns** | fog, milk, barrel, key, lightning |
| **Abstract Nouns** | enthusiasm, pity, ambition, joy |

**EXERCISE 1    Identifying Common Nouns and Proper Nouns**

Underline all of the nouns in the sentences below. If a noun is a proper noun, underline it twice.

EX.    1.    The jogger jumped onto a bus that was going down Broadway.

1.    Dan and his wife Lisa have invented a new way of celebrating

Thanksgiving.

2.    The train traveled across Wyoming and into Utah.

3.    China was hit by a severe earthquake on Tuesday.

4.    A cheetah is known for its speed and beauty.

5.    Our new teacher is an expert on jazz.

6.    The doctor knew that measles had caused the blindness.

7.    In the morning, the mat is rolled up and placed in a small closet.

8.    The Great Wall of China is truly an amazing sight!

9.    That haiku was written by Matsuo Bashō.

10.    The witness rose and placed her right hand on the Bible.

**EXERCISE 2    Identifying Abstract Nouns and Concrete Nouns**

In the sentences below, underline the abstract nouns once and the concrete nouns twice.

EX.    1.    Our first concert was a success.

1.    Oneida certainly has the talent to become a great painter.

2.    Reverend Ross can discuss all the major religions very well.

3.    On Friday the Sargent Memorial Library will be closed.

4.    Suddenly the screen was filled with pictures of robots.

5.    A variety of dips accompanied the vegetables.

6.    For his report, Jonah read a book about the history of airplanes and

locomotives.

7.    People need different kinds of abilities.

8.    Uncle Joe wrote a poem about his dreams.

9.    After the loss, the players showed their disappointment.

10.    Is it true that computers speed up communication?

# COMPOUND NOUNS

**10d** A *compound noun* consists of two or more words used together as a single noun. The parts of a compound noun may be written as one word. They may also be written as two or more words or as a hyphenated word.

| One Word | bodyguard, footprint, newspaper |
|---|---|
| Two or More Words | high school, Kalahari Desert, League of Nations |
| Hyphenated Word | great-grandmother, left-hander |

NOTE  If you are not sure how to write a compound noun, look it up in a dictionary. Some dictionaries may give two correct forms for a word. For example, you may find the word *vice-president* written both with and without the hyphen. As a rule, use the form your dictionary lists first.

## EXERCISE 3   Identifying Compound Nouns

Underline the compound nouns in the sentences below.

EX.   1.   The Gateway Arch is a beautiful structure.

1.   At last, Cheng Ho reached the Persian Gulf.

2.   Your bill of sale is proof that you paid.

3.   The nation watched in horror as the spacecraft fell.

4.   The experiment will test how long the night light will burn.

5.   The new cast will be listed on the bulletin board in the hallway.

6.   I'm taking this course so that I can be a lifeguard next summer.

7.   We were supposed to find the icecap on the map.

8.   You can take my sleeping bag when you go fly-fishing.

9.   Do you know how many patents Thomas Alva Edison held?

10.   Some arrowheads were made of flint and some of bone.

## REVIEW EXERCISE 1

### A. Identifying Common, Proper, and Compound Nouns

In the paragraph below, underline the common nouns once and the proper nouns twice. Circle the compound nouns. [ Note: Some nouns may fit into more than one category.]

EX.   [1] This (newspaper) stated that Samoyeds are useful animals.

[1] At the beginning of the Space Age, scientists placed a white dog inside *Sputnik II.* [2] The dog, Laika, was a Samoyed, a breed known for its sweet disposition.  [3] Samoyeds were originally used by nomadic people in Siberia to herd reindeer and to pull sleds.

[4] However, this animal from the former Soviet Union accomplished a new task.  [5] Laika became the first living creature to orbit our planet.

[6] Laika is also probably the first dog ever to be at an altitude of 1,050 miles above the earth.  [7] We do not know exactly why Laika was chosen, but there are three possible reasons.  [8] First, its husky build and heavy fur coat allow the Samoyed to stand changes in temperature.  [9] Second, the Russians probably wanted a breed of dog from Russia. [10] Third, its strength and intelligence probably helped the Samoyed endure the hardships of the trip.

### B. Classifying Abstract and Concrete Nouns

In the sentences below, underline the abstract nouns once and the concrete nouns twice.

EX.   1.  Do I need talent or luck to become an actor?

1.  My sister and I go to the movies on weekends.

2.  She likes films that are full of romance.

3.  I prefer adventures with characters who show courage.

4.  Is this film about people fighting for their freedom?

5.  The Texans, along with many other people, fought with great bravery at the Alamo.

96

# PRONOUNS

**10e** A *pronoun* is a word used in place of a noun or more than one noun. This noun, called an *antecedent*, gives the pronoun its meaning.

| Personal Pronouns | I, me, my, mine, we, us, our, ours, you, your, yours, he, him, his, she, her, hers, it, its, they, them, their, theirs |
|---|---|
| Reflexive Pronouns | myself, ourselves, yourself, yourselves, himself, herself, itself, themselves |
| Indefinite Pronouns | all, another, any, anyone, both, each, everybody, one, everything, few, many, most, no one, some, several |

EXAMPLES **Miguel** said that **he** spoke three languages. [*Miguel* is the antecedent of the pronoun *he*.]

Did **Kim** leave **her** wallet on the bus?

Go across the **George Washington Bridge. It** will take you into New York City. [*George Washington Bridge* is the antecedent of the pronoun *It*.]

Notice that a pronoun may appear in the same sentence as its antecedent or in a following sentence.

 NOTE Some pronouns, such as possessive forms of pronouns (*my, your,* and *her*) and indefinite pronouns (*all, any,* and *some*) may also be classified as adjectives. Follow your teacher's instructions regarding these forms.

### Identifying Pronouns

Underline all the pronouns in the following paragraph.

EX. [1] Kim invited <u>me</u> over to <u>her</u> house.

[1] Kim introduced me to her parents because I had never met them. [2] Kim's father showed me the used envelopes he collects.

[3] Each is special because it has an advertisement printed on it.

[4] Postage meters print the ads while they are printing the postage.

[5] I had never noticed the ads before! [6] On some envelopes you see only words such as "Use Air Mail." [7] However, I particularly liked the ones with pictures on them. [8] Several included animals, appliances, or airplanes. [9] The next time you get commercial mail, look at it carefully. [10] You can look at the postmark to see if an advertisement is printed next to it.

## EXERCISE    Identifying Pronouns and Antecedents

Underline all the pronouns in the following paragraph. On the numbered lines after the paragraph, write the pronouns and their antecedents.

EX.    [1] Numerous pirates were men, but not all of them.
       1. them—pirates

[1] Piracy was common in nineteenth-century China, and not only men were practicing it. [2] A woman named Hsi Kai Ching Yih earned herself a place in history as a famous pirate. [3] Her husband, Ching Yih, was a pirate off the coast of China. [4] Ching Yih married Hsi Kai in 1807 and promised her half of his property. [5] At the time, his property included six squadrons of ships. [6] Ching Yih was lost at sea, and his wife took command of the fleet. [7] At one time, she controlled almost two thousand ships! [8] They were crewed by a total of over fifty thousand pirates. [9] Madame Ching later retired from her adventures at sea. [10] The emperor of China wanted peace, so he gave her a position of honor and a palace.

1. _____        6. _____

2. _____        7. _____

3. _____        8. _____

4. _____        9. _____

5. _____       10. _____

# ADJECTIVES

**10f    An *adjective* is a word used to modify a noun or a pronoun.**

To *modify* a word means to describe the word or to make its meaning more definite. An adjective modifies a noun or a pronoun by telling *what kind, which one,* or *how many.*

| What kind? | **green** leaves, **slow** bus |
|---|---|
| Which one? | **second** book, **first** one |
| How many? | **forty** people, **three** tacos |

The most frequently used adjectives are *a, an,* and *the.* These words are usually called **articles.** *A* and *an* are **indefinite articles.** They indicate that a noun refers to one of a general group. *A* is used before words beginning with a consonant sound. *An* is used before words beginning with a vowel sound.

EXAMPLES    **A** bell rang.      **An** hour had passed.

*The* is a **definite article.** It indicates that a noun refers to someone or something in particular.

EXAMPLES    **The** bell rang.    **The** hour had passed.

An adjective usually comes before the noun or pronoun it modifies. In some cases, adjectives follow the words they modify. Sometimes, other words separate an adjective from the noun or pronoun that it modifies.

EXAMPLES    The **blue** water attracted us. [adjective comes before noun]
The water, **blue** and **cool**, attracted us. [adjectives follow noun]
The water felt **cool**. [word separates adjective from noun]

## EXERCISE 6   Identifying Adjectives

Underline each adjective in the following sentences. Do not include definite or indefinite articles.

EX.    1.  A <u>magnificent</u> statue stood in the <u>empty</u> hall.

1.  Paul saw many medieval manuscripts in the local museum.

2.  One manuscript, old and torn, was about a legendary hero.

3.  Rodrigo was young, strong, and handsome.

4. He liked fast horses and vigorous activities, including fencing.

5. He became a fierce warrior and a great leader.

6. He fought many long battles in distant countries.

7. In four battles, he carried a jeweled, gleaming sword.

8. Years later, at a splendid ceremony, he became a knight.

9. Proud Rodrigo welcomed relatives and old friends to the ceremony.

10. Knights in colorful clothing and ladies in elegant dresses applauded.

## EXERCISE 7    Revising Sentences by Supplying Adjectives

Supply adjectives for the sentences below. Write the adjectives on the lines in the sentences.

EX.  1.  Matsu lived in a _____ large _____ apartment building.

1. Down the street was a _____ shopping center.

2. One store had _____ clothes.

3. Another store looked _____ .

4. The _____ bus stopped for me.

5. At dawn the streets were _____ and

    _____ .

6. Our _____ steps are _____ , so be careful.

7. _____ people stood impatiently beside the

    _____ sign.

8. Who gave us _____ tickets?

9. You need a _____ jacket and tie for this job.

10. The crowd at the stadium sounded _____ and

    _____ .

# PRONOUNS AND NOUNS USED AS ADJECTIVES

**10g**   **Some words may be used as either pronouns or adjectives. When used as pronouns, these words take the place of nouns. When used as adjectives, they modify nouns.**

| Pronoun | Adjective |
|---|---|
| Take **this**. | Use **this** brush. |
| **Neither** is home. | **Neither** person is home. |

The words *mine, my, your, yours, his, her, hers, its, our, ours, their,* and *theirs* are called pronouns in this book. They are the *possessive* forms of personal pronouns, showing ownership or relationship. Some teachers prefer to call such words adjectives because the words tell *which one* about nouns: *my* radio, *your* ticket. Follow your teacher's instructions in labeling such words.

When a noun is used as an adjective, your teacher may prefer that you call it an adjective. Proper nouns used as adjectives are called *proper adjectives.*

**10h**   **Some words may be used as either nouns or adjectives.**

| | | |
|---|---|---|
| COMMON NOUNS | **autumn** | **water** |
| ADJECTIVES | **autumn** leaves | **water** safety |
| PROPER NOUNS | **New York** | **Navajo** |
| ADJECTIVES | **New York** bank | **Navajo** blanket |

## EXERCISE 8   Identifying Nouns, Pronouns, and Adjectives

Identify each italicized word in the following sentences. Write *n.* for *noun,* *pron.* for *pronoun,* or *adj.* for *adjective* on the line before each sentence.

EX.   _adj._   1. Mario gave his mother an *electric* wok.

_____ 1. Her birthday is *next* week.

_____ 2. Mrs. Vargas said that woks are very *useful.*

_____ 3. Only *some* are electric.

_____ 4. Most woks need a separate *heat* source.

_____ 5. Now she is cooking summer dishes, such as celery *salad.*

_____  6.  That recipe came from a *Chinese* cookbook.

_____  7.  Soon she will make heartier dishes for *winter*.

_____  8.  *That* is my favorite time of year.

_____  9.  Maybe she will make *that* duck dish we like.

_____ 10.  I think it's called *Shanghai* duck.

_____ 11.  Did Hideko bring the *cheese* sandwiches or the chips?

_____ 12.  Kevin and I need *some* help, Ms. Thompson.

_____ 13.  Dr. Kostas is traveling to *Chicago* next Wednesday.

_____ 14.  The weather report warned *Texas* residents about a possible hurricane.

_____ 15.  Do you like *that*?

_____ 16.  *Either* person could work at the concession stand.

_____ 17.  The *bitter* cold caused several pipes to freeze.

_____ 18.  *Summer* is my favorite time of year.

_____ 19.  *Neither* looks good enough to eat.

_____ 20.  The *Thanksgiving* choir program was a success.

## EXERCISE 9    Revising Sentences by Using Appropriate Adjectives

For each sentence below, add at least one common or proper noun used as an adjective. Write your revised sentences on your own paper.

EX.  1.  The cat approached the woman.
    1.  *The Siamese cat approached the young woman.*

1.  The house was built on a road near me.

2.  Trucks rumbled past the store on the corner.

3.  A clerk helped me find a sweater.

4.  Becky gave a speech in front of the students.

5.  On the dresser lay a box.

## REVIEW EXERCISE 2

### A. Identifying Nouns, Pronouns, and Adjectives

In each of the sentences below, tell how the italicized word is used. Write *comm.* for *common noun*, *prop.* for *proper noun*, *comp.* for *compound noun*, *pron.* for *pronoun*, or *adj.* for *adjective*. [Note: Some nouns may fit into more than one category.]

EX. <u>comm.</u> 1. This *ticket* is yours.

_____ 1. You can almost feel the *excitement*!

_____ 2. *Everyone* is waiting to board the submarine.

_____ 3. Is it a *nuclear* submarine?

_____ 4. This ship can stay underwater for *weeks*!

_____ 5. Didn't *Ferdinand Magellan* travel on this route?

_____ 6. This submarine took *twelve* weeks for its journey.

_____ 7. *This* must be as long as a football field!

_____ 8. The galley, *small* but complete, is below the control room.

_____ 9. This ship even has a *recreation room* on it.

_____ 10. I've never seen *anything* like it.

### B. Identifying Abstract and Concrete Nouns

In each of the sentences below, underline the abstract nouns once and the concrete nouns twice.

EX. 1. A <u>day</u> in the <u><u>mountains</u></u> could end your <u>troubles</u>.

1. "Are you ready?" Joe asked Eddie, with excitement in his voice.

2. "Don't we need food and water for the trip?" asked Eddie.

3. Eddie hid his fear when he saw the gigantic mountain.

4. They climbed the mountain with great determination.

5. Because Joe had always wanted to be a mountain climber, his enthusiasm was great .

6. When they reached the top, their spirits soared.

7. As soon as they returned, their mother sighed with relief.

8. "It's an honor to know such brave young men," said their

   neighbor, Sam.

9. Their classmates looked at them with admiration.

10. Joe sat on the front porch and enjoyed his sudden fame.

## C.   Identifying Nouns, Pronouns, and Adjectives

Underline each noun, pronoun, and adjective in the sentences below. Do not include *a, an,* and *the.* In the space above each word, write *n.* for *noun, pron.* for *pronoun,* or *adj.* for *adjective.*

        pron.              adj.       n.

EX.   1.   This has been a wonderful day.

1. A bad storm is headed this way.

2. Summer storms can be powerful.

3. Are those clouds getting darker?

4. Everything will get wet if I don't cover it.

5. Did you see that rainbow in the sky?

6. Tropical rains can last a long time.

7. They come during the rainy season in certain parts of the world.

8. He told me people run for cover when they see the storms.

9. Can the hard-working men and women rebuild their homes?

10. We have always prepared for big storms.

## D.   Working Cooperatively to Write an Advertisement

Working with a partner, create an advertisement to describe and sell a new invention that will help students in school.

1. First, think of what the invention would do and what it might look like. Make your advertisement brief, clear, and interesting. Focus on the most important features of your product, and describe what the product does.

2. Write your advertisement on your own paper. Use at least three nouns and three adjectives in your advertisement. Then underline and label them.

         adj.        n.                  adj.           n.

EX.   End bookshelf clutter forever! The amazing Presso Paperweight

            adj.  n.      n.          n.

will compress huge piles of paper. Buy Presso Paperweight!

# VERBS

**10i A *verb* is a word used to express an action or a state of being.**

Words such as *do, come, go,* and *write* are **action verbs.** Sometimes action verbs express actions that cannot be seen: *believe, understand, love.*

A ***transitive verb*** is an action verb that expresses an action directed toward a person or thing named in the sentence.

EXAMPLES    Lorie **welcomed** the visitors to the game. [The action of the verb *welcomed* is directed toward *visitors.*]
Juan **served** the bread and the herb butter. [The action of the verb *served* is directed toward *bread* and *butter.*]

The action expressed by a transitive verb passes from the doer—the subject—to the receiver of the action. Words that receive the action of a transitive verb are called ***objects***.

An ***intransitive verb*** expresses action (or tells something about the subject) without passing the action from a subject to an object.

EXAMPLES    A cold wind **blew** over the tundra.
We **rode** in silence.

A verb may be transitive in one sentence and intransitive in another.

EXAMPLES    Liang **left** his book. [transitive]
Liang **left** early. [intransitive]

## EXERCISE 10    Identifying Action Verbs

In each of the following sentences, underline the action verb once. If the verb is transitive, underline its object twice.

EX.    1. Tom <u>conducted</u> an <u>experiment</u> in his kitchen.

1. In science class, Mrs. Velade discussed chemical reactions.

2. She provided glasses and various liquids.

3. Tom filled a glass with water.

4. He stirred soda into the water.

5. Another student found a bottle of vinegar nearby.

6. Rosa poured some vinegar into a second glass.

7. No one noticed anything special about the mixtures.

8. Then Tom poured the vinegar into the soda solution.

9. Many small bubbles suddenly rose to the surface.

10. The reaction between the two different liquids created a gas.

## EXERCISE 11　Identifying Transitive and Intransitive Verbs

Underline the verb in each sentence below. On the line before the sentence, write *trans.* if the verb is transitive or *intr.* if it is intransitive.

EX.　_____ 1.　My train tickets <u>arrived</u> today.

_____ 1.　Many families waited at the station.

_____ 2.　Two men boarded the train ahead of me.

_____ 3.　Haruo read my travel plans very carefully.

_____ 4.　The train moved quickly along the smooth track.

_____ 5.　A woman sold food to the hungry passengers.

_____ 6.　After lunch, I slept for about an hour.

_____ 7.　The train reached the station at exactly three o'clock.

_____ 8.　We studied the subway maps on the wall.

_____ 9.　Our visit to Boston ended too soon.

_____ 10.　We took the same train home on Sunday afternoon.

## EXERCISE 12　Using Transitive and Intransitive Verbs

Choose five verbs from the list below. On your own paper, use each verb in two sentences. The verb should be transitive in one sentence and intransitive in the other. After each sentence, label the verb *intr.* for *intransitive* or *trans.* for *transitive*.

| | | |
|---|---|---|
| ate | answered | flew |
| read | remember | cheered |
| study | watched | struck |

EX.　1.　I ate after she did. (intr.)

　　　Danielle ate her salad. (trans.)

# LINKING VERBS

**10j**  A *linking verb* serves as a link between two words. The most commonly used linking verbs are forms of the verb *be*.

| Forms of *Be* | | | |
|---|---|---|---|
| am | can be | will be | may have been |
| are | could be | would be | might have been |
| is | may be | have been | shall have been |
| was | might be | has been | should have been |
| were | shall be | had been | will have been |
| being | should be | could have been | would have been |

Here are some other frequently used linking verbs.

| Other Linking Verbs | | | |
|---|---|---|---|
| appear | grow | seem | stay |
| become | look | smell | taste |
| feel | remain | sound | turn |

The noun, pronoun, or adjective that follows a linking verb completes the meaning of the verb and refers to the noun or pronoun that comes before the verb.

EXAMPLES    The writer **is** Sandra Cisneros. [writer = Sandra Cisneros]
The writer **is** talented. [talented writer]

Many linking verbs can be used as action (nonlinking) verbs as well.

EXAMPLES    Roger **felt** happy this morning. [linking verb—happy Roger]
Roger **felt** the rough fabric. [action verb—object *fabric*]

Even *be* is not always a linking verb. It is sometimes followed by only an adverb.

EXAMPLES    They are **inside**.

To be a linking verb, the verb must be followed by a noun or a pronoun that names the subject, or by an adjective that describes the subject.

**EXERCISE 13   Identifying Linking Verbs and the Words They Link**

In each of the sentences below, underline the linking verb once. Draw two lines under the words that·are linked by the verb.

EX.   1. Sue Ann seems interested in horses. .

1. This ranch in Wyoming is a camp for riders.

2. The riders appeared calm during the show.

3. The campers felt tired after a long day on the trail.

4. The horses are probably hungry and thirsty by now.

5. When the sky grew dark, the campers went into their tents.

6. The pack horses should be ready by now.

7. Food from an open fire tastes wonderful!

8. Even after a day of riding, everyone remained cheerful.

9. I felt sore only on the first day, Friday.

10. Soon the boys and girls were comfortable outdoors.


**EXERCISE 14   Writing Appropriate Linking Verbs**

On the line in each sentence below, write a linking verb. Use a different verb for each sentence. You may use the verbs from the charts on page 107.

EX.   1. The sky _____ looked _____ threatening.

1. The storm _____ scary.

2. That thunder _____ so loud!

3. Nadim _____ nervous as the storm approached.

4. The air _____ moist and heavy.

5. That lightning _____ very close now.

6. You and I _____ safe inside the house.

7. The electricity _____ off for only a few minutes.

8. Severe storms _____ dangerous.

9. The air _____ cool after the rain.

10. The grass _____ wet for a long time.

# VERB PHRASES

**10k** A *verb phrase* consists of a main verb preceded by at least one *helping verb* (also called an *auxiliary verb*). Besides all forms of the verb *be,* helping verbs include

| | | | | |
|---|---|---|---|---|
| can | do | has | might | should |
| could | does | have | must | will |
| did | had | may | shall | would |

Notice how helping verbs work together with main verbs to make a verb phrase.

EXAMPLES  **is** leaving      **may** become      **might have** been
**had** seemed      **should** move      **must have** thought
**shall be** going      **could** jump      **does** sing

Sometimes the parts of a verb phrase are interrupted by other parts of speech.

EXAMPLES  **Did** you **finish** your history paper?
You **could** always **stay** at my house.

NOTE  The word *not* is always an adverb. It is never part of a verb phrase, even when it is joined to a verb as the contraction *–n't.*

EXAMPLES  We **would** not **have left** by that time.
We **would**n't **have left** by that time.

## EXERCISE 15   Identifying Verbs and Verb Phrases

Underline the verbs and verb phrases in the following sentences. [Hint: The parts of a verb phrase may be separated by other words.]

EX.   1.  Our plane should arrive around 2:00 P.M.

1.  We will not be staying in Richmond Friday.

2.  People in Indiana are always talking about basketball!

3.  Well, you should see the trophies at Indiana University.

4.  The state has long been known for its basketball teams.

5.  My sister's team could be playing in the semifinals this year.

6.  Did you watch the game last night on Channel 5?

7.  The game must not have started on time.

8. Well, the team might not have arrived on schedule.

9. Has everyone visited the Basketball Hall of Fame?

10. That building should have been built in Indiana instead of Massachusetts.

11. Do basketball players from Indiana ever become members of professional teams?

12. I haven't been practicing my jump shot.

13. My uncle has never enjoyed contact sports.

14. An interview with a professional team might be exciting.

15. A lot of people from Indiana must really like basketball.

16. The game of basketball was invented in 1891.

17. Wasn't the game developed by a physical education instructor?

18. The new game was played with a soccer ball and two peach baskets.

19. Didn't the first basketball team have nine players?

20. Originally, only one or two players on the team could shoot the ball.

## EXERCISE 16    Writing Verb Phrases

Complete each sentence below by creating a verb phrase that uses the verb in parentheses. Write the verb phrases on your own paper.

EX.   1. I (*shop*) for a birthday present for my brother.
      1. have been shopping

1. My brother (*take*) an English course.

2. Betty (*finish*) a book in an evening.

3. For her birthday, I (*give*) Sally a special photograph.

4. I (*look*) for a good science fiction story.

5. He (*enjoy*) one of those!

6. The teacher (*talk*) to the parent committee.

7. We (*watch*) a film of last week's game.

8. Who (*won*) the Pulitzer Prize this year?

9. The Pyrenees Mountains (*locate*) between Spain and France.

10. Toshi never (*see*) this movie.

## ADVERBS

**10l** **An *adverb* is a word used to modify a verb, an adjective, or another adverb.**

An adverb answers the questions *where, when, how,* or *to what extent* (*how long* or *how much*).

| Where? | Let's go **inside**. <br> Will you stand **there**? |
|---|---|
| When? | We can leave **now**! <br> The rain will stop **soon**. |
| How? | The alarm rang **wildly**. <br> Speak **slowly**. |
| To what extent? | She **hardly** noticed. <br> The path is **quite** steep. |

Adverbs may come before or after the verbs they modify. Sometimes adverbs interrupt parts of a verb phrase. Adverbs may also introduce questions.

EXAMPLES    **Recently** we learned about a new law. [The adverb *recently* modifies the verb *learned,* telling *when* we learned.]
**How** can we **quickly** climb the rope? [The adverb *how* introduces the question and modifies the verb phrase *can climb.* The adverb *quickly* interrupts the verb phrase and tells *how* we climbed.]

If you aren't sure whether a word is an adjective or an adverb, ask yourself what it modifies. If a word modifies a noun or a pronoun, it is an adjective. If it modifies a verb, an adjective, or an adverb, it is an adverb.

EXAMPLES    Jogging is part of my **daily** routine. [*Daily* modifies the noun *routine,* telling *which* one. In this sentence, *daily* is used as an adjective.]
I run **daily**. [*Daily* modifies the verb *run,* telling *when.* In this sentence, *daily* is used as an adverb.]

## EXERCISE 17   Identifying Adverbs

Underline the adverbs in the sentences below. Then draw an arrow to the word or words that each adverb modifies.

EX.   1.   Recently, little rain has fallen.

1.   Newscasters are now warning us about forest fires.

2.   Forest fires can spread rapidly.

3.   Our scout leader often discusses fire safety.

4.   Scouts in this area listen carefully.

5.   We never burn fires in windy weather.

6.   A gust of wind can quickly spread a small fire.

7.   Soon we will find a safe location.

8.   Mr. Stamos always pours water over his fires.

9.   He stirs the coals thoroughly as he pours.

10.   Then he shovels dirt over the wet ashes.

## EXERCISE 18   Revising with Adverb Modifiers

Revise the sentences below by adding one adverb modifier for each italicized word or phrase. Use a different adverb in each item. Write your answers on your own paper.

EX.   1.   *Water* the plants.
         1.   Water the plants weekly.

1.   We *ran* to school.

2.   She *wore* a beautiful coat.

3.   Three guitars *were playing* all at once.

4.   Leticia *dances*.

5.   Severe thunderstorms *are expected*.

6.   The rain *fell*.

7.   We *ate* the tasty apples.

8.   Lamont *quotes* his grandfather.

9.   I *studied* for my math test.

10.   The baby *is crying*.

# OTHER USES OF ADVERBS

**10m Adverbs that modify adjectives often come before the adjectives.**

EXAMPLES This painting is **almost** complete. [The adverb *almost* modifies the adjective *complete*, telling *how complete*.]

This watch is **exceedingly** accurate. [The adverb *exceedingly* modifies the adjective *accurate*, telling *how accurate*.]

The most frequently used adverbs are *too, so,* and *very*. In fact, these words are often overused. Here are some other choices.

| Adverbs That Frequently Modify Adjectives | | |
|---|---|---|
| completely | especially | quite |
| dangerously | extremely | rather |
| definitely | largely | surprisingly |
| dreadfully | mainly | terribly |
| entirely | mostly | unusually |

## EXERCISE 19 Identifying Adverbs That Modify Adjectives

Underline the adverb that modifies an adjective in each sentence below. Draw an arrow to the adjective that the adverb modifies.

EX. 1. The Owens family was <u>rather</u> poor.

1. J. C. Owens was quite unhealthy as a child.

2. His parents were really happy about his running.

3. Running was amazingly good for the boy's health.

4. The Owens' Cleveland home was entirely different from their first home.

5. The boy was too shy to explain that his name was J. C. and not Jesse.

6. In high school, one coach was especially kind to Jesse.

7. Coach Riley noticed that the young man was surprisingly fast.

8. The 1936 Summer Olympics were terribly exciting.

9. Winning four track-and-field gold medals was extremely unusual, so Jesse became a star.

10. Definitely talented, in 1976, Jesse Owens won one of America's highest civilian awards—the Medal of Freedom.

## 10n    Adverbs can modify other adverbs.

EXAMPLES    Don't eat **too** quickly. [The adverb *too* modifies the adverb *quickly,* telling *to what extent.*]
The water covered the town **almost** completely. [The adverb *almost* modifies the adverb *completely,* telling *to what extent.*]

NOTE    Although many adverbs end in *–ly,* the *–ly* ending does not automatically mean that a word is an adverb. Many adjectives also end in *–ly*: a *daily* prayer, a *silly* cartoon, a *lovely* day. Even though some words do not end in *–ly,* they are often used as adverbs. These words include *now, then, far,* and *already.* To identify a word as an adverb, ask yourself two questions.

- Does this word modify a verb, an adjective, or another adverb?
- Does it tell *when, where, how,* or *to what extent?*

## EXERCISE 20    Identifying Adverbs That Modify Other Adverbs

Underline the adverb that modifies other adverbs in each sentence below. Draw an arrow to the other adverbs being modified.

EX.    1.    Cheetahs can move very quickly.

1.    A sloth almost never travels on the ground.

2.    Those armadillos sleep much more than most animals!

3.    A sifaka, a type of lemur, lives almost totally in trees.

4.    You will be able to read this book on animals quite quickly.

5.    Can red kangaroos jump exceedingly high?

6.    Wild turkeys, you know, can run surprisingly fast.

7.    Gray parrots talk much better than other birds.

8.    A few birds fly so slowly that you might expect them to fall from the sky.

9.    One bullfrog jumped quite far during our contest.

10.    The tiny bristlemouth fish lives almost everywhere!

## *PREPOSITIONS*

**10o** A *preposition* **is a word used to show the relationship of a noun or a pronoun to some other word in the sentence.**

EXAMPLES We hung the picture **beside** the sofa.
We hung the picture **above** the sofa.
We hung the picture **near** the sofa.

| Commonly Used Prepositions | | | | |
|---|---|---|---|---|
| aboard | because of | by | like | past |
| above | before | concerning | near | since |
| according to | below | during | next to | through |
| across | beneath | except | of | to |
| against | beside | for | off | toward |
| along | between | from | on | underneath |
| around | beyond | in addition to | out | until |
| as of | but (meaning | inside | over | upon |
| at | *except*) | into | owing to | with |

Many words in the list above can also be adverbs. To be sure that a word is a preposition, ask whether the word relates a noun or a pronoun following it to a word that comes before it.

EXAMPLES One person lagged **behind**. [adverb]
One person lagged **behind** the others. [preposition]

## EXERCISE 21   Distinguishing Prepositions from Adverbs

On the line before each of the following sentences, write *prep.* if the word in italics is a preposition or *adv.* if the word is an adverb.

EX. _prep._ 1. This exhibit has many pictures *of* children.

_____ 1. The name *on* many pictures is Mary Cassatt's.

_____ 2. The sketch for this scene is *beside* the painting.

_____ 3. One woman is sipping tea from a tray that is sitting *near* the chair.

_____ 4. The other woman is sitting just *beyond* her.

_____ 5. Look at the big picture as you go *out*.

_____ 6. Mary Cassatt lived in Paris *for* many years.

_____ 7. Once, she painted a scene of Paris *from* her balcony.

_____ 8. She included her dog, which she loved to have *around*.

_____ 9. The dog has the rails of the balcony to lean *against*.

_____ 10. *According to* a biographer, it was one of the few times she painted a picture of the city.

## EXERCISE 22   Revising Sentences by Using Appropriate Prepositions

Revise the following paragraph by writing an appropriate preposition or compound preposition on the line in each sentence.

EX.    [1] The shield had a picture of a turtle _____*on*_____ it.

[1] Each summer, Native American people _____

many places gather for powwows. [2] In fact, I went to one

_____ Saturday. [3] I stood _____ a

Chippewa dancer. [4] He wore a colorful costume and had beaded,

leather moccasins _____ his feet. [5] He danced

beautifully_____ the regular beat of the drums. [6] My

sister learned some traditional dances _____ a

powwow.  [7] Many Native American people in the Northwest live

and work _____ cities. [8] Those who want to keep their

traditions alive are sometimes caught _____ two

cultures. [9] At the powwows, people dance _____

prizes. [10] Native American culture is remembered and preserved

_____ powwows.

# CONJUNCTIONS AND INTERJECTIONS

**10p** A *conjunction* is a word used to join words or groups of words.

*Coordinating conjunctions* always connect items of the same kind. They may join single words or groups of words. Coordinating conjunctions include *and, but, for, nor, or, so,* and *yet.*

EXAMPLES   songs **and** lyrics [two nouns.]
in sickness **or** in health [two prepositional phrases]
First it rained, **but** the rain stopped quickly. [two complete ideas]

*Correlative conjunctions* also connect items of the same kind. However, unlike coordinating conjunctions, correlatives are always used in pairs. Correlative conjunctions include *both...and, either...or, neither...nor, not only...but also,* and *whether...or.*

EXAMPLES   **Both** dogs **and** cats make good pets. [two nouns]
You should set flowers **not only** on the table **but also** in the basket. [two prepositional phrases]
**Either** borrow a book **or** buy a magazine. [two complete ideas]

A third kind of conjunction—the *subordinating conjunction*—is discussed on page 165.

## EXERCISE 23   Identifying and Classifying Conjunctions

In the following sentences, underline the coordinating conjunctions once and the correlative conjunctions twice. Some sentences contain more than one conjunction.

EX.   1.  I like most fruits, <u>but</u> I don't like <u><u>either</u></u> currants <u><u>or</u></u> blueberries.

1. Most fruits and vegetables are good sources of nutrients.

2. Milk is high in calcium, but it also can be high in fat.

3. Both cereals and pasta are rich in B vitamins yet low in fat.

4. Vitamin C is found not only in oranges, but also in strawberries, green peppers, and tomatoes.

5. I don't know whether to cook this in oil or bake it in the oven.

6. Sara wants neither lettuce nor sprouts on her sandwich.

7. Baked, steamed, or boiled potatoes are low in calories, so don't add butter or sour cream.

8. To make the sauce, use either a blender or an electric mixer.

9. Joel is concerned about additives, so he has started reading food labels.

10. May I have both juice and water with my meal?

---

**10q  An *interjection* is a word used to express emotion. It has no grammatical relation to the rest of the sentence.**

Since an interjection is unrelated to other words in the sentence, it is set off from the rest of the sentence by an exclamation point or a comma.

EXAMPLES    **Hooray!** We won the game!
**Oh,** I guess it's okay.
Dinner was good, but, **ugh,** that dessert was awful.
**No!** Our television picture just disappeared.

---

## EXERCISE 24    Writing Sentences with Interjections

On your own paper, use each of the interjections below to create a sentence.

EX.  1.  ouch
1.  Ouch! That branch scratched me!

1. goodbye            6. ha
2. well               7. yippee
3. yipes              8. shh
4. goodness           9. oh dear
5. wow                10. phew

# CHAPTER REVIEW

## A. Identifying the Parts of Speech

On the line before each sentence, identify the part of speech of the italicized word. Write *n.* for *noun*, *v.* for *verb*, *adv.* for *adverb*, *adj.* for *adjective*, *pron.* for *pronoun*, *conj.* for *conjunction*, *prep.* for *preposition*, or *intj.* for *interjection*.

EX. ___adj.___ 1. Joseph Haydn composed *many* symphonies.

_____ 1. The composer and musician created 104 symphonies, 84 string quartets, *and* many other works.

_____ 2. Did you know that he was *once* expelled from his school?

_____ 3. At the time, Haydn was attending a *choir school* in Vienna.

_____ 4. The choir *sang* in St. Stephen's Cathedral.

_____ 5. In school, a boy with a pigtail stood *in front of* Hyden.

_____ 6. One day, Haydn cut *it* off.

_____ 7. Haydn was seventeen years *old* at the time.

_____ 8. *Well*, the adults at the school were displeased by this.

_____ 9. Haydn was *no* longer a student at that school.

_____ 10. This event did not *seem* to affect his later life, though.

## B. Writing Sentences Using the Same Words as Different Parts of Speech

On your own paper, write two sentences for each of the words below, showing how the word can be used as two different parts of speech. Then label how you used each word.

EX. 1. down
    1. Jonathan looked down. (adv.)
       He tossed the ball down the hill. (prep.)

| | | |
|---|---|---|
| 1. race | 6. milk | 11. for |
| 2. over | 7. dark | 12. jump |
| 3. building | 8. some | 13. both |
| 4. game | 9. well | 14. kick |
| 5. purple | 10. beyond | 15. knot |

## C. Working Cooperatively to Determine Parts of Speech in a Message

You have discovered a letter and a treasure map that have been hidden in an attic for many years. Unfortunately, parts of the letter have crumbled away, leaving numerous holes. Work with a partner to supply a word that makes sense for each hole. Write its part of speech in the space above the line. You may use the following abbreviations: *n.* for *noun*, *v.* for *verb*, *pron.* for *pronoun*, *adj.* for *adjective*, *adv.* for *adverb*, *prep.* for *preposition*, *conj.* for *conjunction*, and *intj.* for *interjection*. [Note: Each part of speech is used at least once. You may wish to read the entire letter before you try to fill in the blanks.]

EX.    Look for a _____ *adj.* *flat* _____ stone.

My dear [1] _____ ,

   I buried [2] _____ bars of gold and a hundred pieces

of silver. If something happens to me, I want [3] _____

to have them. Be sure to follow my [4] _____

exactly, and use the map as a reference. On the map, you will see a

[5] _____ hut. In this hut is a closet. The closet is

[6] _____ feet to the right of the [7] _____.

The floor [8] _____ the closet [9] _____

false. It will lift [10] _____ . Dig [11] _____

about three feet and look for a metal ring. Pull it [12] _____

as hard as [13] _____ can. [14] _____ !

You have discovered the [15] _____ box. The box is

[16] _____ of gold [17] _____ silver. If

you are reading [18] _____ , I might be dead. Good luck!

One of [19] _____ , at least, will get rich.

                                        Your [20] _____ ,

                                        Lemuel

# THE SENTENCE

> **11a  A *sentence* is a group of words that contains a subject and a verb and expresses a complete thought.**
>
> If a group of words does not express a complete thought, it is a *fragment*, or incomplete part, of a sentence.
>
> FRAGMENT   the man in the white coat
> SENTENCE   The man in the white coat is my uncle.
>
> FRAGMENT   standing in line
> SENTENCE   We were standing in line.
>
> FRAGMENT   before you go to the meeting
> SENTENCE   Do you want some lunch before you go to the meeting?
>
> Notice that a sentence always begins with a capital letter and ends with a period, a question mark, or an exclamation point.

## EXERCISE 1   Identifying Complete Sentences and Sentence Fragments

On the line before each word group below, write *sent.* if it is a sentence or *frag.* if it is not a sentence. Add correct capitalization and end punctuation to the sentences.

EX.   *sent.*   1.   W̶ould you like a bowl of soup

_____   1.   waiting for your phone call

_____   2.   help me carry this huge package

_____   3.   after the basketball game was over

_____   4.   three of my favorite animals

_____   5.   did you finish your science project

_____   6.   it doesn't bother me

_____   7.   someday if we are fortunate

_____   8.   the fastest runner on the whole team

_____   9.   there is very little money in the treasury

_____   10.   hoping to win a scholarship to college

## EXERCISE 2    Revising Fragments to Create Complete Sentences

On your own paper, revise each word group below so that it is a complete sentence. Add modifiers and any other words to make the meaning of your completed sentence clear.

EX.    1.  in the center of the room
       1.  *In the center of the room stood a large statue.*

1.  standing in the lobby
2.  nevertheless, I
3.  after the concert
4.  out in the driveway
5.  the men were
6.  climbing to the top of the mountain
7.  it often
8.  this exciting movie
9.  late last night while walking home
10.  four students on the bus
11.  boardsailing in the California surf
12.  in ink on a postcard
13.  want to try the shrimp
14.  now Heidi
15.  feeds her chickens
16.  in almost every letter
17.  were finding shells on the beach
18.  from the two new students
19.  must reach the Evlers
20.  is one of the most dedicated people
21.  to apply for this job
22.  adjusting the throttle
23.  working on a computer
24.  changes in fashions
25.  should write or read
26.  a serious discussion
27.  floating in the pool
28.  therefore, we
29.  just around the corner
30.  wanted the answer

## SUBJECT AND PREDICATE

**11b** **A sentence consists of two parts: the subject and the predicate. The** *subject* **is the part that names the person or thing spoken about in the rest of the sentence. The** *predicate* **is the part that says something about the subject.**

The subject may be one word or a group of words. The *complete subject* contains all the words that name the person or thing spoken about in the rest of the sentence. The complete subject may appear at the beginning, in the middle, or at the end of a sentence.

EXAMPLES
      cmpl. s.
  **The woman in the red car** just got a speeding ticket.
      cmpl. s.
  Did **Phoebe's brother** win the poetry contest?
       cmpl. s.
  Into the water dove **a brown pelican**.

Like the subject, the predicate may be one word or a group of words. The *complete predicate* contains all the words that say something about the subject. Like the complete subject, the complete predicate can appear in many different places in a sentence.

EXAMPLES
        cmpl. pred.
  The woman in the red car **just got a speeding ticket**.
       cmpl. pred.
  **Did** Phoebe's brother **win the poetry contest**?
    cmpl. pred.
  **Into the water dove** a brown pelican.

### EXERCISE 3 Identifying the Complete Subject

Underline the complete subject in each of the following sentences.

EX. 1. <u>What</u> is the source of your information?

1. Martin Miller is a geologist and a photographer.

2. In the September 1993 issue of *Earth* magazine, readers can see examples of his photographs.

3. Did you see his pictures of desert landscapes?

4. In the desert, strong winds can carve deep ridges in the rocks.

5. Similarly, those fierce winds blast clouds of flying sand **against the rocks.**

6. Sand and dust in the wind **leave behind a hard surface of bare rocks.**

7. The sand **is eventually redeposited elsewhere in the desert, often as sand dunes.**

8. Standing in a dramatic row in one of Miller's desert photographs are huge sand dunes.

9. The dunes **are constantly shifting and changing shape because of strong winds.**

10. The powdery dunes **may be compressed into hard layers of sandstone after many thousands of years.**

## EXERCISE 4   Writing Complete Predicates

On your own paper, write ten complete sentences by adding a complete predicate to each of the subjects below. Be sure to use correct capitalization and end punctuation in your sentences.

EX.  1.  the clerk in that store
      1.  The clerk in that store is extremely helpful.

1. one of the buildings on our street
2. my favorite poem
3. a popular tourist attraction in our area
4. dinosaurs
5. several people
6. the most interesting books
7. political leaders
8. a good way to get exercise
9. the escalator at the north end of the mall
10. the artist
11. llamas and alpacas
12. a sifaka, a kind of lemur,
13. your best friend
14. a group of sixth-graders
15. my favorite holiday

# THE SIMPLE SUBJECT AND SIMPLE PREDICATE

**11c** The *simple subject* is the main word or group of words within the complete subject.

| | |
|---|---|
| EXAMPLE | **The letter from Sharon** is on your desk. |
| COMPLETE SUBJECT | The letter from Sharon |
| SIMPLE SUBJECT | letter |
| EXAMPLE | Did **that mysterious Colonel Potter** return my call? |
| COMPLETE SUBJECT | that mysterious Colonel Potter |
| SIMPLE SUBJECT | Colonel Potter |

NOTE  In this book, the term *subject* refers to the simple subject unless otherwise indicated.

## EXERCISE 5  Identifying Complete Subjects and Simple Subjects

In each sentence below, underline the complete subject once, and draw a second line under the simple subject.

EX.  1.  The talented  Ansel Adams  was a photographer, a
       conservationist, and a writer.

1.  Ansel Adams' photographs of Yosemite Valley are very dramatic.

2.  Time after time, Adams filmed the stark beauty of the canyons.

3.  His experiments with light and shutter speed made him unique.

4.  Many talented photographers have tried to duplicate Adams' work, without success.

5.  The photographer wrote in his many books about his photographic techniques.

6.  He often photographed mountains, forests, and rivers.

7.  Adams' style of photography is called *straight photography*.

8.  *Straight photography* shows the subjects of the pictures simply and directly.

9.  Adams established photography departments in several schools.

10. One of these departments is at the San Francisco Art Institute.

**11d    The *simple predicate*, or *verb*, is the main word or group of words within the complete predicate.**

|  |  |
|---|---|
| EXAMPLE | He **wasn't going** to the movie. |
| COMPLETE PREDICATE | wasn't going to the movie |
| SIMPLE PREDICATE | was going |

|  |  |
|---|---|
| EXAMPLE | **In a little while**, the fireworks **should begin**. |
| COMPLETE PREDICATE | should begin in a little while |
| SIMPLE PREDICATE | should begin |

The simple predicate may be a single verb or a verb phrase. A **verb phrase** is a main verb and its helping verbs.

EXAMPLES    is walking        has been called        will have seen

When you look for the simple predicate in a sentence, be sure to include all parts of the verb phrase. Keep in mind the various helping verbs, such as *am*, *is*, *were*, *do*, *have*, *can*, *will*, and *could*.

 In this book, the word *verb* refers to the simple predicate unless otherwise indicated.

## EXERCISE 6    Identifying Complete Predicates and Simple Predicates

In each sentence below, underline the complete predicate once, and draw a second line under the simple predicate. Be sure to include all parts of a verb phrase.

EX.    1.    Ravi <u>was leading the band at practice yesterday</u>.

1.    The high school band has finally gotten new uniforms after many years.

2.    They are black with orange stripes down the pant legs and the sleeves.

3.    A committee raised the money for the uniforms.

4.    They earned almost three thousand dollars through car washes, bake sales, and a flea market.

5.    Everyone in the band helped with these activities.

6.    The band members will appear in their new uniforms tonight.

7.    Dr. Beach has arranged for the appearance of four other high school bands from various parts of the city.

8.    All the band members will march into the stadium in uniform.

9.    Then they will play the "Star-Spangled Banner" together.

10.    Are you going to the concert?

# FINDING THE SUBJECT

The best way to find the subject of a sentence is to find the verb first. Then ask "Who?" or "What?" in front of it.

EXAMPLES   Next week at the library, you can meet the author of *The Pelican Brief*. [The verb is *can meet*. *Who* can meet? *You* can meet. *You* is the subject.]

The fuel for the lantern is in the shed. [The verb is *is*. *What* is in the shed? *Fuel* is in the shed. *Fuel* is the subject.]

**11e   The subject of a verb is never in a prepositional phrase.**

EXAMPLES   The secretary to the principal is Ms. Gómez. [*Secretary* is the subject. The prepositional phrase *to the principal* modifies the subject.]

The car with the flat tire limped into the service station. [*Car* is the subject. The prepositional phrase *with the flat tire* modifies the subject.]

**11f   You can find the subject in a question by turning the question into a statement. Find the verb in the statement and ask "Who?" or "What?" in front of it.**

Questions often begin with a verb, a helping verb, or a word such as *what*, *where*, *when*, *how*, or *why*. The subject usually follows the verb or helping verb.

EXAMPLE   Has the plane left? **becomes** The plane has left. [*What* left? The *plane* left.]

**11g   Do not mistake the word *there* for the subject of a sentence. To find the subject in this type of sentence, omit *there* and ask "Who?" or "What?" before the verb.**

*There* is often used to get a sentence started when the subject comes after the verb.

EXAMPLE   There are many worms in the compost pile. [*What* are in the compost pile? The *worms* are. *Worms* is the subject.]

NOTE   Like *there*, the adverb *here* is often used to get a sentence started. To find the subject in such a sentence, omit *here* and ask "Who?" or "What?" before the verb.

EXAMPLE   Here is your ticket. [*What* is? *Ticket* is. *Ticket* is the subject.]

> **11h** In a request or a command, the subject of a sentence is usually not stated. In such sentences, *you* is the *understood subject*.
>
> REQUEST   Please feed the cat. [*Who* should feed the cat? *You* should feed the cat. *You* is the understood subject.]
>
> COMMAND   Don't talk during his speech. [*Who* shouldn't talk? *You* shouldn't talk. *You* is the understood subject.]
>
> Sometimes a request or command will include a name. Names used in commands or requests are called *nouns of direct address*. They identify the person spoken to or addressed, but they are not subjects. *You* is still the understood subject.
>
> EXAMPLE   Marie, (you) please deliver this note for me.

## EXERCISE 7  Identifying Subjects and Verbs

In the sentences below, underline each subject once. Underline the verb twice. If the understood subject is *you*, write *you* on the line before the sentence.

EX. _____ 1. There are almost forty new houses on this road.

_____ 1. Rodney, return your books to the library.

_____ 2. When will the candidate make a speech here?

_____ 3. Here are the directions to my house.

_____ 4. Take the dog for a walk around the block.

_____ 5. Did your mother enjoy the concert?

_____ 6. There is a new movie at the Fox Theater tonight.

_____ 7. Will you need a ticket to the lecture?

_____ 8. Is Harrisburg the capital of Pennsylvania?

_____ 9. Priscilla, watch the children in the pool.

_____ 10. Be quiet!

_____ 11. Can you play badminton?

_____ 12. The quarterback, along with the coach, left early.

_____ 13. Learn the rules by Wednesday.

_____ 14. Dorothea Dix, with Elizabeth Blackwell, helped the sick.

_____ 15. There was a nail in my shoe.

# COMPOUND SUBJECTS AND COMPOUND VERBS

**11i** A *compound subject* consists of two or more subjects that are joined by a conjunction and have the same verb.

The conjunctions most commonly used to connect the words of a compound subject are *and* and *or*.

EXAMPLE **Lucia** and **Donald** brought refreshments for the team. [*Who* brought refreshments? *Lucia* brought them. *Donald* brought them. *Lucia* and *Donald* form the compound subject.]

When more than two words are included in the compound subject, the conjunction is generally used only between the last two words. Also, the words are separated by commas.

EXAMPLE Lucia**,** Donald**, and** Sophia brought refreshments for the team. [Compound subject: *Lucia, Donald, Sophia*]

Correlative conjunctions may be used with compound subjects.

EXAMPLE **Either** Lucia **or** Donald will bring refreshments for the team. [Compound subject: *Lucia, Donald*]

**11j** A *compound verb* consists of two or more verbs that are joined by a conjunction and have the same subject.

EXAMPLES The photographer **ran** up the aisle and **snapped** the president's picture.
I **listened** to the game on the radio but **missed** the fourth inning.
Our team **won** four games, **lost** two, and **tied** three.
Congress **will** either **approve** the bill or **suggest** some changes.

Notice that in the last sentence, the helping verb *will* is not repeated before the second verb, *suggest*. In compound verbs, the helping verb may or may not be repeated before the second verb if the helper is the same for both verbs.

## EXERCISE 8  Identifying Compound Subjects and Their Verbs

In each of the following sentences, underline the compound subject once and the verb twice.

EX. 1. Birds and lizards might be modern relatives of dinosaurs.

1. Either Tanya or Mae Ellen will win the election.

2. There are your shoes and socks, under your bed.

3. Are Helena and Miguel staying for dinner?

4. In the cold waters of this stream, many trout, bass, and pickerel live.

5. At the bottom of the drawer were needles, thread, and even extra buttons.

6. Bottles of juice and cartons of milk were standing in the cooler.

7. Neither my brother nor my sister can come to the concert on Friday.

8. Only Jeremy and I know the location of the buried treasure.

9. Here are Jim and Sandy at the bus stop, right on time.

10. In April, my sisters and I are visiting colleges in Maine and Utah.

## EXERCISE 9   Identifying Subjects and Compound Verbs

In each sentence below, underline the subject once and the compound verb twice. Be sure to include any helping verbs.

EX. 1.   They <u>visited</u> Canada but <u>did</u> not <u>go</u> to Banff.

1. The fielder shielded her eyes, saw the ball, and moved quickly to her left.

2. I opened the door but saw no one on the porch.

3. Tomorrow morning we will either go to the beach or walk into town for breakfast at the diner.

4. Odessa will direct the play and perform the role of Lady Macbeth.

5. Ray Charles wrote the music and lyrics for his songs and played the piano extremely well.

6. You can come to Puerto Rico, relax on the beach, and visit our great shops and restaurants.

7. At night you can eat dinner and look out at the Caribbean Sea.

8. The new computers at the library have flat-screen monitors and are available for everyone's use.

9. My cousin joined the Houston Museum of Natural Science last year and has gone to many interesting programs there.

10. Could you meet me right after school today or come to my house after soccer practice?

## COMPLEMENTS

> **11k   A *complement* is a word or group of words that completes the meaning of a predicate.**

Notice how the following sentences need the complements to complete the meaning of the predicates. The complement may be a noun, a pronoun, or an adjective, and may be compound. The best way to find the complement in a sentence is to ask who or what receives the action of the verb.

EXAMPLES    Denzel Washington is a great **actor.** [noun]
                    The coach advised **us.** [pronoun]
                    She is always **friendly** and **polite.** [compound adjective]
                    Dr. Ramírez helped **Velma** and **me.** [noun and pronoun]

NOTE    The complement of a sentence is never part of a prepositional phrase.

EXAMPLES    She fed the **dog.** [*Dog* is the complement.]
                She called to the **dog.** [*Dog* is part of the prepositional phrase *to the dog.*]

## EXERCISE 10   Identifying Subjects, Verbs, and Complements

In each of the following sentences, underline the simple subject once and the verb twice. Then put brackets around the complement. [Hint: Some sentences may have a compound complement.]

EX.    1.    Marie rented an old [movie] last night.

1.   Her great-grandfather had recommended the movie to her.

2.   Marie enjoys mysteries and courtroom dramas.

3.   The name of the movie was *Witness for the Prosecution.*

4.   Three very famous actors from Great-Grandpa's era had the leading roles.

5.   Charles Laughton, famous as the hunchback in *The Hunchback of Notre Dame*, played the defense attorney in *Witness for the Prosecution.*

6.   A very famous actor, Tyrone Power, played the defendant.

7.   Marlene Dietrich was one of the most beautiful and most talented women in film history.

8. She played the defendant's wife and the chief witness for the prosecution.

9. Throughout the movie, twists and turns in the plot keep viewers on the edges of their seats.

10. Do not reveal the surprise ending to anyone!

11. We often rent old movies at our house, too.

12. My favorite old movie is *It Happened One Night.*

13. This movie stars Clark Gable and Claudette Colbert.

14. It received the Academy Award for best picture in 1934.

15. The same year, Gable and Colbert each received an Academy Award for best actor and best actress, respectively.

## EXERCISE 11   Writing Sentence Complements

Complete the sentences below by adding a complement to each group of words. Add any other words necessary to make your sentences clear.

EX.   1.  Tomorrow Penny will give ___a speech___ .

1.  Gina sometimes seems _____ .

2.  Do you need_____ or _____ ?

3.  Last Thursday, I finished _____ and _____ .

4.  Barbara won _____ .

5.  This bread tastes _____ .

6.  That painting is really _____ .

7.  Could I borrow your _____ ?

8.  My favorite musician today is _____ .

9.  Is Donald Duck a _____ ?

10.  The best book I ever read was_____ .

11.  Tonight's practice session became _____ but _____ .

12.  Our neighbor brought home _____ .

13.  With paper clips, you can make _____ .

14.  Next Monday I begin my new _____ .

15.  How soon will you finish _____ ?

# THE SUBJECT COMPLEMENT

**11l** A *subject complement* is a noun, pronoun, or adjective that follows a linking verb. It describes or explains the simple subject.

☞ **REFERENCE NOTE:** For more information on linking verbs, see page 107.

There are two kinds of subject complements—the *predicate nominative* and the *predicate adjective*.

**(1) A *predicate nominative* is a noun or pronoun in the predicate that explains or identifies the subject of the sentence.**

EXAMPLES    Termites are dangerous **pests.**
The new attorney general is **she.**
Mario is a very talented **musician.**

**(2) A *predicate adjective* is an adjective in the predicate that modifies the subject of the sentence.**

EXAMPLES    The wind feels **cold.** [cold wind]
The ground is **wet.** [wet ground]

Subject complements may be compound.

EXAMPLES    Two great songwriters were **Richard Rodgers** and **Oscar Hammerstein II.** [compound predicate nominatives]
The pizza is **hot** and **spicy.** [compound predicate adjectives]

To find the subject complement in an interrogative sentence, rearrange the sentence to make a statement.

EXAMPLE    Was Barbra Streisand the director?
Barbra Streisand was the **director.** [predicate nominative]

To find the subject complement in an imperative sentence, insert the understood subject *you*.

EXAMPLE    Be proud of your achievements!
(You) Be **proud** of your achievements! [predicate adjective]

## EXERCISE 12    Identifying Subject Complements

In each of the following sentences, underline the subject complement. On the line before the sentence, write *p.n.* for *predicate nominative* or *p.a.* for *predicate adjective*. [Hint: Some sentences may contain compound subject complements.]

EX.  _p.a._  1. The woods were <u>full</u> of wildflowers and animals.

\_\_\_\_\_  1. Marah is a canoeing counselor at a camp in Maine.

\_\_\_\_\_  2. Most of the campers are boys and girls from big cities.

\_\_\_\_\_  3. At first, some of the new arrivals seem a little scared and shy of the woods of Maine.

\_\_\_\_\_  4. To most of them, canoes seem dangerous.

\_\_\_\_\_  5. Marah is patient with these new wilderness campers.

\_\_\_\_\_  6. She becomes their guide to new experiences.

\_\_\_\_\_  7. Many rivers and river valleys in northern Maine are home to bears, moose, and other wild creatures.

\_\_\_\_\_  8. With Marah's help, children from the city become skilled and knowledgeable about the treasures of the wilderness.

\_\_\_\_\_  9. I was one of Marah's first campers, twelve years ago.

\_\_\_\_\_ 10. Thanks to Marah, I am now a seasoned wilderness traveler and the author of two books about the rivers of Maine.

## EXERCISE 13    Writing Subject Complements

Complete each sentence below by adding a subject complement. Add any other words that you feel are necessary to make your sentences clear. On the line before each word group, identify the complement in your completed sentence. Write _p.n._ for _predicate nominative_ or _p.a._ for _predicate adjective_. [Hint: Some sentences need a compound complement.]

EX.  _p.a._  1. The river was <u>wide</u> and <u>deep</u> .

\_\_\_\_\_  1. Suddenly, the sky became _____ .

\_\_\_\_\_  2. My favorite food is _____ .

\_\_\_\_\_  3. Is that man _____ or _____ ?

\_\_\_\_\_  4. Nancy looked _____ but _____ .

\_\_\_\_\_  5. The winner of the race was _____ .

\_\_\_\_\_  6. Two inventions that changed the world are _____

and _____ .

\_\_\_\_\_  7. Remain _____ to your friends.

\_\_\_\_\_  8. The mountains appear _____ yet _____ .

\_\_\_\_\_  9. Today the weather seems _____ .

\_\_\_\_\_ 10. Is Ms. Ramillo a _____ ?

## OBJECTS

*Objects* are complements that do not refer to the subject.

**11m  A *direct object* is a noun or pronoun that receives the action of the verb or shows the result of the action. It answers the question "Whom?" or "What?" after an action verb.**

EXAMPLES    Gina called **me**. [Gina called *whom*? *Me* is the direct object.]
Hot soup may burn your **throat**. [Hot soup may burn *what*? *Throat* is the direct object.]

Direct objects are never found in prepositional phrases.

EXAMPLES    Yosef rode the **horse**. [*Horse* is the direct object.]
Yosef rode on the **horse**. [*Horse* is part of the prepositional phrase *on the horse*.]

**11n  An *indirect object* is a noun or pronoun that precedes the direct object and usually tells *to whom* or *for whom* (or *to what* or *for what*) the action of the verb is done.**

EXAMPLES    The coach gave **Josh** and **him** awards. [*Josh* and *him* are the compound indirect object of the verb *gave*, telling *to whom the coach gave the awards*. The noun *awards* is the direct object.]
Juan built his **sister** a shelf for her books. [The noun *sister* is the indirect object of the verb *built*, telling *for whom Juan built a shelf*. The noun *shelf* is the direct object.]

If the word *to* or *for* is used, the noun or pronoun following it is part of a prepositional phrase and cannot be an indirect object.

| | |
|---|---|
| PREPOSITIONAL PHRASE | I made a card **for you**. |
| INDIRECT OBJECT | I made **you** a card. |
| PREPOSITIONAL PHRASE | He gave the extra ticket **to Tom**. |
| INDIRECT OBJECT | He gave **Tom** the extra ticket. |

☞ **REFERENCE NOTE:** For more information on action verbs, see page 105.

## EXERCISE 14    Identifying Direct Objects

Underline the direct object in each of the following sentences.

EX.    1.  George's father and mother, Mr. and Mrs. Ristevski, own the Liberty Deli.

1.  Students from the university and staff from the hospital often buy lunch there.

135

2. Early each morning, Mrs. Ristevski bakes the bread for the deli sandwiches.

3. Twice a month, Mr. Ristevski makes his own sausage.

4. During the cold winter months, the neighbors especially like the convenient location of the delicatessen.

5. For twenty-five years the Ristevski family has owned and managed the delicatessen.

## EXERCISE 15   Identifying Direct Objects and Indirect Objects

In each sentence below, underline the direct object once and the indirect object twice. Some sentences may not contain an indirect object. [Hint: Both direct objects and indirect objects may be compound.]

EX.   1.  Ms. Sanchez gave Trudy and us directions to her office.

1.  Can you loan Marley and Pat enough money for their tickets?

2.  He left your jacket in the hall closet.

3.  Dr. Fuller gave the children some good advice about poison ivy.

4.  Please read me the opening paragraph of your composition.

5.  Before the hike, Pierre gave each girl and boy trail maps.

6.  At the wildlife park, we took photographs of zebras and monkeys.

7.  Could you please show me the fastest route to Monterey?

8.  Take Marshall Boulevard to the top of the hill and turn right.

9.  I'll give you this book about interesting sights in Monterey.

10.  Thank you very much, sir.

11.  Amy Tan published her first novel in 1989.

12.  Did you study the life of Sauk chief Black Hawk?

13.  He teaches his students the concepts of t'ai chi ch'uan, a system of self-defense and meditation.

14.  My grandfather visited three cities in the Southwest.

15.  The archaeologist Howard Carter found Tutankhamen's tomb.

# CLASSIFYING SENTENCES BY PURPOSE

**11o** Sentences may be classified as *declarative, imperative, interrogative,* or *exclamatory.*

**(1) A *declarative* sentence makes a statement. All declarative sentences are followed by periods.**

EXAMPLE   The famous painter Arshile Gorky was born in Armenia in 1904.

**(2) An imperative sentence gives a command or makes a request. Imperative sentences are usually followed by periods. Very strong commands, however, may be followed by exclamation points.**

EXAMPLES   Please shut the window.
Don't swim alone.
Watch out for the sharks!

Notice that a command or request has the understood subject *you.*

**(3) An *interrogative* sentence asks a question. Interrogative sentences are followed by question marks.**

EXAMPLE   What is your favorite poem?

**(4) An *exclamatory* sentence expresses strong feeling. Exclamatory sentences are always followed by exclamation points.**

EXAMPLES   That car is rolling down the hill!
What an incredible race that was!
I can't believe I won a trip to Paris!

## EXERCISE 16   Identifying the Four Kinds of Sentences

Add the correct punctuation mark to the end of each of the following sentences. On the line before the sentence, indicate which type of sentence it is. Write *dec.* for *declarative, inter.* for *interrogative, imp.* for *imperative,* or *excl.* for *exclamatory.* [Hint: Some imperative sentences may end in exclamation points.]

EX.   _____imp._____   1. Stop fighting at once !

_____   1. Have you seen all of the Indiana Jones movies

_____   2. The first one, *Raiders of the Lost Ark,* came out in 1981

_____   3. What a fantastic movie it was

———   4.  Although audiences had seen Harrison Ford as Han Solo in
        *Star Wars*, he became a star when he took on the role of
        Indiana Jones

———   5.  Call the video store, and ask if they have *Raiders of the Lost
        Ark* in stock

———   6.  Wow, there must have been at least a billion snakes in that
        scene

———   7.  Are you afraid of snakes

———   8.  Watch out for the falling rocks, Indy

———   9.  Critics did not give the second Indiana Jones movie, *Indiana
        Jones and the Temple of Doom*, the great reviews that they gave
        the first one

———  10.  Did you think that Karen Allen was a better heroine than
        Kate Capshaw

## EXERCISE 17   Writing the Four Kinds of Sentences

You are sitting in a restaurant. Suddenly you notice that the diner at the next
table is a large penguin. On your own paper, write a dialogue that might
take place between you and the penguin. Add stage directions if you wish.
Write ten sentences, and use at least two examples of each of the four kinds
of sentences. Label each of your sentences to identify its classification.

EX.   1.  Me: (with a puzzled expression) We don't usually see penguins in this
        neighborhood. (dec.)

Berry's World reprinted by permission of NEA, Inc.

"What was it like back in the days when people
talked and wrote in complete sentences?"

# CHAPTER REVIEW

## A. Identifying the Parts of a Sentence

In the paragraph below, classify each underlined word according to its function in the sentence. Write *s.* for *subject*, *p.n.* for *predicate nominative*, *d.o.* for *direct object*, *v.* for *verb*, *p.a.* for *predicate adjective*, and *i.o.* for *indirect object*.

EX. Romesh Gunesekera has published a [1] <u>book</u> of short stories. *d.o.*

Romesh Gunesekera is a [1] <u>native</u> of Sri Lanka. [2] <u>Sri Lanka</u> is an island nation located in the Indian Ocean. Gunesekera now [3] <u>lives</u> in London, where he has published [4] <u>*Monkfish Moon.*</u> His book is quite [5] <u>good</u> in its blending of appearance and reality. Its nine short [6] <u>stories</u> give [7] <u>readers</u> several interesting [8] <u>views</u> of life in Sri Lanka. [9] <u>Some</u> of the stories are [10] <u>frightening.</u> They [11] <u>tell</u> of events related to Sri Lanka's long and cruel civil war. Only the [12] <u>setting</u>, however, will seem [13] <u>unfamiliar</u> to readers outside of Sri Lanka. All of the stories contain complex [14] <u>characters</u> and vivid details. Because Gunesekera [15] <u>has based</u> this excellent [16] <u>collection</u> of stories on his native land, he has given the [17] <u>East</u> and the West a new and powerful [18] <u>link</u>. His book [19] <u>is</u> both a masterpiece of literature and a [20] <u>tribute</u> to a beautiful and complex country.

## B. Identifying and Punctuating the Four Kinds of Sentences

Add the correct punctuation mark to the end of each of the following sentences. On the line before the sentence, classify the sentence. Write *dec.* for *declarative, imp.* for *imperative, inter.* for *interrogative,* and *excl.* for *exclamatory.*

EX. _*imp.*_ 1. Please pass the salt

_____ 1. In 1991, Paul Sereno discovered a dinosaur fossil in Argentina

_____ 2. What a fierce animal that dinosaur must have been

_____ 3. Read the article about it in the September 1993 issue of *Earth* magazine

_____ 4. That dinosaur has been given the name *Eoraptor*

_____ 5. Did it live about 228 million years ago

_____ 6. Another dinosaur lived at about the same time

_____ 7. What was its name

_____ 8. It was called *Herrerasaurus,* and Sereno found its fossil in the same rock formation, along with *Eoraptor*

_____ 9. Do you believe that dinosaurs once roamed these woods

_____ 10. Wow, they must have been terrifying

## C.   Writing Sentences

On your own paper, write fifteen sentences according to the guidelines below. Underline the part or parts called for in the guidelines.

EX.   1.   a declarative sentence with a compound verb
   1.   Barbra Streisand <u>produced</u> and <u>directed</u> the movie *The Prince of Tides.*

1.   a declarative sentence with a predicate adjective

2.   an interrogative sentence with a direct object

3.   an interrogative sentence with a compound subject

4.   an imperative sentence with an indirect object and a direct object

5.   an imperative sentence that ends with a period

6.   an imperative sentence that ends with an exclamation point

7.   a declarative sentence with a compound indirect object and a direct object

8.   an exclamatory sentence with a predicate adjective

9.   a sentence that begins with *there* and contains a compound subject

10.   a sentence with the understood subject *you*

11.   a declarative sentence with a predicate nominative

12.   an exclamatory sentence with a compound verb

13.   a declarative sentence with a compound predicate nominative

14.   an interrogative sentence with a compound verb

15.   a sentence with the understood subject *you* and a compound verb

# *PREPOSITIONAL PHRASES*

**12a** A *phrase* is a group of related words that is used as a single part of speech and does not contain both a predicate and its subject.

EXAMPLES    should have listened [verb phrase; no subject]
between Marika and Martin [prepositional phrase; no subject or verb]

**12b** A *prepositional phrase* is a group of words consisting of a preposition, a noun or pronoun that serves as the object of the preposition, and any modifiers of that object.

Some prepositions are made up of more than one word, like *in front of* or *prior to*. Also, an article or some other modifier often appears in a prepositional phrase.

EXAMPLES    Zahara built a model airplane **for her brother**. [The object of the preposition *for* is *brother*. The possessive pronoun *her* modifies *brother*.]
When will she give the birthday present **to him**? [The object of the preposition *to* is *him*.]
Our new bus stop is **in front of the supermarket**. [The object of the preposition *in front of* is *supermarket*. The adjective *the* modifies *supermarket*.]

Objects of prepositions may be compound.

EXAMPLES    Heavy snow fell **throughout the day and night**. [Both *day* and *night* are objects of the preposition *throughout*.]
**In addition to you and me**, six other people are coming. [The preposition *in addition to* has a compound object, *you* and *me*.]
Our new bus stop is **in front of the supermarket and the laundromat**. [The objects of the preposition *in front of* are *supermarket* and *laundromat*. The adjective *the* modifies *supermarket* and *laundromat*.]

 **REFERENCE NOTE:** For a list of commonly used prepositions, see page 115.

## EXERCISE 1   Identifying Prepositions and Their Objects

In each of the following sentences, underline the preposition, and draw an arrow from the preposition to its object.

EX.   1. Our voices echoed loudly <u>inside</u> the empty house.

1. Two of Mr. Johnson's children play the violin.

2. Today, you can buy almost anything from a catalog.

3. That girl with the catcher's mitt plays baseball well.

4. Imagine what the world would be like without television.

5. We spotted a doe and two fawns running across the grassy meadow.

6. The Forty-first and Forty-second Congresses had among their members the first African American representatives and the first African American senator.

7. The coach will award the medals at tonight's sports banquet.

8. Rain has been falling since dawn.

9. According to this article, nearly ten thousand Chinese immigrants helped construct the Central Pacific Railroad.

10. The baseball sailed over the fence, the street, and the parking garage.

## EXERCISE 2   Writing Notes for TV

You are a writer for the show *Wildlife Facts*. Your next program is on snakes. Use the following notes to write ten sentences that might be used for the voice-over for this program. Include at least five prepositional phrases in your sentences. Underline the phrases and draw an arrow from the prepositions to their objects. Write these sentences on your own paper.

EX.   1. True vipers are found in Africa and Eurasia.

### NOTES

1. world's largest poisonous snake—king cobra

2. cobras—Malaysia, China, India, the Philippines

3. true vipers—Africa, Eurasia, and the East Indies

4. pit vipers—facial pits

5. rattlesnake—eats small animals, lifts tail to make sounds

6. African saw-scaled viper—rubs side scales together to produce rasping sound

7. North American sidewinder—moves sideways

8. water moccasin—southern swamps and bayous in North America

9. Indian cobra—hooded, lift up for battle

10. asp—also called Egyptian cobra

# ADJECTIVE PHRASES AND ADVERB PHRASES

**12c** **A prepositional phrase that modifies a noun or pronoun is called an *adjective phrase*.**

Adjective phrases answer the same questions that adjectives answer: *What kind? Which one? How many?* or *How much?* An adjective phrase usually follows the noun or pronoun that it modifies. More than one phrase may modify the same word. An adjective phrase may also modify the object of another prepositional phrase.

EXAMPLES    The names **of the contest winners** will be announced tomorrow. [The phrase *of the contest winners* modifies the noun *names*, telling *which* names.]

Please bring me that big ball **of string in the garage.** [Both phrases modify the noun *ball. Of string* tells *what kind; in the garage* tells *which one.*]

The painting **of the girl with the dog** won first prize. [The phrase *of the girl* modifies the noun *painting*, telling *which painting*. The phrase *with the dog* modifies the object *girl*, telling *which girl.*]

## EXERCISE 3    Identifying Adjective Phrases

Underline each adjective phrase in the sentences below. Draw an arrow to the word it modifies. [Note: Some sentences have more than one adjective phrase.]

EX.   1.   My grandparents tape-recorded stories of our family's history.

1. The walls around us were a brilliant yellow.

2. The flowers along the path are geraniums and petunias.

3. Leon took a picture of a blue heron next to a snowy egret.

4. The heavy winds of the storm spun the weather vane on the roof.

5. The cat ate all of the sardines in the tin.

6. *Hunger of Memory* is an autobiographical story by Richard Rodriguez.

7. The plays in the game were very exciting.

8. Mom opened the can of beans carefully.

9. Which of these books do you want?

10. The castle beside the ocean belonged to Prince Edward.

**12d** An *adverb phrase* is a prepositional phrase that modifies a verb, an adjective, or an adverb.

Adverb phrases answer the same questions that adverbs answer: *When? Where? How? To what extent?* (*How long? How many? How far?*)

EXAMPLES    **Within a few minutes**, the concert will begin. [The phrase *Within a few minutes* modifies the verb phrase *will begin*, telling *when* the concert will begin.]
The water is deeper **on the far end**. [The phrase *on the far end* modifies the adjective *deeper*, telling *where* the water is deeper.]

Like adjective phrases, more than one adverb phrase may modify the same word.

EXAMPLE    **With a final sprint**, Takara won the marathon **by three seconds**. [Both phrases modify the verb *won*. *With a final sprint* tells *how*; *by three seconds* tells *to what extent*.]

## EXERCISE 4   Identifying Adverb Phrases and the Words They Modify

Underline the adverb phrases in the sentences below. Draw an arrow from each phrase to the word or words it modifies. [Note: Some sentences have more than one adverb phrase.]

EX.    1.   After our classes, Germaine and I played basketball in the schoolyard.

1.   Germaine pointed to the dark clouds that were gathering in the sky.

2.   In a few minutes, thunder cracked loudly above our heads.

3.   From the house, we watched the storm.

4.   Lightning flashes appeared repeatedly for an hour.

5.   Soon the lightning seemed closer to the house.

6.   The whirligig was spinning out of control.

7.   I thought the beets and carrots would be ripped out of the ground by the wind.

8.   The rain grew from a drizzle to a downpour.

9.   Germaine's dog Rosamunda hid under the bed.

10.   His sister Elena ran through the house, pretending she was a rescue worker.

# VERBALS AND VERB PHRASES

*Verbals* are formed from verbs. Like verbs, they may be modified by adverbs and may have complements. However, verbals are used as other parts of speech. There are three kinds of verbals: *participles*, *gerunds*, and *infinitives.*

**12e  A *participle* is a verb form that can be used as an adjective.**

EXAMPLE   The divers discovered **sunken** treasure off the coast of Key Largo. [The participle *sunken*, formed from the verb *sink*, modifies the noun *treasure*.]

**(1) *Present participles* end in –*ing*.**

EXAMPLE   The photographer took a picture of the **laughing** baby. [*Laughing* is a present participle modifying the noun *baby*.]

**(2) *Past participles* usually end in –*d* or –*ed*. Other past participles are irregularly formed.**

EXAMPLES   Please pass your **completed** test to the front of the room. [The past participle *completed* modifies the noun *test*.]
Her only son, **grown** and **gone** from home, visits her often. [The irregular past participles *grown* and *gone* modify the noun *son*.]

NOTE   Although participles are forms of verbs, they do not stand alone as verbs. However, a participle may be used with a helping verb to form a verb phrase. When a participle is used in this way, it is part of the verb and is therefore not an adjective.

EXAMPLES   Matthew **has been studying** Spanish.
Her son **is grown** and **has been gone** from home for years.

## EXERCISE 5   Identifying Participles and the Words They Modify

Underline the participles used as adjectives in the following sentences. Then draw an arrow from each participle to the noun or pronoun that it modifies.

EX.   1.  Splashing paint on the canvas, the artist created a masterpiece.

1.  The museum, known for its collection of modern art, has a new exhibit.

2.  Most of the pieces seen in this show are from private collections.

3.  A crowd gathered around a sculpture of a group of people sitting on a bus.

4. The figures, assembled from plaster casts, seemed real.

5. Expressing his opinion loudly, one man obviously did not like the artist's work.

6. Framed and hung on the wall, an enormous picture of a mother and child captured the attention of many people.

7. For a long time, Marissa stood in front of the picture, staring and thinking.

8. Lecturing on the artists of the mid-1900s, the museum guide talked about the work of the sculptor Alexander Calder.

9. Some people believe that Calder's sculptures have a charming quality.

10. Connected with rods and wires and suspended in the air, Calder's mobiles are probably his most popular pieces.

## EXERCISE 6   Choosing Appropriate Participles

On the line in each of the sentences below, write a participle that fits the meaning of the sentence.

EX.   1. The _____*rising*_____ tide washed over the beach.

1. The _____ sun cast a purple haze across the evening sky.

2. _____ her head, the baby fell asleep.

3. The whale, _____ suddenly out of the water, startled the people on the boat.

4. _____ in the sand, the clam was not visible to the hungry sea gulls.

5. We spent the day with our friends at the teen center, _____ .

# PARTICIPIAL PHRASES

**12f** A *participial phrase* is a phrase containing a participle and any complements or modifiers it may have.

A participial phrase should be placed as close as possible to the word it modifies. Otherwise the sentence may not make sense.

EXAMPLES **Hiking in the Sierra Nevada**, Paulo encountered a mountain lion. [The participle is modified by the prepositional phrase *in the Sierra Nevada*.]

Did you see that lioness **carrying her cubs**? [The participle has an object, *cubs*. The possesive pronoun *her* modifies *cubs*.]

The hiker, **acting quickly**, snapped a picture of the lion. [The participle is modified by the adverb *quickly*.]

☞ **REFERENCE NOTE:** The punctuation of participial phrases is discussed on pages 265 and 267. The participle as a dangling modifier is discussed on page 227. Combining sentences by using participles is discussed on page 73.

## EXERCISE 7   Identifying Participial Phrases

Underline the participial phrase in each of the following sentences. Draw an arrow from the participial phrase to the word or words the phrase modifies.

EX.   1.   Listening to the story of the princess and the frog, the children are enchanted.

1. Every Saturday morning, Shanti spends time at the library, telling stories to children.

2. Leaving their children at story hour, the parents run their errands.

3. Shanti reads with the children gathered in a circle around her.

4. The stories, chosen from among Shanti's own childhood favorites, are usually fairy tales and folk tales.

5. Enhanced by Shanti's unique style, each story delights the children.

6. Once, as I passed by the story-hour room, I overheard Shanti speaking gruffly.

7. Speaking in the voices of different characters, she was telling the story of the three little pigs.

8. The children held their breath when the wolf, huffing and puffing with all its might, tried to blow down the house of the third little pig.

9. The house built of bricks did not fall down, of course, and the pig survived.

10. Clapping and cheering at the end, the children showed how much they loved that folk tale.

## EXERCISE 8  Identifying Participles and Participial Phrases

Underline each participle or participial phrase in the paragraph below. Draw an arrow from the participial phrase to the word or words that it modifies.

EX.  [1]  <u>Using an old tale</u>, a poet provides a different view of a familiar character.

[1] Thinking about tomorrow's assignment, I decided to talk about a poem. [2] Skimming through my literature book, I came across an interesting poem titled "The Builders." [3] The poem, written by Sara Henderson Hay, does not actually identify its topic—"The Three Little Pigs." [4] The speaker of the poem is the pig who built his house of bricks, protecting himself from the starving wolf. [5] The pig, recalling recent events, tells the story in a scolding tone. [6] He points out that he told his brothers to build with bricks, but, being stubborn, they wouldn't listen to him. [7] The pig seems to be sorry that his brothers are gone, having been eaten by the wolf. [8] Having heard "The Three Little Pigs" so many times as a child, I found much to say about Hay's poem. [9] Looking for something to use as my first prop, I found a shoebox in my closet. [10] The shoebox, painted with a pattern of small bricks, would represent the pig's house.

# *GERUNDS*

**12g** A *gerund* is a verb form ending in *–ing* that is used as a noun.

| | |
|---|---|
| SUBJECT | **Walking** is good exercise. |
| PREDICATE NOMINATIVE | My favorite activity at the beach is **snorkeling**. |
| DIRECT OBJECT | Mom enjoys **golfing**. |
| OBJECT OF A PREPOSITION | A sturdy, thick-soled shoe is recommended for **hiking**. |

Like nouns, gerunds may be modified by adjectives and adjective phrases.

| | |
|---|---|
| DIRECT OBJECT | I watched **the incredible** diving **of the Olympic gold-medal winner**. [The article *the*, the adjective *incredible*, and the adjective phrase *of the Olympic gold-medal winner* modify the gerund *diving*.] |
| SUBJECT | **The sloppy** writing **of the note** made it impossible to understand. [The article *The*, the adjective *sloppy*, and the adjective phrase *of the note* modify the gerund *writing*.] |

Like verbs, gerunds may also be modified by adverbs and adverb phrases.

| | |
|---|---|
| SUBJECT | Cheering **loudly at the game** gave Geraldo a sore throat. [The gerund *Cheering* is modified by both the adverb *loudly* (telling *how*) and the adverb phrase *at the game* (telling *where*).] |
| DIRECT OBJECT | I would enjoy sitting **quietly for a while**. [The gerund *sitting* is modified by both the adverb *quietly* (telling *how*) and the adverb phrase *for a while* (telling *for how long*).] |

Gerunds, like present participles, end in *–ing*. To be a gerund, a verbal must be used as a noun. In the following sentence, three words end in *–ing*, but only one of them is a gerund.

| | |
|---|---|
| EXAMPLE | **Thinking** about the trip, Earline was **packing** suitable clothes for **sightseeing**. [*Thinking* is a present participle modifying *Earline*. *Packing* is part of the verb phrase *was packing*. Only *sightseeing*, used as the object of the preposition *for*, is a gerund.] |

## EXERCISE 9   Identifying and Classifying Gerunds

Underline the gerunds in the following sentences. On the line before each sentence, identify how each is used. Write *s.* for *subject*, *p.n.* for *predicate nominative*, *d.o.* for *direct object*, or *o.p.* for *object of a preposition*.

EX.   _s_   1.  Fishing relaxes my dad.

_____   1.  Tomás enjoys gardening.

_____   2.  Bicycling is a sport that can be enjoyed at any age.

_____   3.  After the accident, she was bothered by a painful throbbing in her knee.

_____   4.  My favorite part of graduation was the singing, but Dad liked the speeches better.

_____   5.  Running in a marathon is Aretha's goal.

_____   6.  Acting in such plays as *Othello* and *The Emperor Jones* earned national attention for the renowned African American actor Paul Robeson.

_____   7.  On a hot day like today, the only work I want to do is writing.

_____   8.  The new puppies enjoy chasing each other playfully around the house.

_____   9.  When we went to Mexico, we took along a Spanish-English dictionary for translating.

_____  10.  Nestled in our sleeping bags, we heard the howling of a coyote, which sounded lonely to me.

## EXERCISE 10   Writing About Hobbies

On the lines below, write five sentences about hobbies or activities that you enjoy. In each sentence, use a gerund, and underline it. In the space above the gerund, label its use in the sentence. Write *s.* for *subject,* *p.n.* for *predicate nominative,* *d.o.* for *direct object,* or *o.p.* for *object of a preposition.*

EX.   1.  *Playing the Japanese game Go is fun.*

1.  _____

    _____

2.  _____

    _____

3.  _____

    _____

4.  _____

    _____

5.  _____

    _____

## GERUND PHRASES

**12h** A *gerund phrase* contains a gerund and any modifiers or complements it may have.

SUBJECT  **The loud roaring of the wind** could be heard inside the cabin.[The gerund *roaring* is modified by the article *The*, the adjective *loud*, and the prepositional phrase *of the wind*. ]

DIRECT OBJECT  Thelma enjoyed **racing swiftly on her bike**. [The gerund *racing* is modified by the adverb *swiftly* and by the prepositional phrase *on her bike*.]

PREDICATE NOMINATIVE  His hobby is **sending friends old postcards**. [The gerund *sending* has a direct object, *postcards*, and an indirect object, *friends*.]

OBJECT OF A PREPOSITION  She improved her composition by **rewriting the last paragraph**.[The gerund *rewriting* has a direct object, *paragraph*.]

NOTE  Whenever a noun or a pronoun comes before a gerund, the possessive form should be used.

EXAMPLES  The **parrot's** endless squawking made us laugh.
**Her** cooking has really improved.

## EXERCISE 11  Identifying and Classifying Gerund Phrases

Underline the gerund phrases in the following sentences. On the line before each sentence, identify how each phrase is used. Write *s.* for *subject*, *p.n.* for *predicate nominative*, *d.o.* for *direct object*, or *o.p.* for *object of a preposition*.

EX.  _____*s.*_____  1. Traveling to exotic places would be fun.

_____  1. The people on the Samoan island of Upolu in the South Pacific showed their hospitality to the magazine photographer by welcoming her warmly.

_____  2. The photographer's job was taking pictures of the island's scenery for a travel article.

_____  3. She liked talking to the people about their remote South Pacific island.

_____  4. Swimming in the warm waters of Upolu is possible all year.

_____  5.  A popular entertainment on the island is torch dancing.

_____  6.  Tourists enjoy diving from the reef.

_____  7.  Almost one hundred years ago, writer Robert Louis Stevenson found paradise by sailing to the island of Upolu.

_____  8.  Finding an island paradise is the dream of many writers.

_____  9.  After chartering a yacht, Robert Louis Stevenson set sail in search of his dream island.

_____  10.  Flying to Apia, the capital of Western Samoa, is the fastest and simplest way to reach this dream island today.

_____  11.  Driving over Cross Island Road takes you from one coast to the other.

_____  12.  Moving from Los Angeles to Polynesia must be a big change.

_____  13.  Losing your job might cause you to make such a move.

_____  14  A way to honor the local leaders is by taking a Samoan name.

_____  15.  I don't know if I'd like moving to Samoa, but I'd vacation there if I could afford it.

## EXERCISE 12    Working Cooperatively to Write Sentences with Gerund Phrases

Working with a partner, create ten sentences that use the gerund phrases below. Write on your own paper. Underline each gerund phrase, and write above the phrase *s.* for *subject, p.n.* for *predicate nominative, d.o.* for *direct object,* or *o.p.* for *object of a preposition.*

EX.  1.  throwing the javelin

                s.
   1.  <u>Throwing the javelin</u> was the second field event on the schedule.

1.  putting on my running shoes
2.  pole-vaulting at the track meet
3.  pushing off from the starting block
4.  firing the starting gun
5.  passing the baton
6.  running a marathon
7.  crossing the finish line
8.  lying on the grass to rest
9.  landing in the sandpit
10.  cheering for the athletes

# *INFINITIVES AND INFINITIVE PHRASES*

**12i** An *infinitive* is a verb form, usually preceded by *to*, that can be used as a noun, an adjective, or an adverb.

NOUNS    **To sing** with a rock band is Jon's dream. [*To sing* is the subject of the sentence.]

I had hoped **to finish** my story, but Joey's plan was **to leave** early. [*To finish* is the direct object of the verb phrase *had hoped. To leave* is the predicate nominative.]

ADJECTIVE    The person **to ask** is the information director. [*To ask* modifies the noun *person.*]

ADVERB    Eager **to rest**, we sat down on the grass. [*To rest* modifies the adjective *eager.*]

**12j** An *infinitive phrase* consists of an infinitive together with its modifiers and complements.

NOUN    **To find a job quickly** is Rita's goal. [The phrase is the subject of the sentence. The infinitive has a direct object, *job*, and is modified by the adverb *quickly*.]

ADJECTIVE    Roses are the flowers **to give for a special occasion**. [The phrase modifies the predicate nominative *flowers*. The infinitive is modified by the adverb phrase *for a special occasion*.]

ADVERB    He seemed afraid **to say a word**. [The phrase modifies the predicate adjective *afraid* and has a direct object, *word*.]

An infinitive may have a subject. The infinitive, together with its subject, complements, and modifiers, is sometimes called an *infinitive clause*.

EXAMPLE    Mom asked **me to buy milk on my way home.** [*Me* is the subject of the infinitive *to buy*.]

Sometimes the *to* of the infinitive is omitted in a sentence.

EXAMPLE    Will you help me **find** my missing watch?

## EXERCISE 13    Identifying and Classifying Infinitives

Underline the infinitives in the sentences below. On the line before each sentence, identify how each infinitive is used. Write *n.* for *noun*, *adj.* for *adjective*, or *adv.* for *adverb*.

EX.    ___*n.*___   1.   To be a member of the hockey team was important to Chris.

_____ 1. Slow to start, the car was old and unreliable.

_____ 2. Does anyone wish to respond to the mayor's comments?

_____ 3. Dan is the person to follow, because he always knows exactly where he's going.

_____ 4. Mr. Petrakis ran to catch his train so that it would not leave without him.

_____ 5. We left our seats to get some popcorn.

## EXERCISE 14    Identifying and Classifying Infinitive Phrases

Underline the infinitive phrases in the sentences below. On the line before each sentence, identify how the infinitive phrase is used. Write *n.* for *noun*, *adj.* for *adjective*, or *adv.* for *adverb*.

EX.    __n.__   1. To make pizza requires some planning ahead.

_____ 1. Earlier, Luisa and Josh went to get the ingredients at the market.

_____ 2. To prepare the most delicious pizza ever was their objective.

_____ 3. They had already decided to heap lots of fresh vegetables on the pizza.

_____ 4. They needed advice from Luisa's mother on the best way to make the tomato sauce.

_____ 5. She was happy to share her old family recipe with them.

_____ 6. To stretch the dough properly was another technique that she demonstrated for them.

_____ 7. Once the dough was stretched and the sauce was cooked, Luisa and Josh were ready to assemble their pizza.

_____ 8. Josh asked Luisa to ladle the sauce on the dough.

_____ 9. After mushrooms, peppers, artichokes, onions, and cheese were piled on the dough, it was time to bake the pizza in a very hot oven.

_____ 10. Then they invited some friends for dinner, because, Josh said, "Pizza is a food to eat with friends!"

# REVIEW EXERCISE

## A. Identifying and Classifying Prepositional Phrases

Underline all the prepositional phrases in the paragraph below. In the space above each phrase, identify how the phrase is used. Write *adj.* for *adjective* and *adv.* for *adverb.*

                                                                    adj.
EX.   [1] I. M. Pei is just one of the many architects whose work
       enhances city landscapes worldwide.

[1] I. M. Pei, born in Canton, China, in 1917, was the son of a successful Chinese banker. [2] Pei came to the United States to study architectural engineering when he was eighteen years old. [3] Because of a war between China and Japan, Pei could not go home after his college graduation. [4] He obtained a master of architecture degree from Harvard University and, in 1948, joined the staff of an important architectural firm. [5] Before this time, Pei had never designed any actual buildings, but the head of the firm was impressed by Pei's architectural drawings. [6] He wanted Pei on his staff. [7] With this important job, Pei had his chance to alter modern urban environments. [8] Many cities are more beautiful because of Pei's decision to join that firm. [9] Among the buildings he has designed are the Mile High Center in Denver, Colorado, the East Building of the National Gallery of Art, and the Dallas City Hall. [10] If you are looking at Boston's Government Center or Montreal's Place Ville Marie, you are looking at Pei's designs.

## B.   Identifying and Classifying Verbals and Verbal Phrases

Underline the verbal or verbal phrase in each of the following sentences. On the line before each sentence, identify the verbal or verbal phrase. Write *ger.* for *gerund*, *ger. phr.* for *gerund phrase*, *inf.* for *infinitive*, *inf. phr.* for *infinitive phrase*, *part.* for *participle*, or *part. phr.* for *participial phrase*.

EX.    _____*ger. phr.*_____    1.  Imagining a world without computers is
                                     impossible for me.

_____    1.  The photo in the book showed bats hanging upside down.

_____    2.  Although I've tried, I can't seem to take a really good
                        photograph of a sunset.

_____    3.  Theo's one passion is acting.

_____    4.  Lost, the young boy worried that he might never find his
                        way home.

_____    5.  She had a question she wanted to ask.

_____    6.  We came to a tidal pool where we saw crabs, shrimp,
                        and other ocean creatures swimming around.

_____    7.  The fire was about to spread to other buildings when the
                        fire trucks arrived.

_____    8.  Walking beneath the bridge, we could hear the rumble
                        of the train on the tracks above.

_____    9.  It seems obvious, but the only way you'll ever become a
                        better dancer is by dancing more.

_____    10. The growling lion frightened away the birds.

## C.   Writing a Compugram with Verbals and Verbal Phrases

You are on a space team that is exploring Saturn. Once a month, you are allowed to send home an interplanetary compugram (a telegram sent and received by computers) ten sentences long. On your own paper, write a compugram to your friend. Explain what you've been doing. Describe your most exciting discoveries. You may also want to tell your friend what you do for relaxation and entertainment on your days off. Include at least one of each type of verbal and verbal phrase. Underline each verbal or verbal phrase in your sentences. Identify each verbal or verbal phrase by writing *ger.* for *gerund*, *ger. phr.* for *gerund phrase*, *inf.* for *infinitive*, *inf. phr.* for *infinitive phrase*, *part.* for *participle*, or *part. phr.* for *participial phrase*.

                            part. phr.
EX.    Being involved in interplanetary exploration, I have a new appreciation of our
       entire universe.

## APPOSITIVES AND APPOSITIVE PHRASES

**12k** An *appositive* is a noun or a pronoun given beside another noun or pronoun to identify or explain it.

EXAMPLES    My friend **Janet** invited me to her family's cabin. [The noun *Janet* identifies the noun *friend*.]
Linda Ronstadt, a popular **singer**, has recorded an album of Mexican songs. [The noun *singer* explains the noun *Linda Ronstadt*.]

**12l** An *appositive phrase* is made up of the appositive and its modifiers.

EXAMPLES    Joseph, **star pitcher of our baseball team**, sprained his wrist.
The movie *La Bamba* was based on the life of Ritchie Valens, **one of the great rock musicians of the 1950s.**

NOTE    An appositive phrase usually follows the noun or pronoun it refers to. Sometimes, however, the appositive precedes the noun or pronoun explained.

EXAMPLE    **A volunteer worker at the library**, Pamela knows exactly where to look for a book.

Appositives and appositive phrases are usually set off by commas unless the appositive is a single word closely related to the preceding noun or pronoun. Commas are always used with appositives that refer to proper nouns.

ESSENTIAL    Our cat **Snowball** likes to sleep under the couch. [The writer has more than one cat. The appositive is necessary to tell which cat is referred to.]

NONESSENTIAL    Our cat, **Snowball**, likes to sleep under the couch. [The writer has only one cat. The appositive is not necessary to identify the cat.]

## EXERCISE 15    Identifying Appositives and Appositive Phrases

In the following sentences, underline all appositive phrases once. Underline twice the word or words an appositive phrase identifies or explains.

EX.    1. Summer, my favorite time of year, is a great time for hiking.

1. The magazine *Music* is a guide to the enjoyment of classical music.

2. One dessert on the menu, the fresh fruit, is not available today.

3. This article discusses the life and works of Langston Hughes, a poet, novelist, and short-story writer.

4. Tanya wants to become an occupational therapist, a person who treats people with sports injuries and other kinds of injuries.

5. Marjorie, the director of the senior community center, is looking for volunteers to work at the center two days a week.

6. A nuisance to everyone, the mosquitoes seem to be bigger and hungrier this summer.

7. Have you ever played charades, a game in which you have to act out titles for your teammates to guess?

8. My sister Kimiko just got her driver's license.

9. Ina returned the blouse to the store for a refund, twenty-two dollars.

10. What did you think of the movie *Harry Potter and the Goblet of Fire*?

## EXERCISE 16   Adding Appositives

On the line in each of the sentences below, write an appositive or appositive phrase that fits the meaning of the sentence.

EX.   1.   Fluffy, _____*my house cat*_____, lapped some milk and curled up again on my lap.

1. My friend _____ and I are going to the library.

2. Our library, _____, is open on Saturdays.

3. We are giving a presentation, _____, in class.

4. My parents, _____, say television is harmful.

5. We would like to see some research, _____, to decide for ourselves.

6. The jury, _____, reached a verdict.

7. My sister _____ sang in the choir.

8. Is your favorite dish, _____, being served?

9. James asked everyone where his dog _____ had gone.

10. Two students, _____ and _____, won the contest.

## CHAPTER REVIEW

### A. Identifying and Classifying Prepositional Phrases

Underline each prepositional phrase in the paragraph below. Then draw an arrow from the phrase to the word or words it modifies. In the space above the phrase, write *adj.* for *adjective phrase* or *adv.* for *adverb phrase*. A sentence may have more than one phrase.

EX.   [1]  The concerts always start *adv.* with "The Star-Spangled Banner."

[1] Every Friday evening during the summer, something very special happens in our seaside town.  [2] That's when Mr. Turner, who is eighty-four years old, takes his place in front of the Pleasantville Town Band. [3] For forty-six years Mr. Turner has been leading the band in rousing songs that celebrate and reflect the American spirit.  [4] Each Friday night, thousands gather at the Vernon Turner Bandstand and watch Mr. Turner conduct.  [5] Mr. Turner has loved music throughout his life.  [6] As a college student he studied music, and he eventually became a music teacher in the Pleasantville area.  [7] Although Mr. Turner has considered retirement several times, the adoration he receives from band and community members keeps him working.

### B. Identifying Verbals and Appositives

On the line before each of the following sentences, identify the italicized word or word group. Write *prep.* for *preposition*, *part.* for *participle*, *ger.* for *gerund*, *inf.* for *infinitive*, or *app.* for *appositive*.

EX.   __inf.__   1.  Molly wants *to keep* a journal during the summer.

_____   1.  The *stolen* notebook was never recovered, and so the results of his experiments remain a mystery.

_____   2.  Were you planning *to attend* the junior class play?

_____   3.  Hector described his trip, the *one* that he took to Mexico.

_____ 4. *Instead of* taking the bus, let's walk to school today.

_____ 5. Many people associate *knitting* with grandmothers, but my uncle Tim knits sweaters that are works of art.

## C.  Writing Sentences with Phrases

On your own paper, write ten sentences, following the directions given below. Underline your phrase in each sentence. If your phrase is a modifier, draw two lines under the word or words it modifies.

EX.   1. Use an adjective phrase to modify the subject of a sentence.
        1. The tree in front of our house is a weeping cherry tree.

1. Use an adjective phrase to modify the object of a preposition.
2. Use an adverb phrase to modify an adjective.
3. Use an adverb phrase to modify a verb.
4. Use a participial phrase to modify a subject.
5. Use a participial phrase to modify a direct object.
6. Use a gerund phrase as the object of a preposition.
7. Use a gerund phrase as a predicate nominative.
8. Use an infinitive phrase as a noun.
9. Use an infinitive phrase as an adjective.
10. Use an appositive phrase beside a direct object.

## D.  Working Cooperatively to Create a Cluster

Work with a partner to think of situations that are associated with smiles and frowns. On your own paper, fill in a prewriting cluster for smiles and frowns. Use gerund and prepositional phrases, and include at least one infinitive or infinitive phrase in your cluster.

EX.

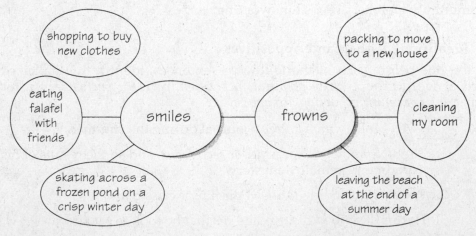

# KINDS OF CLAUSES

**13a**  A *clause* is a group of words that contains a verb and its subject and is used as part of a sentence.

**13b**  An *independent* (or *main*) *clause* expresses a complete thought and can stand by itself as a sentence.

EXAMPLES    Elena is studying astronomy.
            She wants to be an astronaut.

Each independent clause has its own subject and verb and expresses a complete thought. These clauses can be joined by a comma and a coordinating conjunction such as *and, but, or, for, so,* or *yet.* They could also be written with a semicolon between them or with a semicolon followed by a conjunctive adverb and a comma.

EXAMPLES    Elena is studying astronomy, and she wants to be an
            astronaut.
            Elena is studying astronomy; she wants to be an astronaut.
            Elena is studying astronomy; indeed, she wants to be an
            astronaut.

**13c**  A *subordinate* (or *dependent*) *clause* does not express a complete thought and cannot stand alone.

A subordinate clause must be joined to at least one independent clause to express a complete thought. Words such as *whom, because, what, if,* and *when* signal the beginning of a subordinate clause.

SUBORDINATE CLAUSES    if the fog lifts
                       when the show begins
                       whom we have met before

SENTENCES    **If the fog lifts**, we can go sailing.
             Did you ask **when the show begins**?
             Sumio, **whom we have met before**, will take us to
             the site.

## EXERCISE 1    Identifying Independent and Subordinate Clauses

In the following paragraph, identify each italicized clause. On the line before each sentence, write *indep.* for *independent* or *sub.* for *subordinate.*

EX.    [1] __indep.__ Before 2000 B.C. *there were no post offices for the general public.*

[1] _____ Egypt is most likely *where the first postal system was*

161

*developed.* [2] _____ *Postal systems were developed* because ancient governments needed to relay messages. [3] _____ The central government could control provincial administration only *if there was a system of communication linking the capital and the provinces.*

[4] _____ Later postal systems employed relay stations, *which would provide fresh horses and riders.* [5] _____ *Since this idea is so practical,* it was probably thought of quite soon.

[6] _____ Evidence *that postal relay stations were used,* however, is no older than 500 B.C. [7] _____ *The Roman Empire needed a postal system* because it was so enormous in every regard.

[8] _____ The Roman Empire's postal system was important enough *that it was preserved by the succeeding Islamic Empire.*

[9] _____ In the Middle Ages, *additional postal routes were set up privately* so traders could conduct business. [10] _____ *It was not until the middle of the sixteenth century A.D.* that private persons and businesses were allowed to use the government's postal system.

[11] _____ *United Parcel Service and Federal Express are contemporary versions of these privately run postal systems.*

[12] _____ Private citizens' using the postal system was begun in Europe by the prince Thurn und Taxis, *who ran the Imperial postal system of his country.* [13] _____ *This practice began the era of the postage stamp,* which was invented as a way to charge private persons who sent mail. [14] _____ *Before the stamp was invented,* people had to pay to receive mail sent to them. [15] _____ Some people today want to revert to this practice *because they think it would cut down on junk mail.*

# THE ADJECTIVE CLAUSE

**13d   An *adjective clause* is a subordinate clause that modifies a noun or a pronoun.**

An adjective clause follows the word it modifies. If a clause is essential to the meaning of the sentence, it is not set off with commas. If a clause only gives additional information and is nonessential to the meaning of a sentence, it is set off by commas.

EXAMPLES   The pond, **which is a landing place for migrating birds**, lies in a protected area. [The clause *which is a landing place for migrating birds* is not necessary to identify *pond* and is set off by commas.]
Baseball is the sport **that I like best.** [The clause *that I like best* is essential to the meaning of the sentence and, therefore, is not set off by commas.]

Adjective clauses are usually introduced by ***relative pronouns.*** These words relate an adjective clause to the word that the clause modifies.

| Relative Pronouns | | | | |
|---|---|---|---|---|
| that | which | who | whom | whose |

EXAMPLES   Sarah, **who had lived in the Philippines**, still had many friends there. [The relative pronoun *who* relates the adjective clause to *Sarah. Who* is the subject of the adjective clause.]
Stephen Hawking is a scientist **whom I greatly admire.** [The relative pronoun *whom* relates the adjective clause to the subject. *Whom* is the direct object of the verb *admire* in the adjective clause.]
The author, **whose new book was published this week,** spoke to our class. [The relative pronoun *whose* relates the adjective clause to *author. Whose* is used as a possessive pronoun in the adjective clause.]

In many cases, the relative pronoun in the clause may be omitted.

EXAMPLE   Here is the video **you wanted.** [The relative pronoun *that* is understood. *That* relates the adjective clause to *video* and is the direct object in the adjective clause.]

## EXERCISE 2   Identifying Adjective Clauses

Underline the ten adjective clauses in the paragraph below.

EX.   [1]  Cesar Chavez, <u>who was born in 1927</u>, helped migrant workers improve their lives.

[1] Cesar Chavez, who spent much of his life trying to improve the lives of migrant farm workers, believed in the power of nonviolent protests.  [2] His parents owned a store, which they lost in the Great Depression of the 1930s.  [3] The Chavez family moved to California and joined the migrant workers who moved throughout the state, harvesting crops.  [4] Chavez learned firsthand about the miserable conditions which these people had to endure.  [5] He searched for ideas and methods that would improve the lives of farm laborers.  [6] He organized a boycott of California grapes that spread throughout the United States.  [7] The boycott helped workers win a contract, which was the first in the history of farm laborers.  [8] In 1968, Chavez began a fast that lasted twenty-five days.  [9] It was the first of three times he fasted to protest the low pay and poor working conditions of the farm laborer.  [10] Chavez, who died in 1993, saw several improvements in farm labor practices in his lifetime.

## EXERCISE 3   Revising Sentences by Supplying Adjective Clauses

Revise the following pairs of sentences by substituting an adjective clause for one of the sentences. Write the revisions on your own paper.

EX.   1.  We were lucky to see a minke whale. This whale rarely swims into this area.

  1.  We were lucky to see a minke whale, which rarely swims into this area.

1.  Lian planned the menu for the fund-raiser. The fund-raiser was successful.
2.  Two reporters moderated the debate. The reporters are well known.
3.  Amy and Cheng questioned the results of the experiment. This experiment was the first.
4.  The hikers agreed to try a less difficult route. The hikers were tired.
5.  The audience became restless during the presentation. The presentation was long.

# THE ADVERB CLAUSE

**13e** An *adverb clause* is a subordinate clause that modifies a verb, an adjective, or an adverb.

An adverb clause tells *how, when, where, why, how much, to what extent* or *under what condition* the action of the main verb takes place. Adverb clauses are introduced by *subordinating conjunctions*.

| Common Subordinating Conjunctions | | | |
|---|---|---|---|
| after | because | since | when |
| although | before | so that | whenever |
| as | even though | than | where |
| as if | if | though | wherever |
| as long as | in order that | unless | whether |
| as soon as | once | until | while |

EXAMPLES   **After the judge announced her decision**, the attorneys held a press conference. [The adverb clause *after the judge announced her decision* tells *when* the attorneys held a press conference.]
We will go on to the summit **if the good weather holds**. [*If the good weather holds* tells *under what condition* we will go to the summit.]
**Because traffic was so heavy**, the Parks decided to take a different route. [*Because traffic was so heavy* tells *why* the Parks decided to take a different route.]

NOTE   Introductory adverb clauses are usually set off by commas.

EXAMPLE   If you want to come, call me.

## EXERCISE 4   Identifying and Classifying Adverb Clauses

Underline the adverb clause in each of the following sentences. Above each adverb clause, write whether the clause tells *how, when, where, why, how much, to what extent,* or *under what condition*.

EX.   1.  We go camping every year before school starts.
<ins>                                        when                    </ins>

1.  While we were camping in August, we saw a meteor shower.

2.  Meteor showers occur when rock or iron particles called
    meteoroids enter earth's atmosphere from space.

165

3. As these particles enter the earth's atmosphere, they heat up and glow brightly.

4. We call the burning particles "shooting stars" even though they are not really stars.

5. Meteor showers are spectacular because you can see many shooting stars in one night.

6. November is a good month to watch for meteors because the Leonid meteor shower occurs every November.

7. Where space debris is abundant, the showers are more brilliant.

8. Unless you can get away from cities, light pollution makes it hard to see meteors.

9. Once we had driven far enough from the city, we started looking for a campsite.

10. After we viewed the sunset, we watched the sky and saw a fine show.

## EXERCISE 5    Building Sentences That Have Adverb Clauses

On your own paper, write ten sentences, using a clause from the list below in each sentence. Do not use the same subordinate clause twice. In each sentence you create, underline the adverb clause once and the word or words it modifies twice. You may combine two of the clauses below or add words of your own.

EX.    some people are always hungry    the lunch bags appear right away

    1. <u>Because some people are always hungry</u>, the lunch bags <u>appear</u> right away.

after we get to the Museum of Science

where our class goes on an outing

before we will allow radios with speakers

as Mr. Henshaw gets off the bus

once Mr. Favaloro starts talking

while someone makes a joke

as if we agree

if Mr. Henshaw acts like a tour guide

unless we ban radios with speakers

in order that we eat lunch

wherever no one can hear

because we left the parking lot

since some people are always hungry

until we can agree on music

as long as we meet at the cafeteria

whenever we see a video of an animal

so that the bus can leave at nine o'clock

as soon as we eat lunch

although Mr. Favaloro laughs hardest

when we scatter through the museum

# THE NOUN CLAUSE

**13f A *noun clause* is a subordinate clause used as a noun.**

A noun clause may be used as a subject, a complement (predicate nominative, direct object, indirect object), or the object of a preposition.

| | |
|---|---|
| SUBJECT | **What I liked best about my trip to Mexico** was seeing the Aztec ruins. |
| PREDICATE NOMINATIVE | The loser is **whoever has the final piece to the puzzle.** |
| DIRECT OBJECT | We thought we knew **what Kwam's gift would be.** |
| INDIRECT OBJECT | The chef will tell **whoever asks** the recipe for her specialty. |
| OBJECT OF A PREPOSITION | She carefully checked the applications of **whoever applied for the job.** |

Noun clauses are usually introduced by *that, what, whatever, who, whoever, whom,* and *whomever.* Sometimes, however, noun clauses do not have an introductory word.

EXAMPLE   Joey wished he could join the group. [The introductory word *that* is understood.]

## EXERCISE 6   Identifying and Classifying Noun Clauses

Underline each noun clause in the following paragraph. Above it, identify how it is used. Write *s.* for *subject, p.n.* for *predicate nominative, d.o.* for *direct object, i.o.* for *indirect object,* or *o.p.* for *object of a preposition.*

EX.   [1] My sister always said that she did not like animals. *(d. o.)*

[1] What changed her mind was her discovering a baby opossum in our backyard. [2] She realized that it was too tiny to survive on its own. [3] She didn't know what to do with it or who could help her. [4] That our town had a wildlife rescue center proved to be the answer to her problem. [5] My sister carefully wrapped the baby opossum in whatever soft rags were at hand and took it to the center.

[6] The director told her the center would care for the opossum until it was old enough to return to the wild. [7] My sister asked whoever was free many questions. [8] Now she is a volunteer at the center, helping in whatever way she can. [9] A veterinarian is what she wants to be. [10] Whatever animals she treats will be in good hands.

## EXERCISE 7   Writing Sentences by Inserting Noun Clauses

On your own paper, add noun clauses to the sentences below. Then label the function of the noun clause in each sentence.

EX.   1.   Eliza told me _that Ramón is going to the carnival tonight. (d.o.)_
            (Use *that*)

1. _____
   _____ is a sad fact. (Use *that*.)

2. _____
   _____ had better tell me. (Use *whoever*.)

3. _____
   _____ is a good vacation. (Use *what*.)

4. Did you know _____
   _____? (Use *that*.)

5. Mom always gives _____
   _____ a reward. (Use *whoever*.)

6. The teacher limited test items to _____
   _____ . (Use *whatever*.)

7. _____
   _____will probably always be a mystery to me. (Use *where*.)

8. The best answer is _____
   _____ . (Use *whatever*.)

9. Was your question _____
   _____? (Use *how*.)

10. We all wanted to know _____
    _____ . (Use *who*.)

# SENTENCE STRUCTURE

**13g** **According to their structure, sentences are classified as** *simple,* *compound, complex,* **and** *compound-complex.*

**(1)** A *simple sentence* **has one independent clause and no subordinate clauses. It may have a compound subject, a compound verb, and any number of phrases.**

EXAMPLE     After studying Russia and listening to their grandmother's stories, Tanya and Alexis decided to prepare a Russian meal for their friends.

**(2)** A *compound sentence* **has two or more independent clauses but no subordinate clauses.**

In effect, a compound sentence consists of two or more simple sentences joined by a comma and a coordinating conjunction, by a semicolon, or by a semicolon followed by a conjunctive adverb and a comma.

EXAMPLES     They had eaten many of their grandmother's Russian specialties, **but** they had never prepared them.
Tanya's favorite was piroshki; Alexis liked dumplings, latkes, and blini.
They had watched their grandmother prepare these dishes; **consequently,** they knew it was a lot of work.

**(3)** A *complex sentence* **has one independent clause and at least one subordinate clause.**

EXAMPLES     Tanya suggested that they also serve a soup, a salad, and Russian tea.
When they told their grandmother about their plans, she offered to help.

**(4)** A *compound-complex sentence* **contains two or more independent clauses and at least one subordinate clause.**

EXAMPLES     Tanya and Alexis wanted to invite everyone who was interested in their plans, and so they had a long guest list.
Before the party began, the two had spent many hours cooking, and so had their grandmother, who said the feast was first-rate.

## EXERCISE 8   Classifying Sentences According to Structure

Classify each sentence in the paragraph below. On the line before each sentence, write *simp.* for *simple*, *comp.* for *compound*, *cx.* for *complex*, and *cd.-cx.* for *compound-complex*.

EX.   _____cx._____ [1] Machu Picchu, which is located on a mountaintop in Peru, was the capital city for the Incas a thousand years ago.

_____ [1] Built on a peak in the Andes and overlooking a deep canyon, the ancient city contains the ruins of four hundred houses, as well as temples, plazas, and palaces. _____ [2] It was constructed of granite blocks; how the Incas, who had only simple tools, transported this stone up the steep mountain remains a puzzle. _____ [3] A Peruvian legend says that the ancient Incas were helped by angel architects who made the granite fall off cliffs and fly to the building site. _____ [4] Some modern engineers believe this explanation as much as any other! _____ [5] Incas lived in Machu Picchu until the population outgrew the food supply; then they moved the capital to Cuzco, which is on the western slope of the Andes. _____ [6] Machu Picchu was no longer inhabited, but perhaps it was not entirely forgotten. _____ [7] The Spaniards came to Peru hundreds of years after Machu Picchu was abandoned. _____ [8] The Spaniards, who were searching for gold, attempted to seize a convent where Inca women devoted their lives to the service of the Sun God.

_____ [9] They found the convent empty; the women had vanished.

_____ [10] Many Incas believed that the Sun God lifted the women into the sky; but after explorers discovered Machu Picchu in 1911, some people came to believe that the women took refuge there.

# CHAPTER REVIEW

## A. Classifying Subordinate Clauses

Classify each italicized clause in the paragraph below. Write *adj.* for *adjective*, *adv.* for *adverb*, or *n.* for *noun* above the clause.

EX.  [1] *Although rock climbing looks difficult*, it is a sport [2] *that nearly everyone can try*.

                                                 adv.                                               adj.

The variety of the sport is [1] *what makes it open to anyone* [2] *who is interested.* Rock climbing can be climbing [3] *in which the climber stays close to the ground without a rope or special gear,* or it can be big wall-climbing, a feat [4] *that requires much more training.* [5] *Although physical strength and coordination are useful,* expert climbers say [6] *that these are not all there is to climbing.* Determination and courage are also qualities [7] *that a climber must have.* [8] *What you need first of all* is an experienced teacher [9] *with whom you can climb.* [10] *After you have followed an expert up enough rocks,* you may be ready to lead a climb yourself.

## B. Identifying and Classifying Clauses

In the following sentences, underline the subordinate clauses. On the line before each sentence, identify the way each clause is used. Write *s.* for *subject*, *d.o.* for *direct object*, *i.o.* for *indirect object*, *p.n.* for *predicate nominative*, *o.p.* for *object of a preposition*, *adj.* for *adjective*, or *adv.* for *adverb*. [Note: Some sentences have more than one clause.]

EX.   *adv.*   1. <u>When Maryssa gave a report on frogs</u>, the class was fascinated.

_____ 1. I had always thought that frogs were boring.

_____ 2. What Maryssa described showed that she had done a lot of research.

_____ 3. She said that West Africa is home to the world's largest frog, which can grow to a length of three feet.

_____ 4. The smallest known frog is found in Cuba and is only one-half inch long when it is fully grown.

_____ 5. If a person could jump proportionately as far as one small North American frog, the world's long-jump record would be 215 feet.

_____ 6. Because eggs are easy prey, some frogs have developed interesting strategies for protecting their eggs.

_____ 7. It is the male parent of the Darwin's frog in South Africa who guards the eggs.

_____ 8. When the eggs show signs of life, the male frog swallows five to fifteen of them and holds them in his croaking sac until they hatch.

_____ 9. Maryssa also described a male frog who guards newly laid eggs by carrying them wound around his leg.

_____ 10. My favorite story was about the helmet frog, who uses its bony head as a door for its home inside a tree.

## C.  Rewriting a Paragraph to Include a Variety of Sentence Structures

After researching a topic for an essay, you have jotted down the draft of the paragraph below. On your own paper, rewrite the paragraph to improve its style. You will need to vary the sentence structure, and you may want to delete, reword, or add details. Write at least one sentence with each kind of structure: simple, compound, complex, and compound-complex. Be ready to identify the structure of each sentence you write.

1       Dr. Maria Montessori was a pioneer in the field of education.
2    She was also the first woman in Italy to attend medical school. She
3    was born in Italy in 1870. That year Italy became a nation. As a
4    teenager she was interested in mathematics. Her parents suggested
5    she become a teacher. This was practically the only career open to
6    women at that time. She decided that she wanted to attend medical
7    school. She was told this was impossible. She persisted and won
8    entrance to medical school. She even won scholarships. As the only
9    female student, she endured great hardships in medical school. She
10    graduated in 1896. After graduation, she worked at a psychiatric
11    clinic. She became interested in children with learning problems.
12    She came to believe that with the proper education, their lives
13    could improve. She became director of a school for children who
14    were considered hopeless. The progress of the children in her
15    school surprised everyone. She went on to develop theories of
16    education for all children. The equipment she designed for
17    teaching and her ideas about how young children learn are used
18    now in Montessori schools all over the world.

# SUBJECT-VERB AGREEMENT

*Number* is the form of a word that indicates whether the word is singular or plural.

**14a  When a word refers to one person or thing, it is *singular* in number. When a word refers to more than one, it is *plural* in number.**

| SINGULAR | plumber | mouse | I | chopstick |
|----------|---------|-------|---|-----------|
| PLURAL | plumbers | mice | we | chopsticks |

## Classifying Nouns and Pronouns by Number

In the sentences below, identify each italicized word by writing *sing.* for *singular* or *pl.* for *plural* above the word.

EX.   1.   The tiny *peaches* were carved from a *piece* of green jade.
                     *pl.*                          *sing.*

1.   Cleon said that Irene and *he* can rehearse their *scenes* later.

2.   When the ball came flying toward the plate, *Vincente* swung the bat with all *his* strength.

3.   The political *cartoons* are usually on the editorial *page*.

4.   Florence Griffith Joyner has certainly won a lot of *medals* and *awards* in track-and-field events!

5.   An auto *mechanic* can adjust your *brakes* easily.

6.   The new stained-glass *windows* replaced the *ones* that had been damaged during the hailstorm.

7.   Each person in the *class* created colorful *drawings* of people or animals.

8.   An antique silk *kimono* was displayed in a glass *case*.

9.   The driver asked *us* if *we* wanted to stop at Monticello.

10.   Corey is teaching his twin *sisters* how to ride *their* bikes.

**14b    A verb should always agree with its subject in number.**

**(1) Singular subjects take singular verbs.**

EXAMPLE    **Julie kicks** the ball to me. [The singular verb *kicks* agrees with the singular subject *Julie*.]

**(2) Plural subjects take plural verbs.**

EXAMPLE    The **players run** toward the goal. [The plural verb *run* agrees with the plural subject *players*.]

Like single-word verbs, verb phrases also agree with their subjects. However, in a verb phrase, only the first helping (auxiliary) verb changes its form to agree with the subject.

EXAMPLES    **Maribeth has** been working on my campaign.
**Maribeth** and **Eula have** been working on my campaign.

## EXERCISE 2    Identifying Verbs That Agree in Number with Their Subjects

For each sentence below, underline the verb in parentheses that agrees with the subject.

EX.    1.  First, the pilot (*checks*, *check*) the controls.

1.  (*Has*, *Have*) you ever seen Alvin Ailey's ballet?

2.  The Pachecos all (*laughs*, *laugh*) at the same jokes.

3.  These folk tales (*is*, *are*) about how the world began.

4.  First, the students (*picks*, *pick*) up their pencils.

5.  Mama (*has*, *have*) made sopapillas for dessert.

6.  Several trains (*runs*, *run*) on that track.

7.  My youngest cousin (*spins*, *spin*) the dreidel first.

8.  The Indian monetary system (*is*, *are*) based on the rupee, not the dollar.

9.  The two boys (*collects*, *collect*) baseball cards.

10.  Since July, Lorenz (*has*, *have*) painted four pictures.

11.  Bradley (*earns*, *earn*) his blue belt in tae kwon do this year.

12.  Dexter and Paul (*enjoys*, *enjoy*) our school carnivals.

13.  The band from Mexico City (*plays*, *play*) for us frequently.

14.  The Herb Show (*has*, *have*) many interesting booths.

15.  Next week, business leaders (*is*, *are*) hosting a job fair.

# INTERVENING PHRASES

**14c  The number of the subject is not changed by a phrase following the subject.**

Remember that a verb agrees in number with its subject. The subject is never part of a prepositional phrase.

EXAMPLES    That **curtain** behind the actors **is** new. [The verb *is* agrees with the subject *curtain*.]
The **books** on that shelf **are** dictionaries. [The verb *are* agrees with the subject *books*.]

Compound prepositions such as *together with, in addition to, as well as,* and *along with* following the subject do not affect the number of the subject.

EXAMPLES    **Leona**, as well as her parents, **is** visiting us.
The **lettuce**, in addition to the tomatoes, **has** been washed.

## EXERCISE 3   Identifying Subjects and Verbs That Agree in Number

In each of the following sentences, underline the verb form that agrees with the subject. Then underline the subject twice.

EX.    1.   Several cars in the parking lot (*needs, need*) washing.

1.  A pattern of changing colors (*appears, appear*) on the screen when the computer is not in use.

2.  The people from our town (*is, are*) celebrating Nisei Week.

3.  The actor, in addition to the producers, (*calls, call*) the daily meetings.

4.  The pedestrians in this city (*hears, hear*) the muezzin every day.

5.  Two students, together with their teacher, (*is, are*) collecting blankets for flood victims.

6.  The signature below the printed name (*was, were*) difficult to read.

7.  Ben, as well as Aunt Elaine, (*makes, make*) good couscous.

8.  The keys on this keyboard (*feels, feel*) sticky.

9.  A huge bouquet of flowers (*was, were*) delivered to my mother.

10.  The twins, together with Duane, (*is, are*) taking the bus.

11. Roberto Garcia, Jr., a bronze sculptor who lives south of Kingsville, Texas, (*has, have*) an unusual job.

12. All the work on a bronze sculpture (*is, are*) done by Garcia, himself.

13. Bronze, wax, and clay, along with steel, (*is, are*) materials he works with every day.

14. Two clay statues outside his garage (*guards, guard*) his workshop.

15. Sketches, as well as small models, (*makes, make*) up the first step of a new bronze sculpture.

16. A full-size structure of steel and clay (*goes, go*) together next.

17. Mr. Garcia's kiln, at temperatures of about fifteen hundred degrees Farenheit, (*melts, melt*) the wax in a mold.

18. The wax between the mold's layers (*drains, drain*) out.

19. Bronze for the statue (*is, are*) poured into the gap left by the drained wax.

20. Welding, along with sandblasting and grinding, almost (*finishes, finish*) the process.

## EXERCISE 4   Proofreading a Paragraph for Subject-Verb Agreement

In the paragraph below, draw a line through each verb that does not agree with its subject. Write the correct verb form in the space above the incorrect word.

EX.   [1]  A student in my biology class ~~have~~ an interesting terrarium.
                                      *has*

[1] A fish tank, a gift from Pedro's parents, are the container. [2] The plants in it is mostly nonflowering. [3] The moss, as well as the lichens, have spores, not flowers. [4] The mosses near the front comes from the woods near the school. [5] The lichens on the rock is about five years old, according to my biology teacher. [6] The bright red tips on the lichen is partly fungus. [7] One name for the lichens are "British soldiers." [8] In addition to mosses and lichens, a fern thrive in the terrarium. [9] Our teacher, along with us students, want to start a class terrarium. [10] Some students in the class knows where to get a fish tank and some plants.

# AGREEMENT WITH INDEFINITE PRONOUNS

*Indefinite pronouns* are pronouns that do not refer to a specific person or thing.

**14d  The following pronouns are singular:** *each, either, neither, one, everyone, everybody, no one, nobody, anyone, anybody, someone, somebody.*

EXAMPLES  **Neither** of the books **is** difficult. [**Neither** one is difficult.]
**Someone does have** the key.

**14e  The following pronouns are plural:** *several, few, both, many.*

EXAMPLES  **Several** of the books **are** easy.  **Both have** keys to the house.

**14f  The pronouns** *some, all, most, any,* **and** *none* **may be either singular or plural.**

These pronouns are singular when they refer to a singular word and plural when they refer to a plural word.

SINGULAR  **All** of the report **is** factual.
**Most** of the lawn **has** been raked.

PLURAL  **All** of the facts **are** true.
**Most** of the leaves **have** been raked.

The words *any* and *none* may be singular even when they refer to a plural word if the speaker is thinking of each item individually. *Any* and *none* are plural only if the speaker is thinking of several items as a group.

EXAMPLES  **None** of the windows **was** broken. [*Not one window* was broken.]
**None** of the windows **were** large. [*No windows were large.*]
**Is any** of the windows open? [*Is any one window* open?]
**Any** of the windows **are** good places for a plant. [*All the windows* are good places for a plant.]

## EXERCISE 5  Using Indefinite Pronouns Correctly

On your own paper, use each of the following word groups as a subject in a sentence. Underline the subjects once and the verbs twice in your sentences.

EX.  1.  Most of my homework

1.  <u>Most</u> of my homework <u>is finished</u>.

1.  Several of my friends      3.  Everybody in the room

2.  Both Nikki and Emilio      4.  Someone from school

| | |
|---|---|
| 5. Neither of the movies | 13. Some of Mr. Dodd's pecans |
| 6. Somebody upstairs | 14. Most of the movies |
| 7. All of the guitars | 15. Any of the ribbons |
| 8. Everyone at the meeting | 16. No one from our office |
| 9. Many of the puppets | 17. None of the bread |
| 10. Each fish in the tank | 18. Most of her progress |
| 11. None of the streams | 19. Nobody within the class |
| 12. Few among the volunteers | 20. Any of the softball games |

## EXERCISE 6   Proofreading a Paragraph for Subject-Verb Agreement

Draw a line through each verb that does not agree with its subject. Write the correct verb form in the space above the incorrect word. Some sentences may contain no agreement errors.

EX.  [1]  One of my term papers ~~are~~ *is* on Hausa proverbs from the people of northern Nigeria and the Sudan.

[1] All of the proverbs I found makes me really think.  [2] Neither of these two proverbs are easy to understand: "It is not the eye which understands, but the mind" and "Lack of knowledge is darker than the night."  [3] Both proverbs gives insight into how people think. [4] Some proverbs reflects the Hausa way of life.  [5] "A chief is like a trash heap where everyone brings his or her rubbish" seems to show us that the Hausa bring their problems to their leader.  [6] Someone like that chief have to be very patient, I think.  [7] Several proverbs contains words I had to look up in a dictionary.  [8] Most of the unfamiliar words are natural objects, such as cowries and groundnuts.  [9] No one I know have clearly explained the proverb "It is by traveling softly, softly that you will sleep in a distant place." [10] One of my teachers have suggested that I also read the proverbs of the Ashanti, one of the native peoples of West Africa.

# THE COMPOUND SUBJECT

A *compound subject* has two or more nouns or pronouns that are the subject of the same verb.

**14g   Subjects joined by *and* usually take a plural verb.**

EXAMPLES   **Cao** and **I are** building the model together. [Two people are building the model.]

**Light, warmth,** and **water act** together. [Three things act together.]

**14h   Compound subjects that name only one person or thing take a singular verb.**

EXAMPLE   **Red beans** and **rice is** inexpensive and healthful. [*Red beans and rice* is one dish.]

**14i   Singular subjects joined by *or* or *nor* take a singular verb.**

EXAMPLES   **Either Grandfather** or **Julie has** the scissors. [Only one person has the scissors, not both.]

**Neither fog** nor **rain stops** this train! [Neither one stops the train.]

**14j   When a singular subject and a plural subject are joined by *or* or *nor*, the verb agrees with the subject nearer the verb.**

ACCEPTABLE   Either the peaches or the **watermelon is** fine for dessert.
Either the watermelon or the **peaches are** fine for dessert.

BETTER   The **peaches are** fine for dessert, and so **is** the **watermelon**.
The **watermelon is** fine for dessert, and the **peaches are**, too.

You can usually avoid such awkward constructions by rewording the sentence so that each subject has its own verb.

EXAMPLE   Either **Darren is** bringing the children to the ceremony, or his mother and **father are**.

---

**EXERCISE 7   Choosing Verbs That Agree in Number with Their Subjects**

In each of the following sentences, underline the correct form of the verb in parentheses.

EX.   1.  Charles and Pang (*is, are*) on the team.

1.  Either the tuba or the saxophones (*plays, play*) first.

2. Neither my mother nor my father (*is, are*) eager to go.

3. Either Yori or Sheila (*has, have*) extra flyers.

4. Macaroni and cheese (*is, are*) our favorite food.

5. The audience and the actors (*likes, like*) that play.

6. David Ben-Gurion and Golda Meir (*was, were*) prime ministers of Israel.

7. Either Jun or Asa (*has, have*) time to saw the boards.

8. Blocks and a drum (*is, are*) all a two-year-old child needs for entertainment.

9. Neither pencil and paper nor a calculator (*was, were*) available.

10. Rock-and-roll always (*catches, catch*) my sister's attention.

11. Jordan's sketch and Meg's painting (*was, were*) finished.

12. My brother and sister never (*enjoys, enjoy*) arguing.

13. Tents, backpacks, and food (*has, have*) been packed.

14. Neither the pharmacy nor the front desk (*is, are*) answering.

15. (*Was, Were*) chicken and dumplings on the menu today?

16. Both salsa and gazpacho (*requires, require*) tomatoes as ingredients.

17. Patricia, Susan, and Guy (*works, work*) well together.

18. Scissors and paper (*does, do*) need to be on the list.

19. Paula, her brothers, and her sister (*wishes, wish*) to help Mrs. Landowski.

20. Either Mrs. Columbo or Mr. Andrews (*is, are*) able to help them, too.

21. Pencil or pens (*writes, write*) equally well on this type of paper.

22. Bonnie and Rolando (*has, have*) agreed to run for office.

23. How soon (*is, are*) Etta and Albert leaving on vacation?

24. Mark and Coretta (*watches, watch*) the runners carefully.

25. (*Does, Do*) Erica or Han-Ling cast the last vote?

# DOESN'T / DON'T *AND COLLECTIVE NOUNS*

**14k** *Don't* and *doesn't* must agree with their subjects.

*Contractions* are two words combined into one, with one or more letters omitted. *Don't* is the contraction for *do not*. *Doesn't* is the contraction for *does not*.

With the subjects *I* and *you* and with plural subjects, use *don't* (*do not*).

EXAMPLES    I **don't** see anything.    They **don't** care.
You **don't** need one.    Sales **don't** last long.

With other singular subjects, use the singular *doesn't* (*does not*).

EXAMPLES    He **doesn't** work here.    The sweater **doesn't** fit.
This **doesn't** look hard.    Lily **doesn't** feel sick.

**14l** Collective nouns may be either singular or plural.

*Collective nouns* are singular in form, but they name a *group* of persons or things.

| Collective Nouns | | |
|---|---|---|
| army | committee | herd |
| assembly | family | jury |
| audience | fleet | public |
| class | flock | swarm |
| club | group | team |

Use a plural verb with a collective noun when you refer to the individual parts or members of the group acting separately. Use a singular verb when you refer to the group acting together as a unit.

EXAMPLES    The **jury have** not been home yet. [*Jury* is thought of as individuals.]
The **jury has** finally reached a verdict. [*Jury* is thought of as a unit.]

**EXERCISE 8   Using *Doesn't* and *Don't* Correctly**

Use *doesn't* or *don't* correctly to complete each sentence below.

EX.   1.  I ___don't___ need help with this.

1.  We _____ serve any Moroccan food here.

2.  _____ you serve couscous?

3.  Well, our dish _____ contain meat.

4.  You _____ need to use lamb, but it adds good flavor.

5.  These recipes _____ require a special steamer.

6.  The supermarket _____ sell lamb broth.

7.  _____ Jolon need more chickpeas?

8.  The vegetables _____ need a separate bowl.

9.  It _____ look hard to make.

10.  _____ this taste delicious!

11.  Some newspapers _____ have many recipes like this.

12.  _____ you grow some of these vegetables?

13.  Herbs _____ seem to be difficult to grow.

14.  Preparing the garden _____ take long.

15.  _____ overwater the herbs and vegetables.

**EXERCISE 9   Writing Sentences with Collective Nouns**

Select five collective nouns from the chart on the preceding page. On your own paper, write a pair of sentences using each noun. Each pair of sentences should show how the collective noun may be either singular or plural.

EX.   1.  The swarm is huge!
      1.  The swarm are flying in different directions.

## OTHER PROBLEMS IN AGREEMENT

**14m  A verb agrees with its subject, not with its predicate nominative.**

EXAMPLES    The **prize is** two concert tickets.
S   V        P.N.

Two concert **tickets are** the prize.
S   V     P.N.

**14n  When the subject follows the verb, find the subject and make sure that the verb agrees with it.**

The most common cases in which the subject follows the verb are in questions and in sentences beginning with *here* or *there*.

EXAMPLES    Here **is** a **menorah**.
Here **are** some **candles**.

There **is** a new **student** in class.
There **are** new **students** in class.

**Does** the **map** show this road?
**Do** these **roads** appear on the map?

**14o  Words stating an amount are usually singular.**

EXAMPLES    **Six dollars is** a lot for that.
Your **five minutes is** up.

Sometimes, however, the amount is thought of as individual pieces or parts. If so, a plural verb is used.

EXAMPLES    **Two** of the dollars **are** silver dollars.
**Three fourths** of the pencils **are** sharpened.

**14p  *Every* or *many a* before a subject calls for a singular verb.**

EXAMPLES    **Every** shelf **has** a kachina doll on it.
**Many a** doll **was** made of cottonwood root.

**14q  A few nouns, although plural in form, take singular verbs.**

EXAMPLES    The **news is** grim this week.
Unfortunately, **measles is** showing up in young adults.

NOTE    Some nouns that end in –*s* take a plural verb even though they refer to a single item.

EXAMPLES    The **scissors are** on the table.
Your **pants are** clean.

## EXERCISE 10    Identifying Subjects and Verbs That Agree in Number

In each sentence below, underline the verb form that agrees with the subject. Then underline the subject twice.

EX.   1.   A relay team (*is, are*) three people.

1.   Eight miles (*is, are*) a long race.

2.   Two different prizes (*was, were*) given at the party.

3.   Many a trophy (*has, have*) been won by that team!

4.   Politics (*determines, determine*) the choice of team captain.

5.   (*Does, Do*) Ulani have the same coach?

6.   The winner (*is, are*) the first-year runners.

7.   There (*is, are*) professional recruiters in the bleachers today.

8.   Every race (*has, have*) a clear favorite.

9.   Here (*is, are*) the name of the best runner.

10.   Many unknown runners (*has, have*) won the steeplechase.

11.   (*Does, Do*) Gisela have a good chance of winning in the next race?

12.   Where (*is, are*) your friend Rudy now?

13.   That relay team always (*goes, go*) on to the regional meet.

14.   Every heat (*has, have*) six runners in it.

15.   The shorts with green and while stripes (*is, are*) Emilio's.

16.   Why (*does, do*) Caron and Aponte always get here early?

17.   Twenty minutes (*has, have*) passed since the starting gun went off.

18.   Five kilometers (*is, are*) the distance of the cross-country race.

19.   Three of those kilometers (*leads, lead*) up steep hills.

20.   Tonight the news (*covers, cover*) some of the races.

21.   Here (*is, are*) the books you were looking for.

22.   Few varieties of oak tree (*grows, grow*) in our state.

23.   (*Hasn't, Haven't*) Andrés passed his driving test?

24.   Gayle's trousers (*is, are*) a dark shade of green.

25.   There (*is, are*) a new family on our block.

# REVIEW EXERCISE

## A. Choosing Verbs That Agree in Number with Their Subjects

In each of the sentences below, underline the correct form of the verb in parentheses.

EX. 1. The men in the picture (is, <u>are</u>) artists.

1. Each (*has, have*) a brush, some black ink, and a sheet of paper.

2. (*Does, Do*) your sister use a camel's hair brush?

3. The audience (*likes, like*) the bamboo with the drooping leaves.

4. Many in the room (*enjoys, enjoy*) painting.

5. (*Does, Do*) the artists often make their own inks?

6. The ink, the brush, and the silk (*affects, affect*) the finish of a painting done on silk.

7. Either Mr. Tsai or his teacher (*is, are*) demonstrating different kinds of brush strokes.

8. Where (*is, are*) the scrolls that contain all the writing?

9. Neither the words nor the drawing (*is, are*) red.

10. Forty dollars (*seems, seem*) reasonable to me.

11. You (*wasn't, weren't*) home when we telephoned.

12. One of the articles (*is, are*) about N. Scott Momaday.

13. We (*was, were*) talking about these machines in French class.

14. Nobody in these stores (*sells, sell*) my kind of shoe.

15. (*Does, Do*) apples and oranges come in the next shipment?

16. Each of the contestants (*seems, seem*) pleased with the judges' final decision.

17. Theo, Jerry, and Ed (*wants, want*) to work for you.

18. Jeanine and her parents (*gets, get*) all of the mail.

19. Either Gloria or Sandra (*has, have*) a watch with a second hand.

20. The effects of the long dry spell (*was, were*) deadly for crops and cattle.

## B.  Proofreading a Paragraph for Subject-Verb Agreement

In the sentences below, draw a line through each verb that does not agree
with its subject. Write the correct verb form in the space above the incorrect
word. Some sentences have no errors in subject-verb agreement.

EX.   [1]  One of my cousins ~~are~~ a great collector.
          *is*

  [1] The news are full of stories about lucky breaks.  [2] You might

read about how somebody find a rare book in an attic.  [3] Few of

these stories is completely true.  [4] Still, my cousin and I like to hear

them.  [5] We has spent many weekends going to yard sales.  [6] There

is often collections of baseball cards for sale.  [7] These sales offers a

great opportunity for collectors.  [8] People often don't know which

cards are special.  [9] Several of the older cards has greater value today

than ever before.  [10] The cards in my collection was made before

1960.


## C.  Writing Trivia Questions

Your job as a copywriter is to write questions for a television trivia game
show. Your category for the next program is the Olympics. Use reference
books, magazines, or encyclopedias to learn some details about the
Olympics. Then, on your own paper, create fifteen questions from your
notes. Underline the subjects once and the verbs twice in your questions,
and make sure they agree.

EX.    Notes:  games held in Olympia, Greece, every four years between 776 B.C.
              and A.D. 393

      Question:  Where were the first games held?

# PRONOUN-ANTECEDENT AGREEMENT

A pronoun usually refers to a noun or another pronoun that comes before it. The word that a pronoun refers to is called its *antecedent.*

**14r   A pronoun should agree with its antecedent in number and gender.**

Some singular personal pronouns have forms that indicate the gender of the antecedent. Masculine pronouns (*he, him, his*) refer to males. Feminine pronouns (*she, her, hers*) refer to females. Neuter pronouns (*it, its*) refer to things that are neither male nor female, and often to animals.

EXAMPLES   **Sean** took **his** calculator with **him.**
**Mrs. Torres** said that **she** would share **her** lunch.
The **trunk** is missing **its** key.

The gender of other pronouns is determined by the phrase that follows the pronoun.

EXAMPLES   **Neither** of the **women** forgot **her** lines.[*Women*, in the phrase that follows *Neither*, determines the pronoun's gender.]
One **person** left **her** or **his** scarf. [*Person* could be either masculine or feminine.]

**(1) Use a singular pronoun to refer to** *each, either, neither, one, everyone, everybody, no one, nobody, anyone, anybody, someone,* **or** *somebody.*

EXAMPLES   **Each** cast **his** or **her** vote.
**One** of the striped socks lost **its** mate.

**(2) Use a singluar pronoun to refer to two or more singular antecedents joined by** *or* **or** *nor.*

EXAMPLES   Either **Lucia** or **Marna** will explain **her** experiment.
Neither my **father** nor **Rudy** brought **his** camera.

**(3) Two or more antecedents joined by** *and* **should be referred to by a plural pronoun.**

EXAMPLES   **Lionel** and **Laura** were proud of **their** son.
**Mr. Tower**, **Todd**, and I will do **our** best.

## EXERCISE 11    Identifying Antecedents and Writing Pronouns

On the line in each sentence below, write a pronoun that agrees with its antecedent. Underline the antecedent.

EX.    1. <u>Mr. Sharp</u> offered __his__ opinion.

1. No one in the party had forgotten _____ ticket.

2. For many people, this trip to the jungle was _____ first.

3. Flora always carried _____ camera.

4. The train stopped four times on _____ way to the plantation.

5. Neither my sister nor Hazel needed _____ snacks.

6. At the many stops, local people sold _____ goods.

7. One person left _____ hat on the seat.

8. Toshiro and Greg struggled to get _____ seats by the window.

9. The banana plantation ships much of _____ fruit to other countries.

10. One of the men brought _____ puppy on the train.

11. Tara took _____ lamb to the county fair.

12. Our town had _____ centennial celebration last week.

13. Renaldo and Kazuo always go to _____ gymnastic classes.

14. Either Nora or Rosa will invite _____ mother to the open house.

15. Both of the boys went to _____ extra practices to prepare for the Olympic trials.

16. The new motor scooter received _____ first dent.

17. Nobody in our family forgets to wear _____ seat belt when riding in the car.

18. The truck and bicycle had mud all over _____ wheels.

19. Wendy decided that _____ could meet us after all.

20. Did Dr. Bryan agree that she should make _____ speech for our health class?

# CHAPTER REVIEW

## A. Proofreading Sentences for Subject-Verb and Pronoun-Antecedent Agreement

For each error in agreement in the following sentences, draw a line through the incorrect word, and write the correct form above it. If the sentence is correct, write C.

EX. _____ 1. Politics ~~are~~ *is* not as interesting as science.

_____ 1. Where are your report on meteorites?

_____ 2. The students in the front row hears Ms. Swift better than I do.

_____ 3. Somebody in my class forgot to write their name on a paper.

_____ 4. The chart is actually several different photographs put together.

_____ 5. Neither Nancy nor Yolanda want to give their report.

_____ 6. Every comet were seen as an omen of things to come.

_____ 7. Few of my classmates has ever seen an aerial photograph of our city.

_____ 8. Fifteen minutes are a long time to talk!

_____ 9. Do each of the boys want some of this salad?

_____ 10. Each of the women presented their findings separately.

_____ 11. Lori and Yoko, besides arriving early, has brought our dessert.

_____ 12. Many of us agree that Robert Frost is one of America's greatest poets.

_____ 13. Several of my classmates is going to the amusement park today.

_____ 14. Have any of the group members brought the paper and paint for the banners?

_____ 15. Some of the father's answers to his son's questions is funny.

_____ 16. Room and board is included in the summer camp fee.

_____ 17. The garden don't take as much work as I thought it would.

_____ 18. Which questions on the test is hardest for you?

_____ 19. At noon, the posse are leaving to begin the search.

_____ 20. There is twenty students in my Chemistry I class.

## B. Proofreading a Paragraph for Subject-Verb and Pronoun-Antecedent Agreement

In the paragraph below, draw a line through each incorrect verb or pronoun. Write the correct form in the space above the incorrect word. Some sentences have no errors in agreement.

EX.  [1] There *are* ~~is~~ many people in my family.

[1] My entire family visit Nara every summer. [2] Everybody look forward to this trip. [3] My father and grandfather always plays *Go* for one evening. [4] Neither my mother nor my grandmother enjoy the game. [5] She both prefer to walk though the streets of Nara. [6] During the day we all likes to wander in the park. [7] Each of us has their favorite part of the park. [8] Grandfather and Grandmother always spends an hour or two at the statue of Buddha. [9] The most interesting part for me are all the people from many nations. [10] Everyone in the family tries to guess a person's home country.

## C. Writing a Letter to a Pen Pal

After waiting many months, you have finally learned the name and address of your new pen pal. On your own paper, make notes about things you might want this person to know about you. You might tell about your family, your birthday, your age, and what grade you are in. Your new friend might like to know your favorite food, movie, sport, color, or holiday. Use your notes to write ten sentences in a letter to introduce yourself to your pen pal. Be sure to put your address in your letter so your new friend will know where to mail his or her answer. In your sentences, check that your verbs agree with their subjects and that your pronouns agree with their antecedents.

EX.

Mara Aboud
157 Middle St.
Grants Pass, OR 97526

Dear Lani,
My name is Mara, and I'd like to be your new pen pal. I'll tell you about myself.

# REGULAR VERBS

**15a** **The four principal parts of a verb are the** *base form*, **the** *present participle*, **the** *past*, **and the** *past participle*.

EXAMPLES We **walk** to school. [base form of *walk*]
We are **walking** home. [present participle of *walk*]
We **walked** to the store. [past of *walk*]
We have **walked** for hours. [past participle of *walk*]

Notice that the tenses made from the present participle and past participle use helping verbs, such as *am, is, are, has,* and *have.*

**15b** **A** *regular verb* **is a verb that forms its past and past participle by adding** *–d* **or** *–ed* **to the base form.**

| Base Form | Present Participle | Past | Past Participle |
|-----------|--------------------|------|-----------------|
| happen | (is) happening | happened | (have) happened |
| create | (is) creating | created | (have) created |
| carry | (is) carrying | carried | (have) carried |

The present participle of most regular verbs ending in *–e* drops the *–e* before adding *–ing.*

 NOTE A few regular verbs have an alternate past form ending in *–t.* For example, the past form of *burn* is *burned* or *burnt.*

## EXERCISE 1 Writing the Correct Forms of Regular Verbs

For each of the following sentences, decide what the correct form of the italicized verb should be. Write the correct verb form on the line in the sentence.

EX. 1. Last night's train (*arrive*) _____arrived_____ on time.

1. Ashur has (*admit*) _____ that he forgot the flowers.

2. Before she left, Lien (*pledge*) _____ to return.

3. Yes, we have (*create*) _____ a new gumbo.

4. My sister, who loves gardening, is (*plant*) _____ both fruits and vegetables.

5. Although we (*hurry*) _____ , we missed the bus.

6. During World War II, hundreds of Navajos in the U.S. Marines (*work*) _____ as Code Talkers.

7. The club members are (*urge*)_____ us to join.

8. What has (*happen*)_____ to that building?

9. The method that Thelma is (*use*) _____ was developed in India.

10. Yesterday morning the class (*watch*) _____ a film about pollution.

11. The rest of the workers have (*decide*) _____ to follow my suggestion.

12. Every morning last month we (*listen*) _____ to a weather report.

13. Ms. Perkins has (*correct*) _____ the errors.

14. I think that dog is (*follow*) _____ us!

15. The radio station (*play*) _____ my two favorite songs last night.

16. Our neighbor down the street is (*move*) _____ to another town.

17. I (*promise*)_____ that I would feed the cat every morning.

18. Sheila (*search*) _____ for hours, but she could not find her keys.

19. Our art class is (*visit*) _____ the museum today.

20. Because the fans have (*wait*) _____ for a long time, they are getting restless.

**SALLY FORTH**                                    **BY GREG HOWARD**

Sally Forth reprinted with special permission of North America Syndicate, Inc.

# IRREGULAR VERBS

**15c** An *irregular verb* is a verb that forms its past and past participle in some other way than by adding *–d* or *–ed* to the base form.

Irregular verbs form their past and past participle by changing vowels, changing consonants, adding *–en*, or making no change at all.

| Base Form | Past | Past participle |
|---|---|---|
| begin | began | (have) begun |
| go | went | (have) gone |
| take | took | (have) taken |
| set | set | (have) set |

Since most English verbs are regular, people sometimes try to make irregular verbs follow the same pattern. However, words such as *knowed* and *thinked* are considered nonstandard. If you are not sure about the parts of a verb, look in a dictionary which lists the principal parts of irregular verbs.

When the present participle and past participle forms are used as main verbs (simple predicates) in sentences, they always require helping verbs.

| Present Participle | + | Helping Verb | = | Verb Phrase |
|---|---|---|---|---|
| running | | forms | | am running |
| driving | + | of | = | was driving |
| seeing | | *be* | | were seeing |

| Past Participle | + | Helping Verb | = | Verb Phrase |
|---|---|---|---|---|
| run | | forms | | have run |
| driven | + | of | = | has driven |
| seen | | *have* | | had seen |

 **REFERENCE NOTE:** Sometimes a past participle is used with a form of *be*: *was found, is heard, are located.* This use of the verb is called the *passive voice.* See page 199.

| IRREGULAR VERBS FREQUENTLY MISUSED | | | |
|---|---|---|---|
| **Base Form** | **Present Participle** | **Past** | **Past Participle** |
| begin | (is) beginning | began | (have) begun |
| blow | (is) blowing | blew | (have) blown |
| break | (is) breaking | broke | (have) broken |
| bring | (is) bringing | brought | (have) brought |
| burst | (is) bursting | burst | (have) burst |
| choose | (is) choosing | chose | (have) chosen |
| come | (is) coming | came | (have) come |
| dive | (is) diving | dove (*or* dived) | (have) dived |
| do | (is) doing | did | (have) done |
| drink | (is) drinking | drank | (have) drunk |
| drive | (is) driving | drove | (have) driven |
| eat | (is) eating | ate | (have) eaten |
| fall | (is) falling | fell | (have) fallen |
| freeze | (is) freezing | froze | (have) frozen |
| give | (is) giving | gave | (have) given |
| go | (is) going | went | (have) gone |
| grow | (is) growing | grew | (have) grown |
| know | (is) knowing | knew | (have) known |
| make | (is) making | made | (have) made |
| put | (is) putting | put | (have) put |
| ride | (is) riding | rode | (have) ridden |
| ring | (is) ringing | rang | (have) rung |
| run | (is) running | ran | (have) run |
| see | (is) seeing | saw | (have) seen |
| shake | (is) shaking | shook | (have) shaken |
| shrink | (is) shrinking | shrank (*or* shrunk) | (have) shrunk |
| sink | (is) sinking | sank | (have) sunk |
| speak | (is) speaking | spoke | (have) spoken |
| steal | (is) stealing | stole | (have) stolen |
| sting | (is) stinging | stung | (have) stung |

| IRREGULAR VERBS FREQUENTLY MISUSED | | | |
|---|---|---|---|
| **Base Form** | **Present Participle** | **Past** | **Past Participle** |
| strike | (is) striking | struck | (have) struck |
| swear | (is) swearing | swore | (have) sworn |
| swim | (is) swimming | swam | (have) swum |
| take | (is) taking | took | (have) taken |
| tear | (is) tearing | tore | (have) torn |
| throw | (is) throwing | threw | (have) thrown |
| wear | (is) wearing | wore | (have) worn |
| write | (is) writing | wrote | (have) written |

## EXERCISE 2   Writing Forms of Irregular Verbs

Change each of the verb forms below. If the base form is given, change it to the present participle. If the present participle is given, change it to the past form. If the past form is given, change it to the past participle. Use *have* before the past participle form and *is* before the present participle form.

EX.   1.  is diving ___dove___        2.  ran ___have run___

1.  see _____      11.  speak _____

2.  spoke _____    12.  is choosing _____

3.  is freezing _____  13.  wear _____

4.  threw _____     14.  knew _____

5.  is breaking _____  15.  ride _____

6.  brought _____   16.  shook _____

7.  grow _____      17.  is eating _____

8.  drove _____     18.  went _____

9.  is swimming _____  19.  take _____

10.  began _____    20.  drank _____

## EXERCISE 3   Identifying Correct Forms of Irregular Verbs

For each of the following sentences, underline the correct form of the verb in parentheses.

EX.   1.  Those plants have (*grew, grown*) taller.

1.  The class (*chose, chosen*) new officers last week.

2.  Did you know your rear axle has (*broke, broken*)?

3.  An earthquake (*struck, strike*) Antigua earlier today.

4.  I'm afraid your sweater (*shrank, shrunk*) in the wash.

5.  About four inches of rain has (*fell, fallen*) since yesterday.

6.  Anica angrily (*tore, torn*) the letter into bits.

7.  My grandfather has (*wrote, written*) several articles for *National Geographic*.

8.  You can try after Rudy has (*dove, dived*) off the board.

9.  The concert has (*began, begun*), but you have not missed much.

10. Mr. Katz (*shaken, shook*) his head in reply.

## EXERCISE 4   Proofreading a Paragraph for Correct Verb Forms

Proofread the paragraph below. If a sentence contains an incorrect verb form, draw a line through the wrong form and write the correct form above it. Some sentences may have no errors in verb forms.

EX.   1.  Last year we ~~seen~~ *saw* some of the studios in Bombay.

[1] The film industry in India has grew tremendously. [2] Today India's film industry was the largest in the world. [3] Since 1979, India has made more than seven hundred films each year! [4] Only lately have I began to notice the number of Indian films. [5] I had went to an Indian film festival to see a film by Satyajit Ray. [6] I seen several others while I was there. [7] When one film began, I recognized the lead actor. [8] I could have swore that he was in two other films at the same festival. [9] Later, I done a little research on him. [10] He had maked more than a dozen films that year.

## EXERCISE 5   Using Irregular Verbs

On your own paper, write fifteen sentences using verbs from the charts on pages 194-195. Use the participle forms of the verbs in five of your sentences. Underline the verbs you use.

EX.   1.  Frederick <u>has brought</u> us a bushel of potatoes.

# VERB TENSE

**15d The time expressed by a verb is called the *tense* of the verb.**

Every verb in English has six tenses.

| Tense | Examples |
|---|---|
| **Present** | I throw, you throw, he throws, we throw |
| **Past** | I threw, you threw, she threw, they threw |
| **Future** | I will (shall) throw, you will throw, they will throw |
| **Present Perfect** | I have thrown, you have thrown, he has thrown |
| **Past Perfect** | I had thrown, you had thrown, she had thrown |
| **Future Perfect** | I will (shall) have thrown, you will have thrown, we will have thrown |

Each of the six tenses has an additional form, called the *progressive form,* which expresses a continuing action. It consists of a form of the verb *be* plus the present participle of a verb. The progressive is not a separate tense but an additional form of each of the six tenses.

| Form | Examples |
|---|---|
| **Present Progressive** | am/are/is throwing |
| **Past Progressive** | was/were throwing |
| **Future Progressive** | will (shall) be throwing |
| **Present Perfect Progressive** | has/have been throwing |
| **Past Perfect Progressive** | had been throwing |
| **Future Perfect Progressive** | will (shall) have been throwing |

**15e Do not change needlessly from one tense to another.**

NONSTANDARD   Elia drove to the store and buys lunch. [*Drove* is past tense; *buys* is present tense.]

STANDARD   Elia **drove** to the store and **bought** lunch. [*Drove* and *bought* are both past tense.]

## EXERCISE 6    Identifying Verb Tenses

For each sentence below, identify the tense of the verb. Write your answers on your own paper.

EX.    1.  Kam had seen the movie.
       1.  *past perfect*

1.  The team traveled by bus.
2.  Leila has taken her medicine.
3.  The conference will begin on Monday.
4.  We swim on Friday evenings.
5.  Phillip had already seen the movie.

## EXERCISE 7    Proofreading a Paragraph for Consistent Verb Tenses

Decide whether the paragraph below should be written in the present or past tense. Then draw a line through each incorrect verb form, and write the correct form above it.

EX.    [1] I *ate* eat too quickly, so I got these hiccups.

[1] Most times, hiccups are not dangerous, but they are a nuisance. [2] Also; most people found them funny. [3] Yesterday, my hiccups continue for a while, so my friends gave me advice. [4] Maripat tells me to hold my breath and count to ten. [5] Shing says that I should quickly drink a tall glass of water. [6] Other people suggest ideas that sound really strange. [7] My mother says that I should put a pail or a wastebasket over my head and have someone beat on it. [8] My sister gave me the best idea of all. [9] She went into the kitchen and comes back with a paper bag. [10] I place it over my head, and my hiccups vanished.

## EXERCISE 8    Using Verb Tenses and Forms Correctly

On your own paper, write five sentences showing the correct use of the verb *bring*. Use as many different verb tenses and forms as you can. Underline each verb, and label its tense or form.

EX.    1.  Dad <u>is bringing</u> my sister Leta to watch my game. (present progressive)

## ACTIVE AND PASSIVE VOICE

**15f** **A verb in the *active voice* expresses an action done *by* its subject. A verb in the *passive voice* expresses an action done *to* its subject.**

ACTIVE VOICE    Mr. Noor **helped** Sarah. [The subject, *Mr. Noor,* performed the action.]

PASSIVE VOICE    Sarah **was helped** by Mr. Noor. [The subject, *Sarah,* received the action.]

NOTE    In a passive sentence, the verb phrase always includes a form of *be* and the past participle of the main verb. Other helping verbs may also be included.

The passive voice emphasizes the person or thing receiving the action. It may be used when the speaker does not know or does not wish to say who performed the action.

         SUBJECT
PASSIVE VOICE    A window **was broken** by someone last night.
      SUBJECT     OBJECT
ACTIVE VOICE    Someone **broke** a window last night.

In general, you should avoid using the passive voice because it makes your writing sound weak and awkward. Using the active voice helps make your writing direct and forceful.

## EXERCISE 9    Classifying Sentences by Voice

Identify each of the following sentences as active or passive. On the line before each sentence, write *act.* for *active* or *pass.* for *passive.*

EX.    <u>*act.*</u>    1.  Pat Cummings illustrates books.

_____    1.  She has been inspired by Tom Feelings.

_____    2.  Her work is created in Brooklyn.

_____    3.  Cummings uses a variety of materials in her work.

_____    4.  *Jimmy Lee Did It* was illustrated by Cummings.

_____    5.  Our school library owns several of her books.

_____    6.  My sister can be counted among her first big fans.

_____    7.  Sarita was surprised by the invitation.

_____    8.  Was Pat Cummings asked by the art teacher to visit our school?

_____ 9. Did she ever really come?

_____10. The program was enjoyed by all of us.

_____11. I hope we get more programs.

_____12. How many books were suggested?

_____13. Wynona reads several books each month.

_____14. Our teacher wants us to form a book club.

_____15. Did she give you any ideas for a club name?

## EXERCISE 10   Using Verbs in the Active Voice and the Passive Voice

In the cartoon below, Blondie, Dagwood, Daisy, and Mr. Dithers are the subjects and objects of many actions that are occurring. On your own paper, write ten sentences to describe the cartoon. Use the active voice in six sentences and the passive voice in four sentences. After each sentence, write _act._ for _active_ or _pass._ for _passive_ to identify the voice you used.

EX.   1.  Blondie's dog watches the action. (act.)

Blondie reprinted with special permission of King
Features Syndicate, Inc.

# LIE *AND* LAY

**15g** **The verb *lie* means "to rest," "to recline," or "to remain in a lying position." *Lie* rarely takes an object. The verb *lay* means "to put" or "to place" (something). *Lay* usually takes an object.**

EXAMPLES  The dog **is lying** in the doorway.
Sarah **lay** the mat in front of the door.

| PRINCIPAL PARTS OF *LIE* AND *LAY* | | | |
|---|---|---|---|
| **Base Form** | **Present Participle** | **Past** | **Past Participle** |
| lie (to recline) | (is) lying | lay | (have) lain |
| lay (to put) | (is) laying | laid | (have) laid |

NOTE  The verb *lie* may be used to describe the lying position of inanimate objects as well as of people and animals. Even though someone puts an object down, it *lies* (not *lays*) there.

EXAMPLE  Your book **is lying** on the table.

When deciding whether to use *lie* or *lay*, ask yourself two questions.

QUESTION 1:  What do I want to say? Is the meaning "to be in a lying position," or is it "to put something down"?

QUESTION 2:  What time does the verb express, and which principal part is used to show this time?

The following examples show how you can apply these questions to determine which verb—*lie* or *lay*—should be used.

EXAMPLE  That blanket has always (*lain, laid*) on the back of the couch.

QUESTION 1:  Meaning? The meaning is "to be in a lying position." Therefore, the verb should be *lie*.

QUESTION 2:  Principal part? The verb expresses the past, and the sentence requires the past participle with *has*. The past participle of *lie* is *lain*.

ANSWER:  That blanket **has** always **lain** on the back of the couch.

## EXERCISE 11   Choosing the Correct Forms of *Lie* and *Lay*

For each of the following sentences, underline the correct form of *lie* or *lay*.

EX.   1.  The mummy had (*laid*, <u>*lain*</u>) in the ground for centuries.

1.  Early Egyptians sometimes (*laid*, *lay*) bodies in dry sand.

2.  Other mummies have been (*lying*, *laying*) in frozen earth for hundreds of years.

3.  About 2,100 years ago, someone in Hunan, China, had (*lain*, *laid*) the body of a woman in a burial mound.

4.  The mummy (*laid*, *lay*) there until the Chinese government decided to build a hospital on that site.

5.  Native Americans sometimes (*laid*, *lay*) bodies inside dry caves.

6.  One such mummy had (*lain*, *laid*) in a Kentucky cave for two thousand years.

7.  Egyptian embalmers (*lain*, *laid*) strips of linen over their dead.

8.  Often, a person's organs (*lay*, *laid*) inside a separate jar.

9.  The friends of John Paul Jones (*lain*, *laid*) his body in a lead casket that was full of alcohol.

10.  His mummy had (*lain*, *laid*) there for over one hundred years.

11.  Instead of (*lying*, *laying*) down, some mummies are put in a seated position.

12.  Did you know that Egyptian mummies at one point in the process (*lay*, *laid*) in sodium carbonate?

13.  Before being (*laid*, *lain*) in a tomb, mummies were given a treatment lasting seventy days.

14.  The body of King Mer-en-re was found (*lying*, *laying*) in a tomb in 1880.

15.  Besides the mummy, articles from a person's life were (*laid*, *lain*) in the tomb.

## EXERCISE 12   Using *Lie* and *Lay* Correctly

On your own paper, write five sentences using the different forms of *lie* correctly. Then write five sentences using the different forms of *lay* correctly. Use all of the principal parts at least once in your sentences. Underline and label all the forms of *lie* and *lay* in your sentences.

EX.   1.  Chandra <u>laid</u> her pen beside her book. (past)

# SIT *AND* SET *AND* RISE *AND* RAISE

## SIT *AND* SET

**15h** The verb *sit* means "to rest in an upright, seated position." *Sit* almost never takes an object. The verb *set* means "to put" or "to place" (something). *Set* usually takes an object. Notice that *set* does not change form in the past or past participle.

| PRINCIPAL PARTS OF *SIT* AND *SET* | | | |
|---|---|---|---|
| **Base Form** | **Present Participle** | **Past** | **Past Participle** |
| sit (to rest) | (is) sitting | sat | (have) sat |
| set (to put) | (is) setting | set | (have) set |

EXAMPLES   **Sit** here.           **Set** your end down first.
The box **sat** on the table.   The driver **set** it there.

## EXERCISE 13   Using the Forms of *Sit* and *Set*

In each of the following sentences, write the correct form of *sit* or *set* on the line provided.

EX.   1.  Thi and I will both _____*sit*_____ in the back seat.

1. Thi has _____ a pad of paper between us.

2. When I _____ down, I felt a pencil on the seat.

3. We _____ on the floor playing word games and talking about school.

4. Don't _____ your lunch box on the window ledge, or your food will spoil.

5. When the car stopped, I _____ our picnic basket on the table.

6. Thi was reading about Lewis Carroll, but she _____ the book down.

7. We have _____ here for an hour playing *Mischmasch*, one of Carroll's games.

8. I wrote the letters "HTH" on the page and then _____ the pencil beside me.

9. Thi _____ for a long time, trying to think of a word containing that letter combination.

10. When we _____ at lunch the next day, I whispered, "Lighthouse."

---

### *RISE* AND *RAISE*

**15i    The verb *rise* means "to go in an upward direction." *Rise* rarely takes an object. The verb *raise* means "to move something in an upward direction." *Raise* usually takes an object.**

| PRINCIPAL PARTS OF *RISE* AND *RAISE* | | | |
|---|---|---|---|
| **Base Form** | **Present Participle** | **Past** | **Past Participle** |
| rise (to go up) | (is) rising | rose | (have) risen |
| raise (to move something up) | (is) raising | raised | (have) raised |

EXAMPLES    My parents **rise** at about 6:30 most mornings.
I'm glad you **raised** that issue!
The price of oranges will **rise** again.
The store **raised** the price of its fruit.

---

## EXERCISE 14    Using the Forms of *Rise* and *Raise*

Write the correct form of *rise* or *raise* on the line in each sentence below.

EX.    1.  If you add yeast, the dough will _____*rise*_____.

1. Matzo contains no yeast, so the dough does not _____ .

2. My aunt _____ at dawn to start her bread.

3. She has _____ earlier than usual.

4. At dinner, my uncle _____ the napkin and peeked underneath.

5. Before a particularly good dessert, everyone's excitement will

_____ .

# CHAPTER REVIEW

## A. Writing Sentences Using the Correct Forms of Verbs

On your own paper, write twenty sentences using the following verbs.

EX. 1. sunk
　　1. The raft had sunk last summer.

1. laid
2. (have) walked
3. seen
4. swam
5. (had) set
6. lying
7. rose
8. thrown
9. drove
10. (had) used

11. froze
12. (have) shaken
13. (is) bringing
14. stole
15. stung
16. (have) chosen
17. raise
18. began
19. (have) given
20. (is) doing

## B. Proofreading a Paragraph for Correct Verb Forms

In the following paragraph, if a sentence contains an incorrect verb form, cross out the incorrect verb. Then write the correct form above the verb. Some sentences will be correct. Others may have more than one incorrect verb form.

EX. [1] Cochise and Thomas Jeffords ~~beginned~~ *began* a long friendship.

[1] In the late 1800s, the Apache leader Cochise was arrest on a false charge. [2] He escaped and later striked back at the settlers. [3] At one point, his people had killed more than a dozen mail carriers. [4] Thomas Jeffords, the man in charge of the mail, decides to visit Cochise. [5] When they met, he sets his own weapons aside. [6] Then the two men set and talked for days. [7] After this meeting, the men had became good friends, and Jeffords was chose to be the agent for the Apache reservation. [8] The men's friendship lasted

until the chief's death in 1874. [9] Shortly thereafter, Jeffords was

replace by a different agent, and a new leader raised to power among

the Apaches. [10] His name, Geronimo, was soon knew throughout

the United States.

## C.  Writing a Weather Report

You are a weather forecaster on a local television station. For tonight's show, you will be using the weather map that is shown below. When you display the map, you will describe the weather situation to your audience.

1. First, use the weather symbols to determine what the weather is in different parts of the country.

2. Next, make notes on your own paper. Write five sentences about the weather. Use each of the following verbs at least once: *sit*, *lie*, and *rise*.

EX.    1.  A stationary front is sitting over northern Florida.

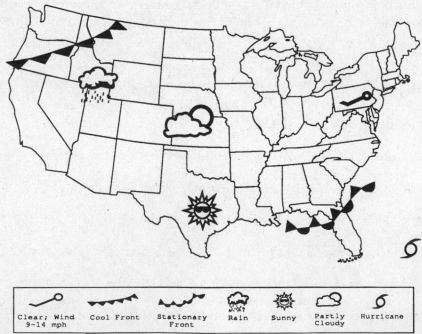

| Clear; Wind 9-14 mph | Cool Front | Stationary Front | Rain | Sunny | Partly Cloudy | Hurricane |

# CASE OF PRONOUNS

*Case* is the form of a noun or pronoun that shows its use in a sentence. In English, there are three cases: *nominative, objective,* and *possessive.*

The form of a noun is the same for the nominative and objective cases.

NOMINATIVE CASE    The **judge** has issued a ruling. [noun used as subject]

  OBJECTIVE CASE    I respect the **judge**. [noun used as direct object]

A noun changes its form only in the possessive case, usually by adding an apostrophe and an *s.*

  POSSESSIVE CASE    The **judge's** ruling was fair.

 **REFERENCE NOTE:** For more about forming possessives with apostrophes, see page 285.

Unlike nouns, most personal pronouns have different forms for the nominative, objective, and possessive cases.

| PERSONAL PRONOUNS | | | |
|---|---|---|---|
| | **Nominative Case** | **Objective Case** | **Possessive Case** |
| **Singular** | I<br>you<br>he, she, it | me<br>you<br>him, her, it | my, mine<br>your, yours<br>his, her, hers, its |
| **Plural** | we<br>you<br>they | us<br>you<br>them | our, ours<br>your, yours<br>their, theirs |

 NOTE   Some teachers prefer to call possessive forms of pronouns (such as *hers, your,* and *their*) adjectives. Follow your teacher's instructions regarding possessive forms.

## EXERCISE 1    Identifying Personal Pronouns and Their Cases

Identify the case of the italicized pronoun in each sentence below. On the line before each sentence, write *nom.* for *nominative*, *obj.* for *objective*, or *poss.* for *possessive*.

EX.    _poss._    1.  Benito Pablo Juárez earned *his* place in history as one of the greatest leaders of Mexico.

_____    1.  *His* birthplace was Oaxaca, Mexico.

_____    2.  In 1847, *he* was elected governor of the Mexican state of Oaxaca.

_____    3.  At that time, the people of Mexico had few freedoms; Santa Anna ruled *them* with an iron hand.

_____    4.  Juárez and other local leaders opposed *him*.

_____    5.  *Their* dreams for greater freedom stalled when Santa Anna sent Juárez out of Mexico.

_____    6.  When Juárez returned to Mexico in 1855, *he* became minister of justice.

_____    7.  *Our* textbook states that one of Juárez's greatest deeds was putting through the Juárez Law.

_____    8.  *It* took away some powers from the army and the clergy and gave more rights to the citizens of Mexico.

_____    9.  Juárez was rewarded in 1861 when the people elected *him* president of Mexico.

_____    10.  Today, *we* credit Juárez for bringing religious freedom and civil rights to the people of Mexico.

## EXERCISE 2    Writing a Poem with Personal Pronouns

On your own paper, write a poem of at least ten lines about how friendship can exist between people who are very different. In your poem, describe the differences between two friends. Use at least two examples of each of the three cases of pronouns. Underline each pronoun that you use.

EX.    I am wildfire.

You are rain.

And yet we are friends.

# NOMINATIVE CASE PRONOUNS

**16a** The *subject of a verb* is always in the nominative case.

EXAMPLES    Do **they** enjoy country music? [*They* is the subject of *Do enjoy.*]

           **He** and **I** watched the show. [*He* and *I* are the two parts of the compound subject of *watched.*]

To choose the correct pronoun for use in a compound subject, try each form of the pronoun separately.

EXAMPLE    Oskar and (*me, I*) play in a band.

          *Me* play in a band. [incorrect use of objective case]

          *I* play in a band. [correct use of nominative case]

ANSWER    Oskar and **I** play in a band.

**16b** A *predicate nominative* is always in the nominative case.

A **predicate nominative** is a noun or pronoun that follows a linking verb and explains or identifies the subject of the sentence. A pronoun used as a predicate nominative always follows a form of the verb *be* or a verb phrase ending in *be* or *been.*

EXAMPLES    The captain of the team is **I**. [*I* follows the linking verb *is* and identifies the subject, *captain.*]

           The owners of the store are Marsha and **he**. [*He* follows the verb *are* and identifies, along with *Marsha*, the subject, *owners.*]

## EXERCISE 3    Identifying Nominative Case Pronouns

Complete each of the following sentences by underlining the correct pronoun or pronoun pair in parentheses.

EX.   1. Elsie and (<u>he</u>, him) are planning an Earth Day project.

1. The contestants on the quiz show were (*him and me, he and I*).

2. The person who called may have been (*she, her*).

3. Naturally, (*she and I, her and me*) will help at the carwash.

4. The most comfortable shoes are (*they, them*).

5. Dr. Ramírez and (*us, we*) are meeting to plan the tournament.

6. Amanda and (*I, me*) are working together on our research reports.

7. The judges for the creative writing contest might be Ms. Robinson and (*them, they*).

8. It was (*we, us*) who donated the set of encyclopedias for the library book sale.

9. Have (*they, them*) visited South America before?

10. Could it have been (*him, he*)?

11. The big winners would be (*she, her*) and Ramona.

12. Did (*I, me*) ever seem this happy before?

13. (*They, Them*) always work together on their boat.

14. (*We, Us*) sat down to think it over.

15. Karen and (*I, me*) joined the soccer team on the same day.

## EXERCISE 4    Proofreading Sentences for Correct Use of Nominative Case Pronouns

If a sentence below contains the wrong form of a pronoun, draw a line through the pronoun, and write the correct form above it. Some sentences are correct.

EX.    1. Juan Carlos the First and ~~her~~ *she* were the rulers of Spain.

1. Our foreign exchange students this year are Kamaria and him.

2. The team member who scored the most points was he.

3. Him and I were both born in Laos.

4. Two successful Cuban American singers are Gloria Estefan and her.

5. Will he and me perform after Juanita?

6. The winners of the award should have been her and I.

7. Was it he who said, "Don't give up yet"?

8. Perhaps you and me should volunteer for cleanup duty.

9. That night, they announced that the winners were us!

10. The drama coach said that he and me could apply for the two jobs as understudies.

## PRONOUNS AS DIRECT OBJECTS

> **16c** The *direct object* of a verb is always in the objective case.
>
> A *direct object* is a noun or pronoun that receives the action of a verb or that shows the result of the action.
>
> EXAMPLES    The officer directed **me** to the right address. [*Me* tells *whom the officer directed.*]
> Teresa gave **them** to her sister. [*Them* tells *what* Teresa gave.]
>
> To choose the correct pronoun for use as a compound direct object, try each form of the pronoun separately.
>
> EXAMPLE    The audience applauded Geraldo and (*I, me*).
> The audience applauded *I*. [**incorrect use of nominative case**]
> The audience applauded *me*. [**correct use of objective case**]
>
> ANSWER    The audience applauded Geraldo and **me**.

### EXERCISE 5    Choosing Correct Pronoun Forms

Complete each sentence below by writing an appropriate pronoun on the line or lines provided. Use a variety of pronouns, but do not use *you* or *it*. Make sure that each pronoun you choose makes sense in the sentence.

EX.    1.    Fran took her brother and _____ me _____ to a concert.

1. Someone called _____ extremely late last night.

2. Please help _____ with the assignment.

3. Did you see _____ at the library?

4. The child answered _____ politely.

5. Professional scouts contacted _____ and _____ after the game.

6. Simon and Rebecca told _____ about their visit to Israel.

7. Tomorrow night my brother will drive _____ to the mall.

8. Dr. Maldonado treated _____ and the other hikers for frostbite.

9. The orchestra leader thanked _____ and _____ for attending the concert.

10. Aunt Maribeth surprised _____ by coming to rehearsal.

## EXERCISE 6    Proofreading for Correct Pronoun Case

Draw a line through each pronoun that is used incorrectly in the paragraph below. Write the correct pronoun in the space above the word. Some sentences are correct.

EX.    [1] They sent Zahara and ~~I~~ me to the regional meeting.

[1] The members of our International Club surprised and pleased Zahara and I at the last meeting.  [2] They chose she and me as representatives for the regional meeting.  [3] They told me it was because Zahara is from East Africa and I am from Santiago, Chile.  [4] Our international experiences have introduced we to many different cultures and beliefs.  [5] Many students in our school, and particularly members of the International Club, have helped her and I in our new surroundings in the United States.  [6] Now they are helping she and I in a whole new way.  [7] They are sending us to the meeting to talk about how the city government might help students from foreign countries.  [8] Zahara and I will tell you and they all about the meeting as soon as we return.  [9] Or can you join she and I at the next meeting of the International Club?  [10] Our meetings are on the first Tuesday of the month; I'm sure you'll enjoy they.  [11] Zahara showed I some African artwork from her country.  [12] I showed she a painting my father had done.  [13] Zahara enjoys museums and often goes to visit they.  [14] I enjoy them, too, but I like soccer games more.  [15] All in all, everyone has treated we very well.

## INDIRECT OBJECTS AND OBJECTS OF PREPOSITIONS

**16d** The *indirect object* of a verb is always in the objective case.

An *indirect object* is a noun or pronoun that tells *to whom* or *for whom* something is done.

EXAMPLES   Hadiya sent **him** a birthday card. [*Him* tells *to whom* Hadiya sent a birthday card.]

Could you make **me** a sandwich? [*Me* tells *for whom* you could make a sandwich.]

To choose the correct pronoun for use in a compound indirect object, try each form of the pronoun separately in the sentence.

EXAMPLE   Emilio Estevez sent Melba and (*she, her*) an autographed photo.

Emilio Estevez sent *she* an autographed photo. [incorrect use of nominative case]

Emilio Estevez sent *her* an autographed photo. [correct use of objective case]

ANSWER   Emilio Estevez sent Melba and **her** an autographed photo.

## EXERCISE 7   Using Pronouns as Indirect Objects

Complete each of the following sentences by writing an appropriate pronoun on the line or lines provided. Use a variety of pronouns, but do not use *you* or *it*.

EX.   1. Did Lorenzo loan his sister and _____him_____ money for the tickets?

1. We gave _____ an award for being such a great coach.

2. Will you loan _____ your copy of the script?

3. When she returned to Somalia, Tabia sent _____ a note.

4. The counselor gave Kareem and _____ some very good advice about scholarships.

5. At lunch, Dolores told _____ and _____ a joke.

6. When I did the job well, the boss offered _____ a better one.

7. She mailed _____ all of our camping equipment.

8. Mattie cooked _____ his favorite meal after the show.

9. Ginette blushed when Alfredo handed _____ the flowers.

10. It took six months for my cousin to write _____ a letter.

---

**16e** The *object of a preposition* is always in the objective case.

A *prepositional phrase* is a group of words consisting of a preposition, a noun or pronoun that serves as the object of the preposition, and any modifiers of that object.

EXAMPLES    for **me**    after Meredith and **him**    in front of **us**

 **REFERENCE NOTE:** For a list of prepositions, see page 115.

---

**EXERCISE 8   Choosing Correct Pronouns as Objects of Prepositions**

Complete each sentence below by underlining the correct pronoun or pair of pronouns in parentheses.

EX.   1.  The musical was directed by (*he and she, him and her*).

1. To my classmates and (*I, me*), Anzu and Ima Asato are very talented twin sisters.

2. They wrote our class musical for (*we, us*).

3. Thanks to (*them, they*), our musical won second place in the city music festival.

4. Perhaps you read the article in the *Kansas City Star* about their family and (*they, them*).

5. Because their father, a member of the Kansas City Symphony, helped them, we should send a thank-you note to (*he, him*).

6. Between (*you and I, you and me*), the music was beautiful.

7. Listen to (*I, me*) while I play the main theme on the piano.

8. Jim and I were lucky that Ima was standing right in front of (*we, us*) in the chorus during the performance.

9. We could listen to (*she, her*) as she sang, and we followed along.

10. The entire cast got tapes of the music from (*they, them*) as gifts on opening night.

# REVIEW EXERCISE

## A. Identifying Correct Pronoun Form

Complete each sentence below by underlining the correct pronoun in parentheses. On the line before the sentence, identify the pronoun's use in the sentence. Write *s.* for *subject*, *p.n.* for *predicate nominative*, *d.o.* for *direct object*, *i.o.* for *indirect object*, or *o.p.* for *object of a preposition*.

EX. __p.n.__ 1. That must be (*her*, <u>*she*</u>) at the door.

_____ 1. Please save two seats for Maisie and (*I*, *me*).

_____ 2. Our coach offered the younger students and (*they*, *them*) some pointers.

_____ 3. Many people thanked Ms. Tan and (*we*, *us*) for our posters in the cafeteria.

_____ 4. You never guessed that the person in the gorilla costume was (*I*, *me*)!

_____ 5. Whenever it rains hard, my sisters and (*I*, *me*) have to put towels around the door.

_____ 6. The Korean family that just moved into the neighborhood thanked (*we*, *us*) for the welcome basket.

_____ 7. Maria shared her grandmother's recipe for salsa with Jamyce and (*he*, *him*).

_____ 8. Somewhere along the way, Shani and (*she*, *her*) misplaced their house keys.

_____ 9. Show Ada May and (*I*, *me*) your drawing when you are finished.

_____ 10. It may have been (*they*, *them*) who sent these flowers.

_____ 11. Was it (*we*, *us*) who had the winning ticket?

_____ 12. Ontario is a place that (*he*, *him*) has always wanted to visit.

_____ 13. Thanks to (*they*, *them*), there are no more mosquitoes in the backyard.

_____ 14. If you hurry, (*I*, *me*) will be able to meet you at the restaurant.

_____ 15. The drama club honored Rita by giving (*she*, *her*) the prize for best play.

## B.   Proofreading for Correct Pronoun Forms

Draw a line through each pronoun that is used incorrectly in the paragraph below. Write the correct pronoun in the space above the word. Some sentences are correct.

EX.   [1] To Mavis and ~~I~~, *me* Ronnie Milsap is the greatest country singer of all time.

[1] Country singer Ronnie Milsap, who is blind, has given we

many memorable songs. [2] When Ronnie was six, his parents sent he

to the Governor Morehead School for the Blind in Raleigh, North

Carolina. [3] There, his classmates and him received excellent

training in music. [4] Ronnie and them learned to play musical

instruments, and he became especially interested in the piano and the

violin. [5] After he left Morehead, he went to college in Georgia.

[6] He entered the music business, and it is him that one can hear

playing the piano on several of Elvis Presley's early hits. [7] By 1973,

many people had heard about he because of his work on Presley's hit

"Kentucky Rain" and many others. [8] In 1973, RCA offered him a

contract to record his own songs. [9] My sister Mavis and me have

collected all twenty-three of the albums he recorded with RCA.

[10] The hit singles "Smoky Mountain Rain" and "Stranger in My

House" are the favorites of both Mavis and I.

## C.   Writing a Friendly Note

On your own paper, write a note to a friend, telling about a movie you recently saw and enjoyed. Describe the major characters and the main events. In your letter, use five nominative and five objective case pronouns correctly. When you have finished writing, underline all of the pronouns. Above each pronoun, identify its use. Write *s.* for *subject*, *p.n.* for *predicate nominative*, *d.o.* for *direct object*, *i.o.* for *indirect object*, or *o.p.* for *object of a preposition*.

EX.   Dear Marvin,
         *s.*                                    *s.*                              *o.p.*
    I just saw a great movie today. You will enjoy all the action in it.

# WHO *AND* WHOM

**16f** Use *who* and *whoever* in the nominative case. Use *whom* and *whomever* in the objective case.

In spoken English, the use of *whom* is becoming less common. In fact, when speaking, you may correctly begin any question with *who*, regardless of the grammar of the sentence.

**16g** The use of *who* or *whom* in a subordinate clause depends on how the pronoun functions in the clause.

When choosing whether to use *who* or *whom* in a subordinate clause, follow these steps.

*Step 1:*  Find the subordinate clause in the sentence.
*Step 2:*  Decide how the pronoun is used in the clause—as subject, predicate nominative, object of the verb, or object of a preposition.
*Step 3:*  Determine the case of the pronoun according to the rules of standard English.
*Step 4:*  Select the correct form of the pronoun.

EXAMPLE  I know (*who, whom*) wrote the note.

*Step 1:*  The clause is (*who, whom*) *wrote the note.*
*Step 2:*  In this clause, the pronoun is used as the subject of the verb *wrote.*
*Step 3:*  A pronoun used as a subject should be in the nominative case.
*Step 4:*  The nominative form is *who.*

ANSWER  I know **who** wrote the note.

No words outside the clause affect the case of the pronoun. In the example above, the entire clause is used as a direct object of the verb *know,* but the pronoun *who* is used as a subject (nominative case) within the clause.

Frequently, *whom* in subordinate clauses is omitted (understood).

EXAMPLE  The man (whom) I voted for is Julian Washington.

**EXERCISE 9** **Classifying Pronouns Used in Subordinate Clauses and Identifying Correct Forms**

Complete each sentence below by underlining the correct pronoun form in parentheses. On the line before the sentence, identify the pronoun's use in the clause. Write *s.* for *subject*, *p.n.* for *predicate nominative*, *d.o.* for *direct object*, or *o.p.* for *object of a preposition*.

EX. **p.n.** 1. Do you know (<u>who</u>, *whom*) they are?

_____ 1. The student for (*who, whom*) I'm saving this seat should arrive shortly.

_____ 2. (*Whoever, Whomever*) you invite to the concert will be happy to go with you.

_____ 3. Did you talk to (*whoever, whomever*) you gave the plates for the party?

_____ 4. Mr. Ignacio is the Navajo artist (*who, whom*) we saw on television last night.

_____ 5. I haven't decided for (*who, whom*) I made this necklace.

_____ 6. Can you predict (*who, whom*) will win the class election?

_____ 7. Please tell me (*who, whom*) the owner of the store is.

_____ 8. The South American ruler (*who, whom*) we are now studying is Juan Perón.

_____ 9. (*Whoever, Whomever*) enters the contest must write a poem.

_____ 10. Tell us (*who, whom*) you saw at the bowling alley last night.

_____ 11. The sentry hailed (*whoever, whomever*) came up the path.

_____ 12. The judges will vote for (*whoever, whomever*) seems to be most worthy.

_____ 13. Can't you see (*who, whom*) really wants it more?

_____ 14. They named (*who, whom*) the winner is.

_____ 15. It's easy to see that (*whoever, whomever*) runs the fastest will arrive the soonest.

_____ 16. We thanked Deniz because he was (*who, whom*) brought the latkes.

_____ 17. Isabel gave the costumes to the actors to (*who, whom*) they were assigned.

_____ 18. Do you know Maribeth, (*who, whom*) I met yesterday?

_____ 19. How did Justin learn (*who, whom*) our new neighbor is?

_____ 20. Ken sent oranges to (*whoever, whomever*) he heard from first.

## APPOSITIVES AND INCOMPLETE CONSTRUCTIONS

**16h Pronouns used with *appositives* are in the same case as the words to which they refer.**

An *appositive* is a noun or pronoun that follows another noun or pronoun to identify or explain it.

EXAMPLES   The judge announced the winners, Bart and **me**. [Since *winners* is the direct object of the verb *announced*, the pronoun *me*, in apposition with *winners*, must be in the objective case.]
**We** runners must train hard. [As subject of the sentence, *We* is in the nominative case. The noun *runners*, which identifies *We*, is the appositive.]

To choose the correct pronoun for use with an appositive or as an appositive, try the sentence with only the pronoun.

EXAMPLE   Two actors, Gina and (*me, I*), won awards on opening night.
Gina and *me* won awards on opening night. [incorrect use of objective case]
Gina and *I* won awards on opening night. [correct use of nominative case]
ANSWER   Two actors, Gina and I, won awards on opening night.

### EXERCISE 10   Identifying Correct Pronouns as Appositives

Complete each of the following sentences by underlining the correct pronoun form in parentheses.

EX.   1.   My cousins, Rachel and (<u>he</u>, him), are visiting from San Juan.

1.   The coach gave the fullbacks, Paulo and (*he, him*), a pep talk.

2.   The doctors thanked the nurses, Jobelle and (*I, me*).

3.   At the end of the concert, the musicians, (*we, us*), played four encores.

4.   Please offer more food to your guests, Charles and (*she, her*).

5.   The best athletes in the class, you and (*he, him*), might be called to the stage.

6.   Several people, the board and (*they, them*), elected a new president last year.

7.   The head cheerleaders, she and (*I, me*), ran the practice.

8.   The school newspaper paid a lot of attention to the basketball players, the forwards and (*we, us*).

9.  The last campers in the water, Manuel and (*I, me*), still reached the raft on time.

10. The task of going for help was given to the best sailors on the lake, (*she, her*) and (*he, him*).

---

**16i**    **When *than* or *as* introduces an incomplete construction, use the form of the pronoun that would be correct if the construction were completed.**

Notice how pronouns change the meaning of sentences with incomplete constructions.

EXAMPLES    I like Cleon better than **she**.
I like Cleon better than **her**.

In the first example, the nominative case pronoun *she* is the subject of an understood verb; *I like Cleon better than she [likes Cleon]*. In the second example, the objective case pronoun *her* is the object of an understood verb; *I like Cleon better than [I like] her*.

---

**EXERCISE 11    Completing Incomplete Constructions and Classifying Pronoun Forms**

Beginning with *than* or *as*, write the understood clause for each of the following sentences, on the line after it. Use the correct form of the pronoun. Then identify the pronoun in the completed clause by writing *s.* for *subject* or *obj.* for *object*. Some items may have more than one correct answer.

EX.    1. Leroy is taller than (*I, me*). than I am (s.) _____

1.  Can you swim to the end of the pool as fast as (*she, her*)?

    _____

2.  You have called Mateo more often than (*I, me*).

    _____

3.  I am just as good a writer as (*he, him*).

    _____

4.  We have known Phoebe longer than (*they, them*).

    _____

5.  Many people pay higher monthly rents than (*we, us*).

    _____

# CHAPTER REVIEW

## A. Correcting Pronoun Forms

Draw a line through each incorrect pronoun in the sentences below. On the line before each sentence, write the correct pronoun form.

EX. _____I_____ 1. Both of the applicants, Johan and me, took part-time jobs.

_____ 1. Katya speaks Spanish far better than her.

_____ 2. Mrs. Macavoy rented a canoe and prepared a picnic for Percy and I.

_____ 3. After the ballgame, the coach and me talked about my pitching.

_____ 4. Us residents of Benton Avenue have begun a neighborhood recycling campaign.

_____ 5. I can't believe that it was him who sent me this beautiful poem!

_____ 6. Do you know yet who you are inviting to the class dance?

_____ 7. The letter may have been written by one of my brothers, Juan or he.

_____ 8. I will give a reward to whomever finds my lost cat.

_____ 9. Have you decided to work for they?

_____ 10. The store owner gave both clerks, Mona and I, generous raises.

_____ 11. Someone should ask we students our opinion.

_____ 12. Wouldn't you like to go with she and me to the party?

_____ 13. To who do you think the principal was speaking?

_____ 14. We invited Helen and Frank to stay, but them wanted to get an early start.

_____ 15. Well, they did a good job, whomever it was.

_____ 16. Her and I have been friends since the first day of school.

_____ 17. Our history teacher told we honor students that we could do extra work.

_____ 18. Sometimes in the evenings my sister and him would sing folk songs together.

_____ 19. Mother wondered whom would speak first.

_____ 20. Us scuba divers like to explore coral reefs.

## B. Proofreading a Paragraph for Correct Pronoun Forms

Draw a line through each pronoun that is used incorrectly in the paragraph below. Write the correct pronoun in the space above the word. Some sentences are correct.

EX. [1] The people ~~whom~~ *who* see the baskets say that they are beautiful.

[1] When my family and me were in South Carolina last summer, we bought a beautiful sweet-grass basket. [2] The women whom make the baskets are African American. [3] Them and their relatives have woven and sewn these beautiful crafts for many years. [4] The people to who credit is given for bringing this art form to the United States were brought here as slaves from West Africa about three hundred years ago. [5] We had never seen sweet-grass baskets before, so we asked the women all about them. [6] Mrs. Washington told my sister and I that the other basket makers and her go to marshy fields to collect the sweet grass that grows wild there. [7] Then they bind together the coarse grass and stitch it into place. [8] The lady to who we spoke said that she takes at least ten hours to sew a basket. [9] Then she told my father and I about new problems that are facing the basket makers. [10] The fields of sweet grass are disappearing, and the art and the tradition of the basket makers might very well disappear with them.

## C. Writing Interview Questions and Answers

As a feature writer for a sports magazine, you are to interview a celebrity sports figure. He or she might be a star in hockey, auto racing, basketball, or any other sport that you choose. On your own paper, write at least ten questions that you would ask about this person's background, accomplishments, and future goals. From magazines, newspapers, and biographies, gather information and details about this person. Use your research to write the answers that the person might give. Be sure to use the correct forms of personal pronouns in your questions and answers.

EX.                          Gordie Howe
    1. Among all the positions, why did you choose to be a goalie?

# COMPARISON OF MODIFIERS

*Positive, comparative,* and *superlative* are the three degrees of comparison for adjectives and adverbs.

| | |
|---|---|
| POSITIVE | Robert told a **funny** joke. |
| COMPARATIVE | Kim told a joke that was **funnier** than Robert's was. |
| SUPERLATIVE | Of all of them, Charlie told the **funniest** joke. |

**17a  A one-syllable modifier regularly forms its comparative and superlative degrees by adding *–er* and *–est*.**

| | |
|---|---|
| POSITIVE | My cat is **wet** from the rain. |
| COMPARATIVE | My dog is **wetter** than my cat is. |
| SUPERLATIVE | My horse is the **wettest** of my three pets. |

**17b  Some two-syllable modifiers form their comparative and superlative degrees by adding *–er* and *–est*. Others form these degrees by using *more* and *most* or *less* and *least*.**

| Positive | Comparative | Superlative |
|---|---|---|
| windy | windier | windiest |
| careful | more careful | most careful |
| anxious | less anxious | least anxious |

NOTE  Some two-syllable modifiers, such as *common,* may use either *–er* and *–est* or *more/less* and *most/least.*

**17c  Modifiers that have more than two syllables form their comparative and superlative degrees with *more/less* and *most/least*.**

| Positive | Comparative | Superlative |
|---|---|---|
| original | more original | most original |
| beautiful | less beautiful | least beautiful |

**17d  Some modifiers use irregular methods of forming their comparative and superlative degrees.**

Do not add *–er* and *–est* or *more/less* and *most/least* to irregularly formed comparisons.

| Positive | Comparative | Superlative |
|---|---|---|
| good | better | best |
| bad | worse | worst |
| many/much | more | most |

## EXERCISE 1    Forming Degrees of Comparison with Modifiers

On the lines below, write the comparative and superlative degrees of each of the following modifiers. Use a dictionary as necessary.

EX.  1. large _____*larger*_____    _____*largest*_____

1. exciting _____    _____

2. happy _____    _____

3. delightful _____    _____

4. little _____    _____

5. quickly _____    _____

6. blue _____    _____

7. afraid _____    _____

8. suspicious _____    _____

9. round _____    _____

10. far _____    _____

## EXERCISE 2    Proofreading for Correct Comparative and Superlative Forms

Underline the comparative or superlative form of the modifier in each sentence below. If the form is incorrect, write the correct form above it.

EX.  1. Avis will be *more careful* carefuller than your last mechanic.

1. Pelé was certainly one of the successfullest soccer players in the world.

2. The judges thought that Alice's poem was originaller than mine.

3. This hurricane was the destructivest that we've had in years!

4. That man looks like the most happy worker in the city.

5. Of all the foods here, sushi is the least likely to contain fat.

6. Which do you like better, traveling by train or by airplane?

7. I'm not sure which of those two is the more safe way to travel.

8. Of all the cities we visited in Japan, Kyoto is the beautifullest.

9. I saw several silk kimonos on sale, but I decided to buy the least expensive one.

10. This trip was even gooder than the one we took last year.

# USES OF COMPARATIVE AND SUPERLATIVE FORMS

**17e** **Use the comparative degree when comparing two things. Use the superlative degree when comparing more than two.**

COMPARATIVE    The little red pepper is **spicier** than the green one.
SUPERLATIVE    This little red pepper is the **spiciest** one of all.

NOTE    In everyday conversation, people sometimes use the superlative degree when comparing two things: *I pitch best with my right hand.*

**17f** **Include the word *other* or *else* when comparing one thing with others that belong in the same group.**

NONSTANDARD    Anaba writes better than any student in her class.
STANDARD    Anaba writes better than any **other** student in her class.

NONSTANDARD    Uncle Luis is funnier than anyone in my family.
STANDARD    Uncle Luis is funnier than anyone **else** in my family.

**17g** **Avoid double comparisons.**

A *double comparison* is incorrect because it contains both *–er* and *more/less* or *–est* and *most/least.*

NONSTANDARD    I think Tom Landry is more older than your father.
STANDARD    I think Tom Landry is **older** than your father.

**17h** **Be sure your comparisons are clear.**

UNCLEAR    The restaurants in Rockport are cheaper than New York City.
CLEAR    The restaurants in Rockport are cheaper than the restaurants in New York City.

## EXERCISE 3   Identifying and Correcting Modifiers

For each of the following sentences, underline the error in the use of modifiers. Rewrite each sentence correctly on the line provided.

EX.   1.   This film is <u>better than any</u> I've seen.

_____

1. Indian films are often more longer than American films.

_____

2. Bombay must contain the greater number of film posters in the world.

_____

3. Tien liked this film more than anyone who saw it.

   _____

4. This comedy is the least funniest in this film festival.

   _____

5. The films of Mr. Satyajit Ray are more seriouser than those of Mr. B. Kapoor.

   _____

6. Of my two sisters, Nora knows most about film directors.

   _____

7. This theater is much less comfortable than yesterday.

   _____

8. The movies made by students are not as polished as experienced directors.

   _____

9. It is certainly more hotter outside than it is in the theater.

   _____

10. Directors in India make more films than directors in any country in the world.

    _____

11. In India, the price of a movie ticket is cheapest than in the United States.

    _____

12. The length of the movie is least important than the entertainment it provides.

    _____

13. Kapoor wants to get the most best stars and the most best music for his movies.

    _____

14. Will Kapoor continue to be India's bigger filmmaker?

    _____

15. One of his movies was the larger production ever made in India.

    _____

# *DANGLING MODIFIERS*

**17i** **A modifying phrase or clause that does not clearly and sensibly modify a word or group of words in a sentence is called a *dangling modifier*.**

When a modifying phrase containing a verbal comes at the beginning of a sentence, the phrase is followed by a comma. Immediately after that comma should come the word that the phrase modifies.

UNCLEAR    Visiting Philadelphia, several museums interested me.
   CLEAR    Visiting Philadelphia, I was interested in several museums.

UNCLEAR    To see Henry Ossawa Tanner's work, a visit to the Philadelphia Museum of Art is necessary.
   CLEAR    To see Henry Ossawa Tanner's work, you must visit the Philadelphia Museum of Art.

To correct a dangling modifier, rearrange the words in the sentence, and add or change words to make the meaning logical and clear.

 DANGLING    Arriving on a holiday, the museum was closed.
CORRECTED    Arriving on a holiday, we found the museum closed.

NOTE    A sentence may appear to have a dangling modifier when *you* is the understood subject. In such cases, the modifier is not dangling; it is modifying the understood subject.

     EXAMPLE    To paint well, (you) spend a lot of time drawing.

**EXERCISE 4**    **Revising Sentences by Eliminating Dangling Modifiers**

On the line after each of the following sentences, indicate how you would revise the sentence to eliminate the dangling modifier. As shown by the example, you need not write the whole sentence.

EX.    1. Looking at one drawing, the signature surprised me.
       *drawing, I was surprised by the signature.*

1. Displayed in one gallery, we enjoyed the Japanese woodcuts. _____

2. To see everything on this floor, a plan is necessary. _____

3. Looking at the watercolors, some looked like oil paintings. _____

_____

4. Hung on several walls, Sharon read placards telling about the artist's life.

_____

5. To prevent damage, many pieces were covered with plastic shields by the officials.

_____

6. There will be a special show next month of local photography.

_____

7. Some winter scenes gave us chills painted in grays and whites.

_____

8. My favorite colors were used in several paintings, which are mainly reds and yellows.

_____

9. Along the New England coast, one group of photographs showed storm scenes.

_____

10. Expecting a large crowd, arrangements were made by the museum to change the viewing hours.

_____

## EXERCISE 5   Writing Sentences with Introductory Modifiers

Write ten complete sentences using the introductory modifiers below. Be sure the word that the phrase modifies immediately follows the comma. Write your sentences on your own paper.

EX.  1. Wearing bug repellent,
         *Wearing bug repellent, we ventured into the woods.*

1. Waving a camera,
2. To create memorable pictures,
3. Working quickly,
4. Covered with mosquito bites,
5. To photograph hummingbirds,
6. After listening to the report,
7. Walking to school,
8. Made from leather,
9. Creeping around the door,
10. To talk on this pay telephone,

## *MISPLACED MODIFIERS*

**17j    A *misplaced modifier* is a phrase or clause that sounds awkward because it modifies the wrong word or group of words.**

Modifying phrases should be placed as near as possible to the word or words they modify.

MISPLACED    The picture was taken at the August Moon Festival of the little girl in a yellow costume.

CORRECTED    The picture **of the little girl in a yellow costume** was taken at the August Moon Festival.

Adjective clauses and adverb clauses should be placed so that they are clearly linked to the words they modify.

MISPLACED    Before you leave, get the atlas from the table that you need.

CORRECTED    Before you leave, get the atlas **that you need** from the table.

### EXERCISE 6    Revising Sentences by Correcting Misplaced Modifiers

Underline the misplaced modifier in each of the following sentences. Indicate where the modifier should appear in the sentence by inserting a caret (∧).

EX.    1.    The detective∧questioned Ms. O'Rourke <u>with the dark beard</u>.

1. Written by Henry David Thoreau, I admire the simple country life portrayed in *Walden*.

2. We could hear the tornado approaching from our basement shelter.

3. Leonora went to her room after her brother had left for the video arcade to do some homework.

4. The car will win an award that is the most fuel-efficient.

5. We read about the candidates who are running for mayor in the Sunday paper.

6. In the sky last night, our astronomy class enjoyed watching a meteor shower.

7. Their dog was waiting at the door looking very excited and wagging its tail.

8. We drove Mr. Mason from his house to the mall, who needed to run an errand.

9. Always a very caring person, Rebecca decided to become a nurse at the age of twelve.

10. The neighbor's dogs frightened the Yamaguchis' new baby barking at night.

11. The salad is in the refrigerator for your lunch.

12. I willingly admit that I might have given up and gone home in her situation.

13. Mrs. Worthington gave some of her prize-winning roses to her neighbor arranged in a white basket.

14. The rusty, green van belongs to our next-door neighbor that is parked in the driveway.

15. Nikki drove the family car wearing sunglasses and a leather cap.

16. The Allentown Community Choir rehearsed a new song paying careful attention to the rhythm.

17. Cheering the loudest, the prize was awarded to the team.

18. During the fire drill, the students were asked to leave the room quietly by the teacher.

19. The puppy sat in the doorway scratching its head.

20. Phoebe got all the supplies from the store that she needed.

21. Granny told me a story about getting caught in a storm sitting in her chair near the window.

22. They fixed the bike's flat quickly working together.

23. I work for my money hard.

24. You can find the photographs that Dad took of your great-grandparents in one of these old photo albums.

25. The old family home sat on a hill needing repair.

## CHAPTER REVIEW

### A. Revising Sentences by Correcting Modifiers

In the sentences below, correct all errors in the use of modifiers. Rewrite each sentence on your own paper.

EX. 1. Yo-Yo Ma must be one of the famousest cellists in the world.
    1. *Yo-Yo Ma must be one of the most famous cellists in the world.*

1. These seats are more better than the ones we had last month.
2. In his seat I told my young cousin to sit quietly.
3. That pianist is better than any musician I've heard.
4. Sitting in the center of the hall, the music surrounded us.
5. The trio is playing the piece that you liked onstage now.
6. There are many families in the audience with children.
7. Later, a chorus will sing the familiarest songs from *The Wizard of Oz*.
8. Having seen the movie, the songs were enjoyed by the children.
9. Which song is your more favorite?
10. Moving her arms gracefully, we watched the conductor.

### B. Using Modifiers Correctly in a Paragraph

In the following paragraph, underline any misplaced or incorrect modifiers. For misplaced modifiers, indicate where the modifier should appear in the sentence by inserting a caret ( ∧ ). For all other errors, write the corrections above the sentence.

EX. [1] Many people ∧ visit Nashville <u>who like music</u>.

[1] Of all the U. S. cities, Nashville is probably the one that is more famous for country music. [2] However, people can enjoy a great variety of music who go there. [3] In 1980, my parents enjoyed a performance of the Royal Laotian Classical Dance Troupe, whose vacation included a visit to Nashville. [4] Before performing, fancy costumes and masks were put on. [5] Then the dancers told traditional stories using their costumes and their bodies. [6] The stories about ancient Laos that they told were more than six hundred years old. [7] The music is played on stringed and percussion

instruments that accompanies the dances.  [8] Originally performed
only for the king of Laos and his court, the Nashville audience
seemed to appreciate the royal dances.  [9] These dances for centuries
have been passed from one generation to the next.  [10] Taking over
Laos in 1975, the royal dancers' safety was threatened by the
Communists.

## C.   Using Modifiers in an Adventure Story

As an author of adventure stories, you have jotted down the following list of
phrases and clauses as prewriting for a new tale. On your own paper, use
ten of the following phrases and clauses correctly to write your opening
paragraph. To make sure that your paragraph does not have any dangling
or misplaced modifiers, underline the modifiers you use, and draw arrows
to the words they modify.

| | |
|---|---|
| speeding down the mountainside | rubbing my bruised leg |
| while enjoying a brief rest | which I discovered by accident |
| to avoid falling in the canyon | from my experience as a rider |
| chased by a wild beast | to avoid being seen |
| that seemed safer | hearing a moaning sound |
| diving into the water | that caused my hair to curl |
| jumping off the speeding freight train | to escape the extreme engine heat |
| that was hidden inside a cave | creeping silently along |
| to save myself from certain disaster | hoping for some daylight |
| which later saved my life | that was under a rotted log |

EX.  that seemed safer
  My eyes darted around frantically as I searched for a path that seemed safer.

# A, AN / BESIDE, BESIDES

This chapter presents an alphabetical list of common problems in English usage. Throughout the chapter, examples are labeled *standard* or *nonstandard*. *Standard English* is the most widely accepted form of English. *Nonstandard English* is language that does not follow the rules and guidelines of standard English.

**a, an**   These *indefinite articles* refer to one of a general group.

EXAMPLES   Jaime ate **a** banana and **an** orange.
Crystal bought **an** umbrella and **a** uniform for work.

Use *a* before words beginning with a consonant sound; use *an* before words beginning with a vowel sound. In the example above, *a* is used before *uniform* because the *u* in *uniform* has a consonant sound.

**affect, effect**   *Affect* is a verb meaning "to influence." *Effect* used as a verb means "to accomplish." Used as a noun, *effect* means "the result of some action."

EXAMPLES   Did the happy story **affect** your mood?
The coach gave a speech to **effect** a change in the team's morale.
The sad story had a negative **effect** on me.

**all the farther, all the faster**   These phrases are used in some parts of the United States to mean "as far as" or "as fast as."

NONSTANDARD   One mile is all the farther he can run.
  STANDARD   One mile is **as far as** he can run.

**among**   See **between, among**.

**and etc.**   *Etc.* is an abbreviation of the Latin phrase *et cetera*, meaning "and other things." Thus, *and etc.* means "and and other things." Do not use *and* with *etc.*

EXAMPLE   During baseball practice, Philip worked on batting, fielding, throwing, *etc.* [not *and etc.*]

**anywheres, everywheres, nowheres, somewheres**   Use these words without the final *s.*

EXAMPLE   I looked **everywhere** for that recipe. [not *everywheres*]

**as**   See **like, as**.

**at**   Do not use *at* after *where.*

NONSTANDARD   I don't know where she's at.
   STANDARD   I don't know **where** she is.

**beside, besides**   *Beside* is a preposition that means "by the side of" someone or something. *Besides* as a preposition means "in addition to." As an adverb, *besides* means "moreover."

EXAMPLES   Lily sat **beside** Natalya on the bus. [preposition]
   **Besides** cleaning his room, he has to wash the dishes. [preposition]
   I don't have enough money for the movie. **Besides**, I haven't finished my homework. [adverb]

## EXERCISE 1   Solving Common Usage Problems

For each sentence below, underline the correct word or expression in parentheses.

EX.   1.   I like to use (*a*, *an*) straw.

1. "This is (*all the farther, as far as*) I can swim," he panted as he climbed into the boat.

2. (*Beside, Besides*) Shanaz, no one did well on the test.

3. The pollution from that factory (*affects, effects*) the air quality of the entire region.

4. Shiloh's puppy follows him (*everywheres, everywhere*).

5. Sometimes I don't know where your head (*is, is at*)!

## EXERCISE 2   Proofreading Sentences for Correct Usage

In each sentence below, draw a line through the error in usage, and write the correct form above it.

EX.   1.   The trunk with Grandma's heirlooms is ~~somewheres~~ in the attic.   *somewhere*

1. I hope Nicholas sits besides me at the play.

2. The missing key was nowheres to be found.

3. Does Rodrigo really practice the trombone for a hour each morning?

4. No one seems to know where our next basketball game is at.

5. Max has to dust the living room, set the table, arrange the flowers, and etc., before the guests arrive.

# BETWEEN, AMONG / FEWER, LESS

**between, among**   Use *between* when you are referring to two things at a time, even though they may be part of a group consisting of more than two. Use *among* when you are thinking of a group rather than of separate things.

EXAMPLES   Place that plant **between** the piano and the chair.
Greetings were exchanged **between** the six guests. [Although there were more than two guests, the guests greeted one another in pairs, or two at a time.]
There was excitement **among** the fans when Irisa scored a goal. [The fans are thought of as a group in this situation.]

**could of**   Do not write *of* with the helping verb *could*. Write *could have*. Also avoid *ought to of, had of, should of, would of, might of*, and *must of*.

EXAMPLES   Jamila **could have** helped you. [not *could of*]
I **ought to have** made souvlakia for dinner. [not *ought to of*]

**discover, invent**   *Discover* means "to be the first to find, see, or learn about something that already exists." *Invent* means "to be the first to do or make something."

EXAMPLES   Edmond Halley **discovered** the comet that bears his name.
The piano was **invented** by Bartolomeo Cristofori in 1709.

**effect, affect**   See **affect, effect**.

**everywheres**   See **anywheres**, etc.

**fewer, less**   *Fewer* is used with plural words. *Less* is used with singular words. *Fewer* tells "how many"; *less* tells "how much."

EXAMPLES   **Fewer** people attended the festival this year.
The festival took up **less** space this year.

## EXERCISE 3   Identifying Correct Usage

For each of the following sentences, underline the correct word or expression in parentheses.

EX.   1.  My ancestors lived (*somewheres*, <u>*somewhere*</u> ) in El Salvador.

1.  We (*should have*, *should of*) left earlier.

2.  Thomas Edison (*discovered*, *invented)* the electric light.

3. Did that hurricane (*affect, effect*) your town?

4. I (*might have, might of*) taken that phone message.

5. Mika sat on the lawn (*among, between*) the dandelions.

6. The heat had a negative (*affect, effect*) on my energy level.

7. When we checked the returns, we were surprised that (*fewer, less*) people donated money this month than last month.

8. Lan (*must have, must of*) rehearsed for hours.

9. I searched (*everywhere, everywheres*) for books about Indira Gandhi, a former prime minister of India.

10. Jonas Salk (*discovered, invented*) a cure for polio.

11. There was (*fewer, less*) room in the car than we had expected.

12. Samuel and Liona (*ought to have, ought to of*) studied harder for their grammar quiz.

13. My grandfather lives in Laos, a country (*among, between*) Vietnam and Thailand.

14. Marco needs to (*affect, effect*) a detailed plan for our project.

15. I had (*less, fewer*) homework assignments than usual, so I (*could have, could of*) helped you.

16. I (*could have, could of*) won the race if only I hadn't gotten a cramp.

17. The television program showed that the four thieves split the stolen money (*among, between*) themselves.

18. Nathaniel has been having·(*fewer, less*) headaches since he improved his diet.

19. Working in their father's shop, the boys (*discovered, invented*) a burglar alarm.

20. Thaddeus (*ought to have, ought to of*) signed up for that class when there was an opening.

# HAD OF / OUGHT TO OF

**had of**   See **could of**.

**had ought, hadn't ought**   Unlike other verbs, *ought* is not used with *had*.

NONSTANDARD   Jake had ought to budget his money; he hadn't ought to spend so much that he can't save any money.

STANDARD   Jake **ought** to budget his money; he **ought not** to spend so much that he can't save any money.

**invent, discover**   See **discover, invent**.

**kind, sort, type**   The words *this, that, these,* and *those* should always agree in number with the words *kind, sort,* and *type*.

EXAMPLE   Is **this type** of music more relaxing than **those** other **types**?

**learn, teach**   *Learn* means "to acquire knowledge." *Teach* means "to instruct" or "to show how."

EXAMPLE   I want to **learn** to speak Italian; do you think you can **teach** me?

**leave, let**   *Leave* means "to go away" or "to depart from." *Let* means "to allow" or "to permit."

NONSTANDARD   Leave Jamal go home.
STANDARD   **Let** Jamal go home.

**less**   See **fewer, less**.

**like, as**   In informal English, the preposition *like* is often used as a conjunction meaning "as." In formal English, use *like* to introduce a prepositional phrase, and use *as* to introduce a subordinate clause.

EXAMPLES   That building looks **like** a castle.
Please do the project **as** our teacher described.

**might of, must of**   See **could of**.

**nowheres**   See **anywheres**, etc.

**of**   Do not use *of* with prepositions such as *inside, off,* or *outside*.

EXAMPLES   I went **inside** the pantry. [not *inside of*]
I took some crackers **off** the top shelf. [not *off of*]
I walked **outside** the building. [not *outside of*]

**ought to of**   See **could of**.

## EXERCISE 4   Identifying Correct Usage

In each sentence below, underline the correct word or expression in parentheses.

EX.   1.  Leon (*had ought, ought*) to attend the spring festival.

1.  Ms. Gabriel will (learn, teach) the class about Martin Luther King, Jr.

2.  Please (let, leave) my puppy play in the yard.

3.  Did you find evidence that this (type, types) of moccasin was worn by many Native Americans?

4.  Wyatt looks (as, like) his older sister.

5.  We walked around (inside, inside of) the White House when we were in Washington, D.C.

## EXERCISE 5   Correcting Errors in Usage

In the sentences below, draw a line through each error, and write the correct form above it. Some sentences contain more than one error.

EX.   1.  Martina climbed ~~off of~~ her bicycle.  *(off)*

1.  I would like to play my cello like Anthony does.

2.  These kind of books learned us all about several kinds of inventions in ancient China.

3.  That cave looked as a good camping spot, so we walked inside of it and looked around.

4.  This kinds of enchilada is spicier than those kind.

5.  We hadn't ought to swim without a lifeguard, even though the camp counselors learned us how to swim.

6.  Please leave me go with you to the Cinco de Mayo parade.

7.  The sea lion has whiskers like a cat does.

8.  Those type of rugs are made in Afghanistan.

9.  The ball flew over the outfield wall and landed outside of the park.

10.  We had ought to wear our rain gear for the hike to the summit.

**should of**   See **could of.**

**some, somewhat**   In writing, do not use *some* for *somewhat* as an adverb.

NONSTANDARD    I enjoyed hiking in the woods some.
STANDARD    I enjoyed hiking in the woods **somewhat.**

**somewheres**   See **anywheres.**

**sort**   See **kind**, etc.

**teach**   See **learn, teach.**

**than, then**   *Than* is a conjunction; *then* is an adverb.

EXAMPLES    That lamp is brighter **than** this one.
I will stop at the market; **then** I will visit you.

**them**   *Them* should not be used as an adjective. Use *those* or *these*.

EXAMPLE    Milagro enjoyed **those** long walks on the beach. [not *them*]

**this here, that there**   The words *here* and *there* are unnecessary after *this* and *that*.

EXAMPLE    I like **this** wallpaper. [not *this here*]
Ida likes **that** style. [not *that there*]

**type**   See **kind**, etc.

**when, where**   Do not use *when* or *where* incorrectly in writing a definition.  Do not use *where* for *that*.

NONSTANDARD    A bialy is when you make a flat breakfast roll.
STANDARD    A bialy is a flat breakfast roll.
STANDARD    I heard in class **that** school is being canceled. [not *where*]

**which, that, who**   The relative pronoun *who* refers to people only; *which* refers to things only; *that* refers to either people or things.

EXAMPLES    Annmarie is the one **who** ordered that sandwich. [person]
That afghan, **which** is in the closet, was a birthday gift. [thing]
Eli was the person **that** I wanted to meet. [person]
The salsa **that** I made is in the refrigerator. [thing]

**would of**   See **could of.**

**EXERCISE 6   Correcting Errors in Usage**

For each sentence below, underline the correct word or expression in parentheses.

EX.   1. (*Them*, *Those*) books are about tropical rain forests.

1. Shina is (*some*, *somewhat*) interested in (*this*, *this here*) topic.

2. Rain forests, (*which*, *who*) have rain almost every day, have no frost.

3. Hundreds of kinds of trees grow in (*these*, *them*) forests.

4. Shina told me (*where*, *that*) the canopy is the tops of the trees, and animals living there climb a long (*way*, *ways*) in search of food.

5. Southeast Asia's rain forest is taller (*than*, *then*) most.

**EXERCISE 7   Correcting Errors in Usage**

In the sentences below, draw a line through each error, and write the correct form above it. Some sentences contain more than one error.

EX.   1. I am ~~some~~ familiar with the Red Cross.  *somewhat*

1. A short ways down the street, people were donating blood.

2. This here blood drive was being run by the Red Cross.

3. Them Red Cross volunteers help people all over the world.

4. Volunteers are when people give their time and services without having to and often without being paid.

5. Red Cross volunteers, which can be found in many countries, are paid with grateful smiles from them people they help.

6. The Red Crescent, who operates in Muslim countries, is part of the same group.

7. When there's a natural disaster, they might have to carry blood and medical supplies a long ways.

8. Often, their work is some dangerous.

9. Red Cross and Red Crescent volunteers often can help better then governments can.

10. My friend Mr. Azakian learned me about these volunteers.

# DOUBLE NEGATIVES

In a **double negative**, two negative words are used when one is sufficient. Avoid double negatives in both writing and speaking.

**hardly, scarcely**   The words *hardly* and *scarcely* both convey a negative meaning. Never use one of these words with another negative word.

EXAMPLES   I **can hardly** believe that my sister is graduating. [not *can't*]
The park **has scarcely** enough swings. [not *hasn't*]

**no, nothing, none**   Do not use one of these words with another negative word.

| | |
|---|---|
| NONSTANDARD | We don't have no library books. |
| STANDARD | We **don't have any** library books. |
| STANDARD | We **have no** library books. |
| NONSTANDARD | I don't want nothing to do with the problem. |
| STANDARD | I **don't want anything** to do with the problem. |
| STANDARD | I **want nothing** to do with the problem. |
| NONSTANDARD | Kareena wanted tickets, but there weren't none left. |
| STANDARD | Kareena wanted tickets, but there **weren't any** left. |
| STANDARD | Kareena wanted tickets, but there **were none** left. |

## EXERCISE 8   Correcting Errors in Usage

Each of the sentences below contains at least one error in usage. Draw a line through each error, and write the correct form above it.

EX.   1.   Hector ~~can't hardly~~ *can hardly* believe he made the team.

1. I didn't have no plans last night, so I went for a long walk.
2. Kali's family owns a wonderful restaurant that hasn't scarcely ever had a slow moment.
3. Ricardo didn't buy nothing at the fruit and vegetable market.
4. Asa and I don't have no time to practice today, and we didn't hardly have any time yesterday.
5. We wanted to build a real wigwam, but there weren't no poles for the frame.

## EXERCISE 9   Proofreading Paragraphs for Double Negatives

In the paragraph below, draw a line through the errors in usage. Write the correct form above the underlined error. Some sentences contain no errors.

EX.   [1]   I ~~can't hardly~~ believe that I have never heard of this poet.
*can't (or can hardly)*

[1] Born in 1917 in Topeka, Kansas, Gwendolyn Brooks didn't hardly live there for long.  [2] She wasn't no adult, but just a teenager, when her poetry was first published in the *Chicago Defender* and *American Childhood*.  [3] At college, and later at the South Side Community Art Center, Gwendolyn didn't miss no chance to improve her writing.  [4] As a result, she didn't hardly surprise people by winning several local poetry contests.  [5] Her poetry hadn't scarcely appeared in *Poetry* magazine before she published her first book of poems, *A Street in Bronzeville*, in 1945.  [6] The critics didn't have nothing but praise for her work, and she received two awards in a row.  [7] Winning the awards meant that she wouldn't have to do nothing but write poetry for a while.

[8] In 1949, Ms. Brooks published *Annie Allen*, which didn't include none of her previous work.  [9] For these new poems, she won nothing no less important than the 1950 Pulitzer Prize in poetry. [10] No other black woman had never won this before.  [11] Ms. Brooks's style became more casual through the 1950s and 1960s, but the change did not take away nothing from her humor and skill. [12] In the 1970s, the themes of her writing were not different from the social issues of the times.  [13] Her children's stories and novels of the 1970s and 1980s didn't reflect these themes no less than her poetry had.  [14] At various times over the years, she went back to college— not as a student, but as a teacher of poetry.  [15] Perhaps nothing couldn't match the honor given to Ms. Brooks in 1968 when she became the poet laureate of Illinois.

# CHAPTER REVIEW

## A. Identifying Errors in Usage

For each sentence below, underline the correct word or expression in parentheses.

EX. 1. The discussion (*between,* <u>*among*</u>) my classmates was about trains.

1. Did you read (*where, that*) railroads have been used since the 1500s?

2. These early (*types, type*) of rails were made of wood.

3. Trains were wagons that had to be pulled (*everywheres, everywhere*) by horses.

4. Steam railroads were (*discovered, invented*) in the 1800s.

5. Steam engines looked much (*like, as*) the diesel engines of today.

6. George Stephenson had a big (*effect, affect*) on this (*kinds, kind*) of transportation.

7. (*This here, This*) man built trains so that people could ride (*inside, inside of*) the cars.

8. Our teacher (*learned, taught*) us about the transcontinental railroad.

9. This (*must have, must of*) been one of the most important projects in U.S. history.

10. The construction of a nationwide railroad system immensely (*effected, affected*) the country's growth.

11. One thing that (*hadn't ought, ought not*) to be ignored is that immigrants (*which, who*) were mostly from China built this railroad.

12. Before the transcontinental railroad, there were (*fewer, less*) people in the West.

13. After the railroad was built, the United States went a long (*way, ways*) in growing as a nation.

14. The transcontinental railroad, (*beside, besides*) transporting people, enabled industries to expand to new areas.

15. For my project on the railroad, I am building (*a, an*) steam engine out of folded paper.

## B.  Using Words Correctly in Sentences

Because your friends respect your opinion, they often ask your advice on how to handle their problems. On your own paper, use fifteen of the words or expressions in this chapter to write sentences suggesting solutions to a few of your friends' problems. Underline the words or expressions you use.

EX.    1.  Learn the rules for using diving equipment before you try diving.

Peanuts reprinted by permission of UFS, Inc.

## C.  Writing a Letter

You are a diver on an expedition. Exploring the sea one morning, you come across a large sunken ship. You and your partner decide to enter it and look around. Later, when you are back on your ship, you decide to sit down and write a letter to a friend, describing your day and all that you saw in the sunken ship. In your letter, use five of the words or expressions covered in this chapter. Underline the words and the expressions that you use.

EX.       Dear Lucia,
          You would have been interested in our discovery today.

# SENTENCES, PRONOUN I, AND INTERJECTION O

**19a   Capitalize the first word in every sentence.**

EXAMPLES     The bus is late.
We may be late for the game.

Traditionally, the first word of a line of poetry is capitalized.

EXAMPLE     We wandered freely in the park
Until the summer sky grew dark.

 Some writers do not always follow these capitalization rules. If you are quoting, use letters exactly as the author uses them in the source of the quotation.

☞ **REFERENCE NOTE:** For more information about using capital letters in quotations, see page 281.

**19b   Capitalize the pronoun *I* and the interjection *O*.**

Although it is rarely used, *O* is always capitalized. Generally, it is reserved for invocations and is followed by the name of the person or thing being addressed. You will more often use the interjection *oh*, which is not capitalized unless it is the first word of the sentence.

EXAMPLES     When **I** wake up my brother, **I** sometimes say, "**O** Sleepyhead, you will miss your bus."
We paddled safely through, but **oh**, what a struggle we had!

---

## EXERCISE 1   Capitalizing Sentences in a Paragraph

In the following paragraph, circle the words that should begin with a capital letter.

EX.     (my) favorite section of the orchestra is the percussion section

1     drums, castanets, and xylophones are all percussion

2   instruments.  the player strikes these instruments in some way to

3   make a sound.  for striking, the player may use sticks, mallets, or

4   sometimes brushes.  pitch, though, is not adjustable on some

5   percussion instruments.  for a xylophone, the length of the bars

6   determines the pitch when you play it, but many drums are tuned

7   by a player. have you ever watched the timpanist tune a

8   kettledrum? the player adjusts the skin of the drum to make the

9   pitch higher or lower. in order to do this, the player uses a special

10  key to loosen or tighten the tuning pegs. i love to hear the

11  timpani in *Thus Spoke Zarathustra*. next year I hope to learn to

12  play the timpani in our school orchestra.

## EXERCISE 2    Correcting Capitalization Errors in Sentences

In the sentences below, underline the words that have errors in capitalization.

EX.   1.  If i could have three wishes, one would be "Give me three more
          wishes, o genie!"

1.  Do some holy books often address their readers, "o faithful believers"?

2.  the first snowfall is beautiful, but Oh, how i wish it were spring!

3.  We laughed when he said the punch line, "So i bit him."

4.  have you ever heard anyone say, "Woe is me!"?

5.  The team chanted, "o you Tigers! go! go! go!"

6.  are you buying cookies this year from the Girl Scouts?

7.  we studied the works of the Danish poet Johannes Ewald.

8.  Adolfo López Mateos was, i believe, president of Mexico from 1958–64.

9.  the Chinese poet Li Po lived from A.D. 701–762.

10. have you ever heard of the first-century Greek critic Longinus?

# PROPER NOUNS AND ADJECTIVES

**19c   Capitalize proper nouns and proper adjectives.**

A *common noun* names one of a group of people, places, or things. A *proper noun* names a particular person, place, or thing. *Proper adjectives* are formed from proper nouns.

 **REFERENCE NOTE:**   For more about proper nouns, see page 93. For more about proper adjectives, see page 101.

Common nouns are not capitalized unless they begin a sentence or a direct quotation, or are included in a title. Proper nouns are always capitalized.

| Common Nouns | Proper Nouns | Proper Adjectives |
|---|---|---|
| a country | Mexico | Mexican artist |
| a ruler | Napoleon | Napoleonic period |
| a city | Paris | Parisian styles |
| a poet | Dante | Dantean verses |

Some proper nouns consist of more than one word. In these names, short prepositions (generally fewer than five letters) and articles are not capitalized.

EXAMPLES   Statue of Liberty        Alexander the Great

 Proper nouns and adjectives sometimes lose their capitals through frequent usage.

EXAMPLES   china        pasteurize        sandwich

## EXERCISE 3   Identifying Correct Capitalization

For each of the following pairs of phrases, write the letter of the correct phrase on the line provided.

EX. _____ 1. a. visit a University
            b. visit Stanford University

_____ 1. a. last tuesday
            b. last Tuesday

_____ 2. a. the Brooklyn Bridge
            b. a Bridge in New York City

_____ 3. a. Kanes county
            b. Kanes County

_____ 4. a. Mississippi River
            b. Mississippi river

_____ 5. a. a european tour        _____ 8. a. nation's laws
           b. a trip through Europe               b. mexican laws

_____ 6. a. a famous film actor      _____ 9. a. Cajun dishes
           b. actor danny glover                 b. cajun dishes

_____ 7. a. a man named Eric the Red    _____ 10. a. World Trade Center
           b. a man named Eric The Red            b. World Trade center

## EXERCISE 4   Correcting Errors in Capitalization

In the sentences below, underline each error in capitalization. Write your correction in the space above the error.

                 *October*                            *New York City*

EX.   1.   Last <u>october</u>, my brother Earl and I went to <u>new york city</u>.

1.   We took a bus from newark, new jersey, after lunch.

2.   When we arrived at the greyhound station, we took another bus.

3.   The bus went to Central park.

4.   Sharika led the group of canadian tourists through the egyptian exhibit at the museum.

5.   Many people were dressed in the latest italian styles.

6.   We got off the bus and walked to lexington avenue.

7.   On the way, we stopped to talk with a man called binti, an African Artist.

8.   He had recently arrived from zanzibar, an island off the coast of africa.

9.   He was selling persian rugs and tapestries.

10.   The rugs had pictures of the united nations seal.

11.   Every ten years, the bureau of the census counts the U.S. population.

12.   Tagalog is the language used by the austronesian people of the same name.

13.   The ukrainian Sculptor archipenko was born in 1887.

14.   The Lammermuir hills are in the borders and lothian regions of Scotland.

15.   Laos, formerly a state of french indochina, is in southeast Asia.

# PEOPLE AND PLACES

**19d**  **Capitalize the names of people.**

EXAMPLES    Maya Angelou, Herman Melville, Joyce Chen, Eva Perón

**19e**  **Capitalize geographical names.**

| Type of Name | Examples |
|---|---|
| continents | South America, Australia |
| countries | Sri Lanka, Israel, Albania |
| cities, towns | Oklahoma City, Acton |
| counties, townships | Essex County, Niles Township |
| states | Arizona, North Carolina |
| islands | Staten Island, Key West |
| bodies of water | Bay of Fundy, Pacific Ocean |
| streets, highways | South Marshall Street, Ford Boulevard |
| parks and forests | Natchez National Park, Sherwood Forest |
| mountains | Andes Mountains, Mount Everest |
| regions | the South, the Northwest |

 Words such as *east*, *west*, *north*, and *south* are not capitalized when they indicate directions.

EXAMPLES    Drive **south** two miles and take a left. [direction]
Citrus fruits grow throughout the **South**. [region]

However, these words are capitalized when they name a particular place.

EXAMPLES    in the No thwest        by the South

 In a hyphenated street number, the second part of the number is not capitalized.

EXAMPLE    West Ninety-third Street

## EXERCISE 5    Correcting Errors in Capitalization

In the sentences below, underline each error in capitalization. Write
your correction in the space above the error.

EX.   1.   The <u>appalachian mountains</u> stretch from <u>georgia</u> to <u>maine</u>.

Appalachian Mountains               Georgia    Maine

1.   The country of argentina is in the southern part of south america.

2.   Just South of the city of new orleans, the mississippi river empties
     into the Gulf of Mexico.

3.   The novelist jorge amado was born in brazil in 1912.

4.   We traveled to the southwest to study the varieties of cactus that
     grow there.

5.   When the bus reaches herald square, how much farther will I ride
     to Thirty-Fifth Street?

6.   As you know, cochise was a famous American indian.

7.   The hetch hetchy valley is located in yosemite national park.

8.   Mountains known as the alps tower over much of europe.

9.   The states of new jersey and pennsylvania are separated by the
     delaware river.

10.   We visited my friend Ramón in jefferson city, the capital of
      missouri.

11.   Why did we count fifteen streets between Eleventh Street and
      Twenty-First Street?

12.   Penzance is a port in cornwall in the southwest part of England.

13.   The urubamba river, flowing through peru, joins a second river to
      become the Ucayali River.

14.   Have you ever visited the Dinaric alps Northeast of Italy?

15.   The Little Karroo mountains are part of the Drakensburg
      mountains in south africa.

# GROUPS, EVENTS, AND NATIONALITIES

**19f** **Capitalize the names of organizations, teams, businesses, institutions, and government bodies.**

| Type of Name | Examples |
|---|---|
| organizations | American Legion |
| teams | Houston Oilers |
| businesses | Ford Motor Company |
| government bodies | Department of Agriculture |
| institutions | University of Rochester |

NOTE Do not capitalize words such as *hotel, theater, college, high school, post office,* and *courthouse* unless they are part of a proper name.

EXAMPLES    Gloucester High School
my high school

**19g** **Capitalize the names of historical events and periods, special events, and calendar items.**

| Type of Name | Examples |
|---|---|
| historical events, periods | World War I, Middle Ages |
| special events | Olympic Games, Summerfest |
| calendar items | Monday, May, Arbor Day |

NOTE Do not capitalize the name of a season unless it is personified or used in the name of a special event.

EXAMPLES    We felt Winter's rule.
the annual Dartmouth Winter Carnival

**19h** **Capitalize the names of nationalities, races, and peoples.**

EXAMPLES  Spanish, Caucasian, Asian, Cherokee, Zulu

NOTE The words *black* and *white* may or may not be capitalized when they refer to races.

EXAMPLE    Both Blacks and Whites [*or* blacks and whites] have
worked to protect our civil rights.

## EXERCISE 6   Proofreading Sentences for Correct Capitalization

In the sentences below, underline each error in capitalization. Write your correction in the space above the error.

Johnson         Bell Telephone

EX.   1.   My neighbor, Mr. <u>johnson</u>, works for <u>bell</u> telephone.

1.   Our local bank, first federal savings, is closed on thanksgiving day.

2.   Many doctors belong to the American medical association.

3.   One well-known egyptian leader was anwar sadat.

4.   People celebrated the end of world war I on armistice day.

5.   After he graduated from the university of maryland, John Lucas played basketball for the houston rockets.

6.   The Veterans of Foreign Wars helps soldiers from world wars I and II.

7.   In Canada, Christmas day is the day before Boxing day.

8.   Among Spanish leaders of the Middle ages, el cid was quite famous.

9.   We gladly said farewell to summer and her long, hot days.

10.   Fans throughout the stadium cheered the team from the university of arizona.

## EXERCISE 7   Identifying Correct Capitalization

For each of the pairs of phrases below, write the letter of the correct phrase on the line provided.

EX.   <u>a.</u>   1.   a.  the Chicago Bulls
               b.  the New York mets

_____   1.   a.  a pleasant stay at the Bellevue hotel
            b.  a pleasant stay at the Bellevue Hotel

_____   2.   a.  a Service Bureau
            b.  the Internal Revenue Service

_____   3.   a.  an Italian opera
            b.  a french artist

_____   4.   a.  raced in the New York City Marathon
            b.  raced in the Marathon

_____   5.   a.  Stone age humans
            b.  Iron Age humans

# OBJECT, STRUCTURES, AND SCHOOL SUBJECTS

**19i    Capitalize brand names and trade names.**

EXAMPLES    Chicken of the Sea, Apple, Xerox

NOTE    Do not capitalize a common noun that follows a brand name:
Chicken of the Sea tuna, Apple computer.

**19j    Capitalize the names of ships, monuments, awards, planets, and other particular places or things.**

| Type of Name | Examples |
|---|---|
| ships, trains | the *Mayflower*, the *Orient Express* |
| aircraft, spacecraft, missiles | *Hindenburg, Apollo I, Patriot* |
| monuments, memorials | Bunker Hill Monument, Martin Luther King, Jr., Memorial Center |
| buildings | Town Hall, Lincoln Center |
| awards | Nobel Prize |
| planets, stars | Mercury, the North Star |

**19k    Do not capitalize names of school subjects, except for languages or course names followed by a number.**

EXAMPLE    Besides math and art, I'm taking Italian and History 102.

## EXERCISE 8    Proofreading Sentences for Correct Capitalization

In the following sentences, underline each error in capitalization. Write your correction in the space above the error.

EX.    1. Our school recently bought a <u>macintosh</u> computer.
                                     Macintosh (above *macintosh*)

1. The *Spirit of st. louis* was Charles Lindbergh's Airplane.

2. The Passenger Ship named *titanic* struck an iceberg.

3. Did *Gone with the Wind,* the famous movie that was set during the american civil war, win an academy award?

4. I am giving my sister a timex watch for Graduation.

5.  The First Star you see at night is often the planet venus.

6.  Roberto has to choose between Algebra II and American History.

7.  Did the spacecraft called *skylab* travel to any Planets?

8.  When you're in washington, d.c., be sure to visit the white house and the vietnam veterans war memorial.

9.  The french novelist Jules Verne wrote about a fictitious submarine called *nautilus*, piloted by Captain nemo.

10. The Poet Richard Wilbur won the pulitzer prize in 1957 and in 1989.

11. Have you checked the records on file at city hall?

12. Scientists wonder what the environments of saturn and pluto might be like.

13. Did Rayjean tell you the old joke about who is buried in grant's tomb?

14. The Bay area rapid transit system helps workers get to their jobs.

15. Chuck won the most valuable player award again this year.

## EXERCISE 9   Writing Sentences Using Correct Capitalization

You are a reporter covering the International Trade Fair in Tokyo, Japan. You are writing down notes that you can later use in an article. On your own paper, write ten sentences. In your sentences, include at least two of the rules for capitalization covered in this lesson. You might include types of products, companies represented, and awards won.

EX.   1.  The U.S. Waterbed Co. won the Most Unusual New Product Award for its collapsible waterbed.

## *TITLES*

**19l** **Capitalize titles.**

**(1) Capitalize the title of a person when it comes before a name.**

EXAMPLES    **Dr.** Schweitzer, **Senator** Boxer, **Ms.** Katz

Do not capitalize a title that is used alone or that follows a person's name. Often, these titles are preceded by *a* or *the*.

EXAMPLES    A president whom I admire was Abraham Lincoln.
My friend Samantha is vice-president of the Stamp Club.

When a title is used alone in a direct address, it is usually capitalized.

EXAMPLES    I would like to interview you, **Senator.**  Thanks, **Doctor.**

EXCEPTIONS Yes, **Sir** [or sir].  I will, **Ma'am** [or ma'am].

**(2) Capitalize words showing family relationship when used with a person's name, but *not* when preceded by a possessive.**

EXAMPLES    **Grandmother** Smith  **Aunt** Tanya  my grandfather  your father

**(3) Capitalize the first and last words and all important words in titles of books, periodicals, poems, stories, historical documents, movies, television programs, works of art, and short musical compositions.**

Unimportant words in titles include articles (*a, an, the*), coordinating conjunctions (*and, but, for, nor, or, so, yet*), and prepositions of fewer than five letters (*by, for, on, with*).

| Type of Name | Examples |
|---|---|
| books | *A Tale of Two Cities* |
| periodicals | the *Chicago Tribune* |
| poems | "The Hollow Men" |
| stories | "The Open Window" |
| historical documents | **Bill of Rights** |
| movies | *In the Line of Fire* |
| television programs | *Sixty Minutes* |
| works of art | *View of Toledo* |
| short musical works | "A Minor Variation" |

## EXERCISE 10    Proofreading Sentences for Correct Capitalization

In the sentences below, underline each error in capitalization. Write your correction in the space above the error.

EX.    1.    Annie Lennox was interviewed in that issue of *rolling stone.* [Rolling Stone]

1.    In 2004, senator John Kerry lost the election to president George Bush.

2.    Uncle dan gave me a copy of Dorothy Parker's story, "a telephone call."

3.    I read a review of Tom Clancy's book, *the teeth of the tiger,* in the Sunday paper.

4.    My Cousin Adrienne and I have learned to play Willie Nelson's song "stranger" on the piano.

5.    I got interested in poetry only after I read "break, break, break" by Tennyson.

6.    "I gave it to your Father," said professor Jones.

7.    Let's get the march issue of *harper's.*

8.    I don't remember who wrote the declaration of independence, but I know that john hancock signed it.

9.    constable's painting *wivenhoe park, essex* is of the actual Wivenhoe Park.

10.    My Mother hopes to write a book called *cooking for others,* about her days at *La Cantina.*

11.    Have they read any of the books by doctor Joyce Brothers?

12.    Please ask Gerry to find out how many Presidents have been elected since 1900.

13.    King john of england did not want to sign the magna carta.

14.    Grandma moses painted *Out for Christmas trees* in 1987.

15.    The musical *Sunday In The Park With George* is based on the life of the French painter Georges Seurat.

# CHAPTER REVIEW

## A. Correcting Errors in Capitalization

In the sentences below, underline each error in capitalization. Write your correction in the space above the error.

EX. 1. When ~~i~~ finish ~~High School~~, I want to go to ~~allegheny college~~.
 *(corrections above: I / high school / Allegheny College)*

1. Yes, doctor, i did read the article about you in *the denver post*.

2. The japanese city of hiroshima is located on a large Bay.

3. In philadelphia, the franklin institute is on benjamin franklin parkway.

4. Ana's Uncle Georgio wrote an article about the Spacecraft *challenger*.

5. When you're in the northwest, be sure to visit the city of seattle.

6. candace bergen, a television star, spoke at the spring women's conference at the University where my aunt Flo teaches.

7. We received a letter from governor rick perry of texas.

8. I bought this perdue chicken at hal's market on Fifty-Third Street.

9. Was this house really the inspiration for Nathaniel Hawthorne's book *the house of the seven gables?*

10. My Grandmother always says, "Waste not, want not."

11. Shall I take Biology I, English I, or Algebra?

12. West Indian music combines African, spanish, and other styles.

13. The National science fair is scheduled for early in the winter.

14. Marlene's new poem begins, "Say, Let me tell you a story."

15. Is Thanksgiving day always celebrated on a thursday ?

## B. Proofreading a Paragraph for Correct Capitalization

In the paragraph below, all capital letters have been omitted. Underline each word that should be capitalized. Write your correction in the space above the word.

EX. [1] ~~next tuesday~~ the students at ~~west chester junior high~~
 *(corrections above: Next Tuesday / West Chester Junior High)*

will celebrate ~~earth day~~.
 *(correction above: Earth Day)*

[1] my friend bobby ray robinson and i are making an exhibit called "steel from trash." [2] last week, we drove east on route 30 to interview doctor ramón martínez of the lukens steel company in the city of coatesville. [3] he assured us that his company is very interested in purchasing clean, used steel cans from the residents of west chester. [4] when bobby ray heard that, he said, "Let's get this recycling project off the ground!" [5] we are thinking about writing a letter to the *west chester gazette*.

## C.  Working with a Partner to Report on a Space Journey

The year is 2110, and you and your partner are newspaper reporters. Your editor has asked you to accompany an astronaut as she journeys into space. The purpose of your trip is to interview the astronaut, gathering details about her childhood and education, her training as an astronaut, the goals of her mission, and her hopes for the future.

1.  Working together, use reference books and science magazines to make notes about current space missions. Add science fiction details to put your journey clearly into future times. Create character details for the astronaut. What might she have studied in school? How might she have trained for this mission?

2.  On your own paper, write a news story based on your notes. Identify the name of the spacecraft, the name of the astronaut's school and hometown, the astronaut's cultural background, and the planets or stars the astronaut plans to visit. Be sure to capitalize correctly.

3.  Be sure to include the name of your newspaper and your editor.

EX.   Astronaut June Villarmo is proof of how important Science 102 can be!

# END MARKS AND ABBREVIATIONS

*End marks* are used to show the purpose of a sentence.

**20a    A period follows a statement (or declarative sentence).**

EXAMPLE    My father speaks Yiddish fluently**.**

**20b    A question mark follows a question (or interrogative sentence).**

EXAMPLE    Can you open this jar**?**

**20c    An exclamation point follows an exclamation.**

EXAMPLE    What a terrible storm that was**!**

**20d    Either a period or an exclamation point may follow an imperative sentence.**

EXAMPLES    Please wait here**.** [a request]
Don't touch that**!** [a command]

**20e    A period usually follows an abbreviation.**

| Abbreviations with Periods | |
|---|---|
| Personal Names | I. M. Pei, H. H. Munroe |
| Titles Used with Names | Mrs., Ms., Mr., Dr., Jr., Sr. |
| States | Calif., N.H., Wash. |
| Organizations and Companies | Co., Inc., Assn. |
| Addresses | St., Rd., Ave., P.O. Box |
| Times | A.M., P.M., B.C., A.D. |
| **Abbreviations Without Periods** | |
| Government Agencies | HUD, IRS, FBI, WHO |
| States followed by ZIP Codes | Encinitas, CA 92024 |
| Units of Measure | mg, cm, g, pt, gal, lb |
| Other Organizations | NASA, YMCA, NAACP |

## EXERCISE 1 Adding End Marks to Sentences

Write the end mark that should appear at the end of each sentence below.

EX. 1. On what day does the Vietnamese holiday Tet begin**?**

1. We will be fine if the rain doesn't start

2. How wonderful it is to meet you at last

3. Where do you leave newspapers for recycling

4. Tamara will proofread my book report

5. Were those pots made by a Maricopa potter

6. Please hold the door for me

7. How can we fix this bicycle

8. Stop that noise immediately

9. What a great interview Laurence Yep gave

10. This dog doesn't seem to have a license or rabies tag

11. Which museum will we visit on this field trip

12. Return these books to the library, please

13. A seismograph records earthquake data

14. Don't jump off a seesaw too quickly

15. Why can't we go to lunch together

## EXERCISE 2 Proofreading for the Correct Use of Abbreviations

Add or delete periods where needed in the items below. On the line before each name or phrase, write C if the name or phrase is correct.

EX. _____ 1. Mrs. Violette A. Johnson

_____ 1. is 12 cm. long

_____ 2. at 311 Catalpa Dr

_____ 3. U S Senator Joseph Montoya

_____ 4. Ed Begley, Jr

_____ 5. West Warwick, RI 02893

_____ 6. inside FBI headquarters

_____ 7. weighs 6 g

_____ 8. at 2:30 AM

_____ 9. E L Baines Enterprises, Inc

_____ 10. the room is 6 ft 6 in long

_____ 11. Dr Laura Stans

_____ 12. in the third century BC

_____ 13. Juan Sánchez, Sr.

_____ 14. by 3:00 P.M.

_____ 15. Ms. J R Peale

_____ 16. with the I.R.S.

_____ 17. San Diego, Calif

_____ 18. San Diego, CA 92119

_____ 19. 18 mg.

_____ 20. PO Box 87

## COMMAS IN A SERIES

**20f   Use commas to separate items in a series.**

EXAMPLES   I will have hummus, tahini, and pita bread. [words]
They found locusts in their car, on their porch, and even in
their kitchen. [phrases]
The drawings that Tena had dreamed about, that she had
struggled to create, and that she had carefully matted were
sold in a week.  [clauses]

**(1) If all items in a series are joined by *and* or *or*, do not use commas to separate them.**

EXAMPLE   The bronco kicked and bucked and reared.

**(2) Semicolons usually separate independent clauses in a series. Commas may separate short independent clauses, however.**

EXAMPLES   We arrived well before dawn; we scrubbed the walls and
ceilings; and we painted the rooms a pale blue.
We arrived, we cleaned, and we painted.

**20g   Use commas to separate two or more adjectives preceding a noun.**

EXAMPLE   This sari is a fine, beautiful silk.

When the last adjective in a series is thought of as part of the noun, the
comma before the adjective is omitted. Compound nouns like *orange juice*
and *lunch box* are considered single units.

EXAMPLE   My father grabbed his steel lunch box.

Try inserting *and* between the adjectives in a series. If *and* fits
sensibly, use a comma. For example, *fine and beautiful* sounds
sensible, so a comma is used. *And* cannot be logically inserted in
*steel lunch box*, however.

**REFERENCE NOTE**: For more about compound nouns, see
page 95.

## EXERCISE 3   Proofreading Sentences for the Correct Use of Commas

Add commas where needed in the following sentences. On the line before
each sentence, write *C* if the sentence is correct.

EX.   _____ 1.  We rode through forests, up mountains, and across a desert.

_____ 1.  French, Spanish and German will be offered next year.

_____ 2. Look for shrubs that are short rounded and dense.

_____ 3. Duane stared across the vast cornfields.

_____ 4. Invite Tyree to sing to dance or to tell jokes.

_____ 5. Jennifer sputtered coughed and finally took a deep breath.

_____ 6. Heat drought and poor soil were our biggest obstacles.

_____ 7. Someone drove up saw your sign and left a dollar.

_____ 8. We invited all of our aunts uncles and cousins.

_____ 9. Aretha was so determined to find her ring that she searched in the house in the yard and even out in the orchard.

_____ 10. Our bus soon began to produce clouds of black greasy smoke.

_____ 11. The poets that we studied included Robert Frost and Zora Neale Hurston.

_____ 12. The salsa that my mother makes is thick red and spicy.

_____ 13. You would have time to visit São Paulo stop in Rio de Janeiro and still meet your cousin in Recife.

_____ 14. All you have to do is nod and smile and keep quiet.

_____ 15. People write from right to left in Egypt Iran and Israel.

_____ 16. We sat on the metal fire escape to enjoy the cool air.

_____ 17. That character has appeared in books plays poems and films.

_____ 18. This is a person who is honest fearless and admired.

_____ 19. Shanghai seemed stylish successful and busy when we visited last year.

_____ 20. Postcards books and magazines are for sale in this store.

Peanuts reprinted by permission of UFS, Inc.

# COMMAS WITH COMPOUND SENTENCES

**20h** Use commas before *and, but, for, or, nor, so,* and *yet* when they join independent clauses.

EXAMPLE    Chico dove for the ball**, but** Shing reached it first.

NOTE    A comma is always used before *for, so,* and *yet* when they join two independent clauses. The comma may be omitted, however, when the independent clauses are very short; before *and, but, or* or *nor;* and when there is no possibility of misunderstanding.

EXAMPLE    Dad washed and I dried.

Do not be misled by compound verbs, which often make a sentence look as if it contains two independent clauses.

SIMPLE SENTENCE    Lian **sharpened** her pencil and **sat** down to write. [one subject with a compound verb]

COMPOUND SENTENCE    First Lian sharpened her pencil**, and** then she began to write. [two independent clauses]

## EXERCISE 4    Correcting Compound Sentences by Adding Commas

For each of the following sentences, add commas where needed. On the line before the sentence, write *C* if the sentence is correct.

EX.    _C_    1.  Amy climbed on her horse, but then she had to wait for us.

_____    1.  The falafel contained no meat yet it was very filling.

_____    2.  A dark cloud approached from the east and gradually filled up the sky.

_____    3.  The river was crowded for today was market day.

_____    4.  The first pictures of Venus came in and they were startling.

_____    5.  You can read for an hour or you can make the salad.

_____    6.  Amy could not even see her hand nor could she find the light switch.

_____    7.  Before the show started, Chad climbed on stage and tested the microphones.

_____    8.  I wasn't wearing repellent yet the mosquitoes didn't bite me.

_____ 9. Neither my cousin in Ohio nor my cousin in Texas drives yet.

_____ 10. The calendar is very old and it is made of stone.

_____ 11. How far did you have to go for the milk and eggs?

_____ 12. We haven't started school yet but we will begin on Monday.

_____ 13. Charlotte laughed but I didn't.

_____ 14. Douglas lost his dollar so he had to go home.

_____ 15. The sign said we had to pay ten dollars but the woman at the gate let us in for free.

## EXERCISE 5    Combining Sentences

On your own paper, rewrite each pair of sentences as a single compound sentence. Use a comma and *and, but, for, nor, or, so,* or *yet.*

EX.    1.  We could go to a movie. We could rent one.

    1.  We could go to a movie, or we could rent one.

1. We can go to the station now. The bus doesn't leave for two hours.
2. I swam for hours. I wasn't tired.
3. The fiesta began on Thursday. It continued for three days.
4. I studied hard for this quiz. I am as ready as I can be.
5. Most dogs aren't allowed in here. Guide dogs are always welcome.
6. I fed that plant and watered it. It still won't grow.
7. Long ago, that woman died of smallpox. She wasn't allowed to be buried with the other townspeople.
8. Some beads were made of shell. These are made of bone.
9. Put the spoiled food in the compost heap. Grind it up in the disposal.
10. This letter is very fragile. It was written almost two hundred years ago.
11. We left the party early. We were not having fun.
12. Put covers on your textbooks. They will stay clean.
13. Volunteers stacked sandbags along the riverbank. The river flowed over the sandbags.
14. Maxine was our best hockey player. She wanted to try out for the track team.
15. Roland likes apples. Abby prefers peaches.

# COMMAS WITH NONESSENTIAL WORDS

**20i** **Use commas to set off nonessential clauses and nonessential participial phrases**.

A *nonessential* (or *nonrestrictive*) clause or participial phrase adds information that is not necessary to the main idea in the sentence.

NONESSENTIAL PHRASE  The cook, **smiling broadly,** bowed at us.
NONESSENTIAL CLAUSE  This fabric, **which is tie-dyed,** came from East Africa.

When a clause or phrase is necessary to the meaning of a sentence—that is, when it tells *which one*—the clause or phrase is *essential* (or *restrictive*), and commas are not used.

ESSENTIAL PHRASE  The car **sitting on the trailer** is a dragster. [*Which* car?]
ESSENTIAL CLAUSE  The book **that I reserved** is for a report. [*Which* book?]

 NOTE  An adjective clause beginning with *that* is usually essential.

## EXERCISE 6  Using Commas Correctly

On the line before each sentence, identify each italicized phrase or clause by writing *e.* for *essential* or *n.e.* for *nonessential.* Insert commas where necessary.

EX.  _n.e._  1.  The speech was by Chief Joseph, a Nez Perce chief.

_____  1.  This manuscript *which is very old* belongs in a museum.

_____  2.  The kimchi *that Bob makes* is spicier than mine.

_____  3.  Don't you wonder why that diamond *lost for centuries* should suddenly turn up here?

_____  4.  The mural *that you liked* was painted by Diego Rivera.

_____  5.  Lobster Newburg *which was named for a man named Wenberg* is made with a delicious sauce.

_____  6.  This little menorah is the one *that we light during Hanukkah*.

_____  7.  Ricardo owns a brown-and-white horse *which looks like an appaloosa to me*.

_____  8.  Circle any words *that you don't understand*.

_____ 9. Geothermal energy *already popular in Denmark* is gradually finding supporters in the United States.

_____ 10. The woman *on the camel* is a Mongolian sheepherder.

_____ 11. Juan de la Cierva is one of the two men *who perfected the helicopter.*

_____ 12. The novel The Age of Innocence *which was written by Edith Wharton* has been made into a movie.

_____ 13. A band of dust *which some scientists blame on the eruption of Mt. Pinatubo* is now circling the globe.

_____ 14. The large dog *on the right* is a Great Dane.

_____ 15. Labor Day *which the Mexicans celebrate on May 1* is a festive holiday.

_____ 16. The Braille alphabet *which consists of patterns of raised dots* was named for its inventor.

_____ 17. The statue shows Thomas Gallaudet *for whom Gallaudet College is named.*

_____ 18. Millions of people perished as a result of the Black Death *which was a form of bubonic plague.*

_____ 19. Early hockey teams *playing on frozen lakes* sometimes had thirty players on a team.

_____ 20. The lucky astronauts were the ones *who rode in Apollo 11.*

_____ 21. Nancy lives next door to the new recreation center *which is made of red brick.*

_____ 22. Turn the handle *attached to the left side* to operate the jack-in-the-box.

_____ 23. A jaguar is a fierce forest cat *resembling a leopard.*

_____ 24. Professor Dunlap *who teaches driver safety* is originally from New Hampshire.

_____ 25. Quicksand will quickly swallow any heavy object *falling into it.*

# COMMAS WITH INTRODUCTORY WORDS

**20j** Use a comma after words such as *well, yes, no,* and *why* when they begin a sentence.

EXAMPLES   **No,** we won't be late.
**Well,** it's finally finished.

**20k** Use a comma after an introductory participial phrase.

EXAMPLE   **Jumping up,** Carlotta grabbed the ball.

**20l** Use a comma after a series of introductory prepositional phrases.

A short introductory prepositional phrase does not require a comma unless the comma is necessary to make the meaning clear.

EXAMPLES   **In the front of the store,** two clerks were ringing up purchases.
**After dinner** we talked for hours.
**After dinner,** time seemed to stand still. [The comma is needed to avoid reading "*dinner time*"]

**20m** Use a comma after an introductory adverb clause.

EXAMPLES   **When you're finished,** please help me here.

**20n** Use commas to separate items in dates and addresses.

EXAMPLES   On **September 5, 1968,** a star was born!
I will be at **54 Howard Lane, Bartow, FL 33830.**

**20o** Use a comma after the salutation of a friendly letter and after the closing of any letter.

EXAMPLES   Dear Ms. Hoy**,**          Sincerely yours**,**

**20p** Use a comma after a name followed by an abbreviation such as Jr., Sr., and M.D.

EXAMPLES   Martin Luther King**,** Jr.          Ben Casey**,** M.D.

## EXERCISE 7   Adding Commas with Introductory Elements

In each of the following sentences, add commas where needed. On the line before the sentence, write *C* if the sentence is correct.

EX.   _____ 1.  Washing my clothes in the river, I saw an alligator.

_____ 1.  In the back of the closet Jared noticed a small door.

_____  2.  Yes the writer Miguel Angel Asturias did win a Nobel Prize.

_____  3.  Singing at the top of her lungs Heather attracted quite a bit of attention.

_____  4.  Before you leave, look at this picture of Lou Gehrig.

_____  5.  As you read the chapter ask yourself questions about it.

_____  6.  Next to the kayak a much larger boat was being built.

_____  7.  At noon everyone took a short break for lunch.

_____  8.  Climbing over the fence Guido noticed a nest of rabbits.

_____  9.  Before you lock up check the alarm system.

_____ 10.  Why one of my friends made it for me.

_____ 11.  Say do you know Frieda?

_____ 12.  Because Mother worked all day, she is tired tonight.

_____ 13.  However we know that you did the best job that you could.

_____ 14.  At the sound of the bell everyone should leave the building.

_____ 15.  Why do onions make a person's eyes water?

## EXERCISE 8    Using Commas Correctly

On your own paper, rewrite the sentences below, inserting commas where needed.

EX.    1.  March 9 1943 was a truly memorable day.
       1.  March 9, 1943, was a truly memorable day.

1.  On September 9 1957 Congress established the Commission on Civil Rights.

2.  A terrible blizzard struck New York City on March 11 1888.

3.  In a letter to the editor of our school paper Duncan wrote about our lunchroom schedule.

4.  You can write to the American Hockey League at 425 Union Street West Springfield MA 01089.

5.  After we moved into our new house we met our neighbor Harriet Barlow Ph.D.

6.  This note arrived yesterday: "Dear Aunt Jo Thanks. Kisses Kim."

7.  I need the address of Fran Ahola M.D. of Dayton Ohio.

8.  On April 7 1992 Debra began her job as office assistant.

9.  Wow what an exciting concert that was last night!

10.  Why was the letter dated May 28 1900 so late in being delivered?

## COMMAS WITH SENTENCE INTERRUPTERS

**20q   Use commas to set off elements that interrupt the sentence.**

Two commas are used around an interrupting element—one before the "interrupter" and one after. If the interrupter comes at the beginning or the end of the sentence, only one comma is needed.

EXAMPLES   Roberto Clemente, **the ball player,** once lived there.
**Furthermore,** the whales are protected.
I need some help, **Kai.**

**(1) Appositives and appositive phrases are usually set off by commas.**

EXAMPLES   Inez, **my pen pal,** is an artist.
The documentary told about spelunkers, **people who explore caves for a hobby**.

If an appositive is closely related to the word preceding it, it should not be set off by commas.

EXAMPLE   I am looking for my friend **Greg**.

**(2) Words used in direct address are set off by commas.**

EXAMPLES   **Mrs. Ignacio,** your cab is here.
I know, **Mai,** that you will do your best.
We want to thank you, **Jolon**.

**(3) Parenthetical expressions are set off by commas.**

*Parenthetical expressions* are side remarks that add information or relate ideas.

EXAMPLES   The bronze lion, **in fact,** is quite common.
**For instance,** look at this butterfly.

**EXERCISE 9    Proofreading Sentences for the Correct Use of Commas**

For each of the following sentences, underline the appositive word or phrase. Add commas where needed.

EX.   1.   The animal, a guanaco, is related to the camel.

1.   My sister Kate knows all about camels and guanacos.

2. East of the Andes a mountain range in South America live the guanacos.

3. Another relative of the camel the alpaca is also used for wool.

4. Alpacas descendants of the guanaco are bred for their wool.

5. The bigger animals the llamas are becoming popular pets.

6. Llama wool a very coarse fiber is used for making rope.

7. Llamas sturdy animals are also used as pack animals.

8. The country that I visited Peru still uses llamas.

9. Another pack animal the dromedary lives in Asia and Africa.

10. Dromedaries the camels with one hump can carry heavy loads.

## EXERCISE 10   Punctuating Sentence Interrupters

In the sentences below, add commas where needed.

EX.   1.  Mah-jong, I believe, is an ancient game.

1. To be honest I never understood the appeal.

2. Please tell me what you think Ms. Karas.

3. My grandmother for example loved her sports car.

4. Uncle Marco do you remember the 1960s?

5. The beauty of the orchid I suppose isn't in its scent.

6. By the way did everyone in the 1920s love jazz?

7. I understand Keiko that you want a new kimono.

8. Nevertheless I refuse to use pesticide.

9. *Alice in Wonderland* was written in English; it has however been translated into many other languages.

10. Like all fads of course pet rocks lost popularity.

11. Toni Morrison my favorite author won the Nobel Prize in literature in 1993.

12. At any rate a majority of the senators will vote to pass the legislation.

13. One of these days Marcia we must find your jacket.

14. What happened at the end of the movie Dennis?

15. My aunt Mae an avid gardener loves her roses.

## REVIEW EXERCISE

### A. Proofreading Sentences for Correct Use of Commas

In the sentences below, insert commas where needed.

EX. 1. Caves, after all, can be rich sources of history.

1. I have visited caves in Virginia Pennsylvania and Kentucky.

2. In some caves scientists have found traces of ancient tools.

3. Thousands of years before Columbus arrived people were living in North American caves.

4. Scientists have found these caves and sometimes people discover tools inside them.

5. Some caves had walls some had roofs and some had separate rooms.

6. The tools which were made of stone were buried in the dirt.

7. They were preserved naturally by the hot dry air.

8. In limestone caves in the Southwest archaeologists even found mummies.

9. In one cave pet dogs were found buried next to bones.

10. Indeed these early people had baskets blankets and pets.

### B. Proofreading a Paragraph for Correct Use of Commas

In the following paragraph, insert commas where needed.

EX. [1] This park, I think, was designed by Olmsted.

[1] Frederick Law Olmsted was born on April 26 1882. [2] He began life in Hartford Connecticut. [3] He went to college at Yale University and he studied agriculture and engineering. [4] After he graduated he traveled through Europe to study gardens. [5] When he returned he became both the architect and the superintendent of Central Park in New York City. [6] He went on to design parks in Boston Chicago Detroit and Montreal. [7] Why did you know that the University of California in Berkeley California had Olmsted design

its campus? [8] It is certainly a beautiful place. [9] Olmsted's son

another Frederick also designed parks. [10] In fact he designed a

whole system of parks for Boston Massachusetts.

## C.  Writing Brief Descriptions

You are writing to someone your age who is moving to your area. This person will be attending your school. You have included a list of some of the activities and clubs available at school that you think this person would like to know about. Write brief descriptions of four of these activities or clubs.

1.  First, choose four school activities or clubs.

2.  Choose three details about each of them. Write at least two sentences about each activity or club, and use at least one comma in each sentence.

EX.    1.    *One club you might like, the Chess Club, meets twice a month.*

1._____

_____

_____

_____

2._____

_____

_____

_____

3._____

_____

_____

_____

4._____

_____

_____

_____

# SEMICOLONS

**20r** **Use a semicolon between independent clauses if they are not joined by** *and, but, or, nor, for, so,* **or** *yet.*

EXAMPLES   Selma pressed the button and waited; nothing happened.
Our bathroom leads a double life; it's also a darkroom.

**20s** **Use a semicolon between independent clauses joined by conjunctive adverbs or transitional expressions.**

| Commonly Used Conjunctive Adverbs | | | |
|---|---|---|---|
| accordingly | furthermore | meanwhile | otherwise |
| also | however | moreover | still |
| besides | indeed | nevertheless | then |
| consequently | instead | next | therefore |
| **Commonly Used Transitional Expressions** | | | |
| as a result | for instance | in fact | on the other hand |
| for example | in addition | in other words | that is |

EXAMPLES   I have a cat; **therefore,** I have cat hair on my clothes much of the time.
Stacking wood is no fun; **on the other hand,** it is good exercise.

**20t** **A semicolon (rather than a comma) may be needed to separate independent clauses joined by a coordinating conjunction when there are commas within the clauses.**

CONFUSING   You must bring boots, socks, and a backpack, but fruit, nuts, and a cup would be nice.

CLEAR   You must bring boots, socks, and a backpack; but fruit, nuts, and a cup would be nice.

**20u** **Use a semicolon between items in a series if the items contain commas.**

EXAMPLE   I have lived in Beaufort, North Carolina; New Orleans, Louisiana; Evanston, Illinois; and Gloucester, Massachusetts.

## EXERCISE 11    Using Semicolons Correctly

In each sentence below, add the missing semicolon.

EX.    1.    The flag of the United States has fifty stars; each star stands for a
state.

1.    Almost everyone recognizes our country's flag however, few
recognize our state's flag.

2.    All states have flags some are quite beautiful.

3.    Some have pictures on them the flag of California, for example,
shows a bear.

4.    Arkansas was our twenty-fifth state as a result, its flag has
twenty-five white stars on it to show the states.

5.    The Arkansas flag is red, white, and blue and it has three blue
stars beneath the name *Arkansas* representing Spain, France, and
the United States.

6.    Texas has had many flags flown over it at one point France, Spain,
and Mexico all claimed it.

7.    Ohio's flag is different from other flags it is swallow-tailed instead
of rectangular.

8.    The Ohio flag's stripes represent roads and waterways its stars
represent the original states and its circle represents the
Northwest Territory.

9.    The flag of West Virginia shows a wreath of rhododendron, the
state flower a cap of liberty and a ribbon with the state name.

10.    The American Legion in Alaska sponsored a flag-design contest
Benny Benson, from the Jesse Lee Mission Home, was the winner.

11.    This thirteen-year-old boy designed Alaska's flag the flag shows
the constellation known as the Big Dipper.

12.    Alaska became the forty-ninth state on January 3 the year was
1959.

13.    Michigan and Arkansas became states at the same time on the
Arkansas flag, a pair of stars on the blue band represents this
relationship.

14.    Some flags use stars to show that they were once territories others
use circles.

15.    The state of Washington was named for George Washington he
was our first president.

## COLONS

**20v   Use a colon to mean "note what follows."**

**(1)  Use a colon before a list of items, especially after expressions like *the following* and *as follows*.**

EXAMPLES   Your test will contain the following items: definitions, multiple-choice questions, and two essay questions.
Please bring these when you come: two sharp pencils, a calculator, and one sheet of scratch paper.

 NOTE   Do not use a colon before a list that follows a verb or a preposition.

INCORRECT   Pay special attention to: the size, the shape of the tail, and the shape of the bill.

CORRECT   Pay special attention to these features: the size, the shape of the tail, and the shape of the bill.

**(2)  Use a colon before a long, formal statement or a long quotation.**

EXAMPLE   This is how I feel about friends: "By helping you today, I give you the chance to help me tomorrow."

**20w  Use a colon in certain conventional situations.**

**(1)  Use a colon between the hour and the minute.**

EXAMPLES   The film starts at 7:00 P.M.      Try to call before 10:00 A.M.

**(2)  Use a colon between chapter and verse in referring to passages from the Bible.**

EXAMPLES   Genesis 43:29–34          James 3:7–11

**(3)  Use a colon after the salutation of a business letter.**

EXAMPLES   Dear Mr. Blanco:          Dear Personnel Manager:

## EXERCISE 12   Adding Colons to Sentences

In each of the following sentences, add the missing colon.

EX.   1.  Make sure that the names of the following cities are on your tickets: Portland, Seattle, and Vancouver.

1.  Many couples include Ruth 1 16 in their wedding ceremonies.

2. These are my favorite breakfast foods waffles, fresh fruit, and orange juice.

3. Every morning, Dad rides the 7 45 commuter train into town.

4. You will need these items before beginning bobsled training a helmet, gloves, and kneepads.

5. We will dismiss classes at 2 30 P.M. on school days before holidays.

6. We should ask these people to help with the science project David, Susan, Anna, and Tony.

7. Please write "Dear Sir or Madam" for your business letter salutation.

8. This year's transportation show includes a variety of vehicles cars, trucks, vans, and motorcycles.

9. Do you have these things on the grocery list onions, apples, paper towels, soap?

10. Mathew has appeared in two plays *The Diary of Anne Frank* and *High Noon*.

## EXERCISE 13    Using Colons Correctly

Proofread the following business letter. Add, delete, or replace punctuation as necessary.

1    Dear Ms. Reynolds,

2      I am writing to confirm your speaking engagement at our church

3    on Sunday, April 10. Pastor Reeves will open the proceedings at

4    3;00 P.M. with a reading of Isaiah 40.28–31.

5      We have the following audiovisual equipment available for your

6    use, a slide projector, a VCR, and an audiocassette player. Please let

7    me know if you require any other equipment or supplies.

8                                    Sincerely:

9                                    Maureen A. Brown

# CHAPTER REVIEW

## A. Proofreading Sentences for Correct Use of Commas

For each of the sentences below, add commas where needed.

EX. 1. Mary Cassatt , I heard , was an interesting woman.

1. Well she was born just before midnight on May 22 1844.

2. Shortly after that her family moved to Allegheny City Pennsylvania.

3. At the age of seven she moved to France with her family.

4. The three other children in the family were Lydia Alexander and Robert.

5. When Mary was a young woman she returned to Paris to study art.

6. She drew she painted and she met other artists.

7. Many of her early works in fact were destroyed in a fire that hit Chicago on October 8 1871.

8. One of her most famous paintings *The Bath* shows a mother bathing a child.

9. Besides working at her art Cassatt strongly supported women's rights.

10. In her later years however her eyesight failed and this failure forced her to stop painting.

## B. Using End Marks, Commas, Semicolons, and Colons Correctly in a Paragraph

Add the missing punctuation to the following paragraph.

1      July 15 1993 was a red-letter day we started driving across the

2    United States For the past two years my family has talked about

3    making this trip and we finally did it On our first day we drove by

4    these cities Providence Rhode Island Hartford Connecticut Albany

5    New York and Cleveland Ohio Why did we drive so far Well we

6    had seen all these places before When we crossed the Mississippi

7    River we slowed down and started sightseeing We reached Arizona

8    my favorite state during the last week in July We all loved the state

9    indeed we stayed there two weeks Arizona has a lot to see Navajo

10   and Hopi communities Grand Canyon National Park and several

11   national monuments

## C.   Proofreading a Letter

Add the missing punctuation to the business letter below.

1                                          590 Washington Street
2                                          Waverly PA 18471
3                                          October 10 1994
4    Dr Tonya Powell
5    426 Lane Drive
6    Bangor PA 18013

7    Dear Dr Powell
8        I understand that you are seeking volunteers for the
9    Community Supper which you hold every Wednesday evening
10   between 6 30 and 8 00 P M Our class advisor Ms Rice explained
11   your program and asked for volunteers.
12       Many students were interested consequently we can fully staff
13   the supper during the months of November December and
14   January Will you need additional volunteers after that date If you
15   will, just let us know Your volunteers for November will include
16   the following four students Margaret Lee Flavio Torres Rebecca
17   Solomon and me
18       We have all been told what to expect Dr. Powell According to
19   Ms Rice you need people to cook to serve and to clean up
20   afterward Everyone who volunteered is willing to do any of those
21   tasks, I believe We are delighted to be able to help and we look
22   forward to meeting you As you requested we will arrive at 6 15
23   the first night for an orientation tour
24                                         Sincerely
25                                         Farah Davis
                                           Farah Davis

# UNDERLINING (ITALICS)

**21a** Use underlining (italics) for titles of books, plays, periodicals, films, television programs, works of art, long musical compositions, ships, aircraft, and spacecraft.

| Type of Name | Examples |
|---|---|
| Books | *Annie John, A Separate Peace* |
| Plays | *Raisin in the Sun, Macbeth* |
| Periodicals | *International Herald Tribune, Smithsonian* |
| Films | *Casablanca, Glory* |
| Television Programs | *Nightline, Entertainment Tonight* |
| Works of Art | *The Footballer, Urban Freeways* |
| Long Musical Compositions | *Treemonisha, Messiah* |
| Ships | *Titanic, Columbia* |
| Aircraft | *Spirit of Columbus, Air Force One* |
| Spacecraft | *Apollo 12, Sputnik II* |

**NOTE** The article *the* is often written before a title but is not capitalized unless it is part of the official title. The official title of a book is found on the title page. The official title of a newspaper or periodical is found on the masthead, which usually appears on the editorial page.

EXAMPLE   I read the editorial in **the** *Houston Post.*

**21b** Use underlining (italics) for words, letters, and figures referred to as such and for foreign words.

EXAMPLES   The words *bite* and *bight* are homophones.

The word does not have an *e* at the end.

There are two digits in *10.*

Do you like to eat *akara?*

## EXERCISE 1  Using Underlining (Italics) Correctly

For each sentence below, underline the word or item that should be italicized.

EX.  1.  Which actor played the policeman in the film <u>Casablanca</u>?

1.  The song is about a train called The City of New Orleans.

2.  Many artists and photographers have done funny versions of the painting American Gothic.

3.  Tonight Channel 5 is showing two different episodes of Star Trek.

4.  Electricity had just arrived in this town the year that Sputnik I was launched.

5.  I don't think you spell the name with a k at the end.

6.  My parents took these pictures on board the Queen Elizabeth 2.

7.  Did you read the interesting editorial in The Des Moines Register last Wednesday?

8.  After we read the play Hamlet, we'll see the movie, which is on video.

9.  I enjoyed the book Nisei, which is by Bill Hosokawa.

10.  The word kvetch, which means to complain, actually comes from Yiddish.

## EXERCISE 2  Proofreading Sentences for the Correct Use of Underlining (Italics)

In the sentences below, underline each word or item that should be italicized.

EX.  1.  Mom looked in <u>Newsweek</u> to see what's available in entertainment.

1.  Friday Night Lights, based on the movie, got good reviews.

2.  The book Harry Potter and the Goblet of Fire is as popular as the movie Harry Potter and the Goblet of Fire.

3.  A new production of the old opera Xerxes is opening in Santa Fe.

4.  The classic book, Jane Eyre, has been made into a movie several times.

5.  Mom said that if we don't want to go out, we can stay home and watch re-runs of I Love Lucy.

# *QUOTATION MARKS*

**21c** **Use quotation marks to enclose a direct quotation—a person's exact words.**

EXAMPLE   "Wait here," said the officer, "until the woman with the flag waves you on."

**21d** **A direct quotation begins with a capital letter.**

EXAMPLE   Shane said, "The earlier arrowheads were larger than the later ones."

**21e** **When the expression identifying the speaker interrupts a quoted sentence, the second part of the quotation begins with a small letter.**

EXAMPLE   "The clay," said Kelly, "comes from an area near the bottom of the cliffs."

When the second part of a divided quotation is a sentence, it begins with a capital letter.

EXAMPLE   "Look at this," said Mr. Park. "It is a piece of amber."

**21f** **A direct quotation is set off from the rest of the sentence by a comma, a question mark, or an exclamation point, but not by a period.**

EXAMPLES   "They will ask for time out," whispered Palani.
"What good will that do?" asked Jason.
"We won!" shouted Teresa.

**21g** **A period or a comma should always be placed inside the closing quotation marks.**

EXAMPLES   Kwam said, "That's a beautiful serape."
"My grandmother gave it to me," said Flora.

**21h** **A question mark or an exclamation point should be placed inside the closing quotation marks when the quotation itself is a question or an exclamation. Otherwise, it should be placed outside.**

EXAMPLES   "Who has an extra pencil?" I asked.   [The quotation is a question.]
Why did you say, "Space aliens did it"?   [The sentence, not the quotation, is a question.]

When both the sentence and a quotation at the end of the sentence are questions (or exclamations), only one question mark (or exclamation point) is used. It is placed inside the closing quotation marks.

EXAMPLE   Did Arthur ask, "Who's in charge here?"

## EXERCISE 3    Punctuating Quotations

For each sentence below, insert quotation marks and other marks of punctuation where needed.

EX.   1.  "Who was Daniel Hale Williams?" asked Marty.

1.  Dr. Williams was the doctor said Virgil who founded the first interracial hospital in this country

2.  He did more than that explained Lori He also started the first training school for African American nurses

3.  What did people do before that asked one student Were they treated at home

4.  They were either treated at home said Brian or they were put into dirty wards

5.  This doctor even performed heart surgery exclaimed Lina That was unheard of in 1893

## EXERCISE 4    Proofreading Sentences for the Use of Quotation Marks

In the sentences below, correctly punctuate and capitalize all direct quotations. If a sentence is correct, write C on the line before the sentence.

EX.   _____ 1.  "Look out for the cars!" yelled Karas

_____ 1.  We came Ming said to celebrate Kosciuszko Day

_____ 2.  Hey, Mark Angelo whispered did you finish your homework

_____ 3.  Will you help me asked Lani

_____ 4.  What a great way to decorate the invitations exclaimed Gan

_____ 5.  You were right she said the store opens at eight o'clock

## Using Quotation Marks

On your own paper, create five sentences that each illustrate a rule from this lesson. Then label the sentences with the correct rule number.

EX.   1.  "Did you know," asked Marta, "that I was chosen?" (21c)

**21i   When a quotation consists of several sentences, put quotation marks only at the beginning and the end of the whole quotation.**

EXAMPLE   "Now, you're galloping toward the first barrel. You know you're going to turn and go around it, but the horse doesn't know. So you squeeze with your right knee, " said Ron.

**21j   When you write dialogue (conversation), begin a new paragraph every time the speaker changes.**

EXAMPLE   Chad looked nervous as he said, "You guys are not going to believe what I saw last night. Coming home from practice, I saw this thing glowing in the sky, just above the horizon."
"Did you think it was a UFO?" asked Jodie.
"I don't know what it was, but it sure was strange."
"Look," said Umeko, "let's call the state police. They'll know if anyone else reported it."

**21k   Use quotation marks to enclose the titles of short works such as short stories, poems, articles, songs, episodes of television programs, and chapters and other parts of books.**

EXAMPLE   Did she sing "Love is the Thing" at the concert?

**21l   Use single quotation marks to enclose a quotation within a quotation and to punctuate the title of a short work used within a quotation.**

EXAMPLES   Luana said, "I spoke to the principal, and she said, 'Remember that everyone has the right of free speech.' "
"Have you ever read the poem 'Refugee in America'?" asked Juan.

**EXERCISE 6   Punctuating Quotations**

In each of the following sentences, insert quotation marks where needed.

EX.   1. " That poem, called ' Preciosa and the Wind,' is by Federico García Lorca," said Ms. Lee.

1. Who said He who hesitates is lost? asked Ali.

2. When she walks in said Belinda, we'll sing Happy Birthday.

3. Before you leave, read the article called The New Youth Brigades.

4. The first day is the hardest, said Byron. After that you get used to eating less salt.

5. Did your mother say Patti is always welcome? asked Patti.

6.  Kathy handed me the book and said, The funniest chapter is the one called The Solar Democrat.

7.  Is the title of that poem The Silent Crowd?

8.  The reviewer said, This book would have been better if it had been shorter. In fact, it might have been wonderful.

9.  Did Nikki Giovanni write the poem Knoxville, Tennessee, or did someone else?

10.  And then, said Julia, someone started singing The Bear Went Over the Mountain. It was wild!

11.  Nathan, Billy asked did you know that there really are dragons in the world?

12.  No there aren't countered Nathan.

13.  Yes, I read about the Komodo dragon, the forest dragon, and the bearded dragon in the article Amazing Real-life Dragons, answered Nathan.

14.  Kiu asked, did Ms. Jeffery say Include material about the Haitian artist Roosevelt in your report?

15.  Jerome wants a copy of the brochure Careers in Computers and Electronic Engineering.

## EXERCISE 7    Punctuating Paragraphs

On your own paper, rewrite the passage below, adding paragraph breaks and quotation marks where needed.

EX.    [1]  Now listen up! said Ms. Vacca.
       1. "Now listen up!" said Ms. Vacca.

[1] Today you will learn something new, said Ms. Vacca. [2] You will learn how to check your spelling with your computer. [3] That's what I need, said Amir. [4] I'm not a really good speller. [5] Ms. Vacca said, This program can help you. [6] However, it won't find certain kinds of mistakes. [7] What kinds won't it find? asked Sopa.
[8] Sometimes, said Ms. Vacca, you can misspell one word by writing another word correctly. [9] You mean, like writing "t-h-e-i-r" instead of "t-h-e-r-e"? asked Amir. [10] That's exactly what I mean, said Ms. Vacca, and most computers won't catch that kind of mistake.

# APOSTROPHES

The *possessive case* of a noun or a pronoun shows ownership or relationship.

| Ownership | Relationship |
|---|---|
| **Toby's** poncho | a **night's** sleep |
| **my** homework | **dogs'** leashes |
| **everyone's** award | **anyone's** guess |

**21m** **To form the possessive case of a singular noun, add an apostrophe and an *s*.**

EXAMPLES   the teacher**'s** desk    Jess**'s** grades    this morning**'s** paper

**NOTE**   A proper noun ending in *s* may take only an apostrophe to form the possessive case if the addition of *'s* would make the name awkward to say.

EXAMPLES   Miss Rawlings' book    Jesus' teachings    Diaz' home

**21n** **To form the possessive case of a plural noun ending in s, add only the apostrophe.**

EXAMPLES   students' names    two-days' growth    the Stones' home

**21o** **To form the possessive case of a plural noun that does not end in s, add an apostrophe and an *s*.**

EXAMPLES   sheep**'s** coats       men**'s** barracks       teeth**'s** hardness

**NOTE**   Do not use an apostrophe to form the plural of a noun. Remember that the apostrophe shows ownership or relationship.

INCORRECT   Two players' have red jerseys.
CORRECT   Two **players** have red jerseys
CORRECT   The two **players'** jerseys are red.

**21p** **Do not use an apostrophe with possessive personal pronouns.**

EXAMPLES   Is this book **yours**?       Is the marker **hers**?

## EXERCISE 8    Proofreading for the Use of Apostrophes for Singular Possessives

In the paragraph below, underline each word that needs an apostrophe, and insert the apostrophe. Some sentences have no errors in the use of apostrophes.

EX.    [1] These <u>families'</u> homes were in West Virginia.

[1] The coal miners lives were different from mine. [2] About half of the workers houses had once belonged to the company. [3] Now local families own them. [4] In this community, the mens jobs were basically farming and mining. [5] The womens tasks included factory work, farming, and child care. [6] I visited one mine and was allowed to go down into the mines tunnels. [7] The ones that I visited were about four hundred feet underground. [8] All the miners talk was cheerful until an alarm rang. [9] Everyones face then became serious as we rode to the surface. [10] Although the days work was cut short, no one was hurt.

## EXERCISE 9    Writing Possessives

On your own paper, rewrite each of the expressions below by adding an apostrophe to create the correct possessive form.

EX.    1.    the shoes of the dancer
       1.    *the dancer's shoes*

1.  the desk of the boss
2.  the games of the children
3.  the beds of the soldiers
4.  the color of the tooth
5.  the kimono that belongs to somebody

6.  the popcorn of Ms. Thomas
7.  the food of the geese
8.  the chairs of the speakers
9.  the streets of the city
10. the tortillas of the customer

# OTHER USES OF THE APOSTROPHE

A *contraction* is a shortened form of a word, a number, or a group of words.

**21q  Use an apostrophe to show where letters, numbers, or words have been omitted (left out) in a contraction.**

| Common Contractions | |
|---|---|
| you are ...............you're | they have...................they've |
| 1995 .........................'95 | she had..........................she'd |
| she will................she'll | where is ..................where's |
| of the clock......o'clock | who will.....................who'll |
| I will........................I'll | I would.............................I'd |

The word *not* can be shortened to *n't* and added to a verb, usually without any change in the spelling of the verb.

EXAMPLES  are not..........aren't          could not.........couldn't
                 has not ........hasn't          should not ....shouldn't
EXCEPTIONS  will not ........won't          cannot....................can't

Be careful not to confuse contractions with possessive pronouns.

| Contractions | Possessive Pronouns |
|---|---|
| **It's** late. [It is] | **Its** voice was loud. |
| **You're** here! [You are] | **Your** chili was spicy! |
| **Who's** there? [Who is] | **Whose** jacket is this? |
| **There's** the car. [There is] | The red ones are **theirs**. |

**21r  Use an apostrophe and an *s* to form the plurals of letters, of numerals, and of words referred to as words.**

EXAMPLES  Dot your *i*'s and cross your *t*'s.
                 No, there are two *1*'s and two *2*'s.
                 Try not to begin all sentences with *then*'s.

## EXERCISE 10    Using Apostrophes Correctly

In the sentences below, underline each word that needs an apostrophe, and insert the apostrophe. On the line before the sentence, write *C* if the sentence is correct.

EX. _____ 1. The boat you're looking at is handmade.

_____ 1. Stay for a while, and well look through the whole museum.

_____ 2. Youll notice that most of the boats are made from animal skins.

_____ 3. Theyre stretched over frames that are made from wood or bone.

_____ 4. The kayak that youre looking at holds just one person.

_____ 5. The bigger boat on your left isnt a kayak, though.

_____ 6. You can tell that boat is an umiak because its hull is much larger.

_____ 7. Some linguists spell *kayak* with *q*s instead of *k*s.

_____ 8. These boats havent been used in many years.

_____ 9. Which of these kayaks was theirs?

_____ 10. Whos talking to your friend about the Inuit hunters?

## EXERCISE 11    Writing Contractions

On the line before each sentence below, write a contraction for the italicized word or word pair.

EX. ___Who's___ 1. *Who is* that woman?

_____ 1. I *do not* remember her first name, but her last name was Taylor.

_____ 2. I think *it is* a picture of Anna Edson Taylor.

_____ 3. I *cannot* guess why she went over Niagara Falls in a barrel.

_____ 4. *I am* sure she just wanted to prove that it could be done.

_____ 5. I *will not* say if she was brave or if she was foolish.

## CHAPTER REVIEW

**A.  Proofreading for the Correct Use of Apostrophes, Quotation Marks, and Underlining (Italics)**

Rewrite each of the following sentences, using apostrophes, quotation marks, and underlining correctly. [Note: A sentence may contain more than one error.]

EX.  1.  The English words their and theyre sound the same, said Inez.

"The English words their and they're sound the same," said Inez.

1.  For homework, we are supposed to read the chapter called Cells in the book called Real Life. _____

_____

2.  Whos going to play lead guitar? asked Irina. May I? _____

_____

3.  Have you ever, asked Jamal, heard the song called Texas Flood? _____

_____

4.  This letter was probably written during the 1800s, said Mr. Koski. It uses words like verily and beshrew. No one writes like that today. _____

_____

_____

5.  I love this new jacket! shouted Ms. MacPherson. Lets buy one! _____

_____

6.  Was Harry kidding me? asked Selma. Did anyone really write a book called A Wrinkle in Time? _____

_____

_____

7.  Some people make their capital qs look like large 2s. _____

_____

8.  Brads parents are going to be pleased because he got an A and two Bs. _____

_____

9.  Theres a picture of the new ocean liner Queen Mary in this
    volume of the New Encyclopaedia Britannica. _____

    _____

10. Sofie asked, Why would anyone even try to say The sixth sheiks
    sheep is sick? _____

    _____

11. The three broadcasters reports did not agree about the game. _____

    _____

12. What do you want to do with yesterdays menus? _____

    _____

13. Two managers employee rules were being discussed. _____

    _____

14. Walt, have you read that article about Miriam Makeba, titled
    Mama Africa? asked Abby. Its about her U.S. tours. _____

    _____

15. Yes, answered Walt. I heard her perform with Paul Simon in 1987. _____

    _____

## B.  Writing a Dialogue

On your own paper, create a dialogue based on the following old joke. Write
the dialogue in sentence form with direct quotations, and be sure to use
quotation marks and other marks of punctuation correctly. In addition to
punctuation marks, you will need to add dialogue tags to identify who is
speaking (*shouted Al; said Earline*).

Three people were riding on a loud subway. They couldn't hear
each other very well. When Al said it was *windy*, Tranh thought that
Al had said *Wednesday*. Tranh then remarked that today was
Thursday, not Wednesday. Then Earline spoke up. She thought that
Tranh had said *thirsty*, and she admitted that she was thirsty, too.

EX.   "Tranh, it is windy today," shouted Al.

# THE DICTIONARY

A dictionary entry is divided into several parts. Study the parts of the sample dictionary entry below.

**hap•py** (hap′ē), *adj.,* **–pi•er, –pi•est** [Old English *haep,* convenient, suitable] **1.** having a feeling of pleasure [a *happy* person] **2.** giving a feeling of pleasure [a *happy* birthday] **3.** lucky; suitable and fitting [a *happy* chance] **4.** INFORMAL silly or too quick to act [see *slap-happy*] **–hap′pi•ly,** *adv.* **–hap′pi•ness,** *n.*

SYN. *Happy* suggests "a feeling of pleasure." *Glad* suggests "a reaction of pleasure." *Cheerful* means "showing bright spirits." *Joyful* and *joyous* mean "feeling very happy." *ANT.* sad, melancholy.

1. **Entry word.** The entry word shows the correct spelling of a word. An alternate spelling may also be shown. The entry word shows how the word should be divided into syllables and may also show if the word should be capitalized.
2. **Pronunciation.** The pronunciation is shown using accent marks, phonetic symbols, or diacritical marks. Each *phonetic symbol* represents a specific sound. *Diacritical marks* are special symbols placed above letters to show how those letters sound.
3. **Part-of-speech labels.** These labels are usually abbreviated and show how the entry word should be used in a sentence. Some words may be used as more than one part of speech. In such a case, a part-of-speech label is also given either before or after the set of definitions that matches each label.
4. **Other forms.** Sometimes a dictionary shows spellings of plural forms of nouns, tenses of verbs, or the comparative forms of adjectives and adverbs.

5.  **Etymology.** The *etymology* tells how a word (or its parts) entered the English language. The etymology also shows how the word has changed over time.
6.  **Definitions.** If there is more than one meaning, definitions are numbered or lettered.
7.  **Sample of usage.** Some dictionaries include sample phrases to illustrate particular meanings of words.
8.  **Special usage labels.** These labels identify how a word is used (*Slang*), how common a word is (*Rare*), or how a word is used in a special field, such as botany (*Bot.*).
9.  **Related word forms.** These are forms of the entry word created by adding suffixes or prefixes. Sometimes dictionaries also list common phrases in which the word and its related forms appear.
10. **Synonyms and antonyms.** Words similar in meaning are *synonyms*. Words opposite in meaning are *antonyms*. Many dictionaries list synonyms and antonyms at the ends of some word entries.

## EXERCISE 1   Using a Dictionary

Use a dictionary to answer the questions below.

EX.    1.  How many syllables are in the word *retaliation*? _____five_____

1.  How is the word *delirious* divided into syllables? _____

2.  What is the spelling for the plural form of *flamingo*? _____

3.  Give three different meanings for the word *mean.* _____

_____

4.  What is the past tense of *arise*? _____

5.  What is the etymology of the word *maverick*? _____

_____

## EXERCISE 2   Writing Words with Alternate Spellings

For each of the words below, write the alternate spelling on the line after the word.

EX.   1.  archaeology _*archeology*_

1.  catalog _____        4.  ameba _____

2.  theater _____        5.  enroll _____

3.  yogurt _____

# SPELLING RULES

---

### *ie* and *ei*

**22a   Write *ie* when the sound is long *e*, except after *c*.**

EXAMPLES   chief, believe, piece, relief, receive, deceit
EXCEPTIONS   either, neither, leisure, seize, weird

**22b   Write *ei* when the sound is not long *e*, especially when the sound is long *a*.**

EXAMPLES   weight, height, veil, neighbor, eight, reign
EXCEPTIONS   lie, pie, tie, friend, mischief

---

## EXERCISE 3   Writing Words with *ie* and *ei*

On the line in each word below, write the letters *ie* or *ei* to spell each word correctly. Use a dictionary as needed.

EX.   1. for _ei_ gn

1. n _____ ce
2. th _____ r
3. f _____ ld
4. fr _____ ght
5. h _____ r

6. gr _____ f
7. br _____ f
8. sh _____ ld
9. de _____ ve
10. ach _____ ve

11. b _____ ge
12. c _____ ling
13. misch _____ f
14. y _____ ld
15. conc _____ t

---

### *–cede*, *–ceed*, and *–sede*

**22c   In English, the only word ending in *–sede* is *supersede*. The only words ending in *–ceed* are *exceed*, *proceed*, and *succeed*. All other words with this sound end in *–cede*.**

EXAMPLES   concede, recede, precede, secede, intercede

---

## EXERCISE 4   Proofreading a Paragraph to Correct Spelling Errors

The following paragraph contains ten spelling errors. Underline the misspelled words. Write the correct spelling above each misspelled word.

EX.   [1] In the <u>preceeding</u> week, Alexis and I visited the Carnegie
     *preceding*
Science Center.

[1] The staff of the Carnegie Science Center has succeded in creating a museum that is truly an "amusement park for the mind." [2] The museum has recieved rave reviews from the residents of Pittsburgh. [3] It has also gained worldwide publicity because of its many foriegn visitors. [4] Visitors to the Science Center can liesurely examine more than two hundred and fifty hands-on exhibits. [5] They can then procede to either the planetarium or the aquarium. [6] Believe me, niether Alexis nor I had ever been to such an exciting aquarium. [7] The giant tank rises to a great hieght. [8] Swimming together in the tank are thousands of fish and many wierd creatures from the deep. [9] The fish seem very freindly and calm, although we did see a brief battle between two barracudas. [10] We also saw a giant tortoise that must have wieghed two hundred pounds.

**BORN LOSER® by Art Sansom**

Born Loser reprinted by permission of NEA, Inc.

# PREFIXES AND SUFFIXES

A *prefix* is a letter or a group of letters added to the beginning of a word to change the word's meaning. A *suffix* is a letter or a group of letters added to the end of a word to change its meaning.

**22d  When adding a prefix to a word, do not change the spelling of the word itself.**

EXAMPLES  mis + spell = **mis**spell       im + possible = **im**possible
over + ripe = **over**ripe       un + rehearsed = **un**rehearsed

**22e  When adding the suffix *–ness* or *–ly* to a word, do not change the spelling of the word itself.**

EXAMPLES  fair + ness = fair**ness**        open + ness = open**ness**
soft + ly = soft**ly**        real + ly = real**ly**

EXCEPTION  For most words that end in *y*, change the *y* to *i* before *–ly* or *–ness*.

EXAMPLES  happy + ness = happ**iness**      busy + ly = bus**ily**

**22f  Drop the final silent *e* before a suffix beginning with a vowel.**

*Vowels* are the letters *a, e, i, o, u*, and sometimes *y*. All other letters of the alphabet are *consonants*.

EXAMPLES  gentle + est = gentl**est**       skate + ing = skat**ing**
note + able = not**able**       race + er = rac**er**

EXCEPTION  In words ending in *ce* and *ge*, keep the silent *e* before a suffix beginning with *a* or *o*.

EXAMPLES  notice + able = notic**eable**
courage + ous = courag**eous**

**22g  Keep the final *e* before a suffix beginning with a consonant.**

EXAMPLES  hope + less = hop**eless**       late + ness = lat**eness**
grace + ful = grac**eful**       sure + ly = sur**ely**

EXCEPTIONS  argue + ment = argu**ment**      true + ly = tru**ly**

## EXERCISE 5  Spelling Words with Prefixes and Suffixes

On the line after each partial word equation below, write the word, including the prefix or suffix that is given.

EX.   1.  final + ly    _finally_

1.  thick + ness      _____    11.  il + legal        _____
2.  a + rise          _____    12.  up + set         _____
3.  un + noticed      _____    13.  dis + satisfy    _____
4.  cheerful + ly     _____    14.  im + mortal      _____
5.  ir + responsible  _____    15.  easy + ly        _____
6.  return + able     _____    16.  anti + toxin     _____
7.  baby + ish        _____    17.  waste + ful      _____
8.  joy + ous         _____    18.  haste + y        _____
9.  state + ing       _____    19.  en + counter     _____
10. outrage + ous     _____    20.  rake + ed        _____

## EXERCISE 6  Spelling Words with Suffixes

On the line after each partial word equation below, write the word, including the suffix that is given.

EX.   1.  ride + ing    _riding_

1.  admire + able    _____    11.  brown + ness    _____
2.  quick + ly       _____    12.  bake + er       _____
3.  large + est      _____    13.  joke + ing      _____
4.  primary + ly     _____    14.  argue + ment    _____
5.  aviate + or      _____    15.  nine + ty       _____
6.  bossy + ness     _____    16.  range + ing     _____
7.  rise + ing       _____    17.  mighty + ly     _____
8.  peace + able     _____    18.  change + able   _____
9.  skate + er       _____    19.  lazy + ly       _____
10. usual + ly       _____    20.  mis + state     _____

## *SUFFIXES*

**22h** **For words ending in *y* preceded by a consonant, change the *y* to *i* before any suffix that does not begin with *i*; keep the *y* before a suffix that does begin with *i*.**

EXAMPLES    mystery + ous = myster**ious**        easy + ly = eas**ily**
                 dry + ing + dry**ing**                   hurry + ing = hurr**ying**
EXCEPTIONS  dry + ness = dry**ness**                 sly + ly = sl**yly**

**22i** **Words ending in *y* preceded by a vowel do not change their spelling before a suffix.**

EXAMPLES    boy + hood = boy**hood**            pray + ed = pra**yed**
EXCEPTIONS  say + ed = sa**id**                     day + ly = dai**ly**

**22j** **Double the final consonant before adding *–ing*, *–ed*, *–er*, or *–est* to a one-syllable word that ends in a single consonant preceded by a single vowel.**

EXAMPLES    step + ing = ste**pping**            hit + er = hi**tter**
                 ship + ed = shi**pped**              sad + est = sa**ddest**

With a one-syllable word ending in a single consonant that is not preceded by a single vowel, do not double the consonant before adding *–ing*, *–ed*, *–er*, or *–est*.

EXAMPLES    wail + ing = wailing              near + er = nearer
                 seem + ed = seemed              cool + est = coolest

## EXERCISE 7   Spelling Words with Suffixes

On your own paper, write each of the following words, including the suffix that is given.

EX.   1. dim + er
         1. *dimmer*

1. crazy + ness
2. spin + ing
3. wait + ed
4. hot + er
5. crusty + est
6. stray + ed
7. drop + ing
8. clear + est
9. worry + ed
10. hazy + er
11. pay + ing
12. vary + ous
13. play + ed
14. swim + er
15. snap + ed
16. big + est
17. fool + ing
18. warm + er
19. try + ing
20. glory + ous

# REVIEW EXERCISE

**Proofreading to Correct Spelling in a Paragraph**

In the paragraph below, underline the twenty spelling errors. Write the correct spelling above each incorrect word.

EX.  [1] Sparky Rucker is <u>makeing</u> history interesting.
*making*

[1] Rucker, an African American storyteller from Tennessee, has been delighting audeinces for many years. [2] In his new show, which is called *Concieved in Liberty*, he discusses fameous historycal figures and tells stories about the culture and music of West Africans who were brought to the United States as slaves. [3] His shows usualy contain many songs; this show includes "Amazeing Grace" and "Hambone." [4] Through his work, Rucker has succeded in teaching many people about their African American heritage. [5] In the process, he has truely been makeing history more real. [6] In many of his shows, he explains the meannings of such slave songs as "Follow the Drinking Gourd." [7] Rucker has sayed that this song was realy a map of the Underground Railroad. [8] Its first line is "Follow the drinking gourd, for the old man is waitting to carry you to Canaan." [9] The drinking gourd is the Big Dipper, and Canaan is Canada, the land where the couragous slaves hopeed to gain their freedom. [10] Storytelling was not unatural in Rucker's family. [11] He remembers his aunts and uncles telling some of the same stories in varyous ways. [12] He often includes hand-clapping rhythms as well. [13] His beleif that no one can easyly separate politics and culture shows in his storytelling.

## PLURALS OF NOUNS

**22k   Form the plurals of most nouns by adding –s.**

| SINGULAR | shoe | date | desk | donkey | radio | hymn |
|---|---|---|---|---|---|---|
| PLURAL | shoes | dates | desks | donkeys | radios | hymns |

**22l   Form the plurals of nouns ending in s, x, z, ch, or sh by adding –es.**

| SINGULAR | glass | tax | waltz | lunch | dish |
|---|---|---|---|---|---|
| PLURAL | glasses | taxes | waltzes | lunches | dishes |

NOTE   Proper nouns usually follow these rules, too.

EXAMPLES   the Espinozas          the Bendexes
the Jenkinses          the Moskowitzes

## EXERCISE 8   Spelling the Plurals of Nouns

On the line after each noun, write the correct plural form.

EX.   1. ax     _axes_

1. bench _____
2. stereo _____
3. box _____
4. Cortez _____
5. wish _____
6. class _____
7. kiss _____
8. rash _____
9. grass _____
10. nickel _____
11. piano _____
12. Katz _____
13. Delgado _____

14. rodeo _____
15. area _____
16. tray _____
17. Vélez _____
18. switch _____
19. pencil _____
20. mask _____
21. moth _____
22. donkey _____
23. fizz _____
24. guess _____
25. Kirkpatrick _____

**22m Form the plurals of nouns ending in *y* preceded by a consonant by changing the *y* to *i* and adding *–es*.**

SINGULAR    story      berry      army       sky      jury
PLURAL      stor**ies**   berr**ies**   arm**ies**   sk**ies**   jur**ies**

EXCEPTION    With proper nouns, simply add *–s*.

EXAMPLES    the Reilly**s**, the Brodsky**s**

**22n Form the plurals of nouns ending in *y* preceded by a vowel by adding *–s*.**

SINGULAR    tray      key      Sunday      boy      play
PLURAL      tray**s**   key**s**   Sunday**s**   boy**s**   play**s**

**22o Form the plurals of most nouns ending in *f* by adding *–s*. The plurals of some nouns ending in *f* or *fe* are formed by changing the *f* to *v* and adding either *–s* or *–es*.**

SINGULAR    roof      belief      reef      knife      wife      leaf
PLURAL      roof**s**   belief**s**   reef**s**   kni**ves**   wi**ves**   lea**ves**

NOTE    When you are not sure how to spell the plural of a noun ending in *f* or *fe*, look in a dictionary.

## EXERCISE 9    Spelling the Plurals of Nouns

On the line after each noun, write the correct plural form.

EX.    1. baby    *babies*

1. theory    _____
2. calf      _____
3. bay       _____
4. cherry    _____
5. life      _____
6. valley    _____
7. Tuesday   _____
8. shelf     _____
9. injury    _____
10. toy      _____

11. gulf        _____
12. Sablosky    _____
13. honey       _____
14. reply       _____
15. filly       _____
16. thief       _____
17. day         _____
18. raspberry   _____
19. Daly        _____
20. scarf       _____

**22p  Form the plurals of nouns ending in _o_ preceded by a vowel by adding _–s_. The plurals of many nouns ending in _o_ preceded by a consonant are formed by adding _–es_.**

| SINGULAR | stereo | zoo | hero | tomato |
|---|---|---|---|---|
| PLURAL | stereos | zoos | hero**es** | tomato**es** |

| EXCEPTIONS | tuxedo | tuxedos | hello | hellos |
|---|---|---|---|---|

Form the plurals of most musical terms ending in _o_ by adding _–s_.

| SINGULAR | solo | cello | soprano | contralto |
|---|---|---|---|---|
| PLURAL | solo**s** | cello**s** | soprano**s** | contralto**s** |

**NOTE**  To form the plurals of some nouns ending in _o_ preceded by a consonant, you may add either _–s_ or _–es_.

| SINGULAR | flamingo | grotto | volcano |
|---|---|---|---|
| PLURAL | flamingo**s** | grotto**s** | volcano**s** |
| | _or_ | _or_ | _or_ |
| | flamingo**es** | grotto**es** | volcano**es** |

**22q  The plurals of a few nouns are formed in irregular ways.**

| SINGULAR | child | man | tooth | goose | mouse |
|---|---|---|---|---|---|
| PLURAL | child**ren** | m**en** | t**ee**th | g**ee**se | m**ice** |

**22r  Form the plural of a compound noun consisting of a noun plus a modifier by making the modified noun plural.**

| SINGULAR | sister-in-law | man-of-war | stock market |
|---|---|---|---|
| PLURAL | sister**s**-in-law | m**en**-of-war | stock market**s** |

## EXERCISE 10   Spelling the Plurals of Nouns

On the line after each noun, write the correct plural form.

EX.   1.  radio ___radios___

1.  veto _____

2.  gaucho _____

3.  woman _____

4.  studio _____

5.  father-in-law _____

6.  blue jay _____

7.  foot _____

8.  baby sitter _____

9.  potato _____

10.  video _____

## EXERCISE 11    Proofreading to Correct Spelling in a Paragraph

In the paragraph below, underline the fifteen errors in spelling. Write the correct spelling above each misspelled word.

EX.    [1] All of the <u>childs</u> in the international chorus visited our school.
*children*

[1] Because they have naturally high voices, most of the singers are sopranoes, and only a few are altoes. [2] During the concert, echos of soaring voices, almost like those of Baltimore oriolees or other singing birds, filled the hall. [3] The singers were accompanied by two womans who played grand pianoes and two mans who played piccoloes. [4] Afterwards, the singers met with members of our school chorus to tour our practice studioes. [5] Then we all had lunch on the patioes, which were only a few foots away from the music wing and the art department. [6] Two mans from a television station interviewed the singers and taped videoes for tonight's news broadcast. [7] Two radio stations are planning to play excerptes from the concert on separate broadcasts next week. [8] Tonight, several members of the chorus will sing soloes during the City Symphony's performance.

## EXERCISE 12    Using Plurals Correctly

On your own paper, write a sentence, using the plural form of each word below.

EX.    1. foot
      1. *Please wear shoes to protect your feet.*

1. hobo      3. great-uncle   5. cargo            7. rodeo      9. mosquito
2. ox         4. banjo         6. maid of honor   8. lingo     10. Congo snake

# CHAPTER REVIEW

## A. Correcting Spelling Errors in Sentences

Underline all misspelled words in each sentence below. Then write each misspelled word correctly in the space above the word.

EX. 1. Tamara and Louis had a <u>breif</u> meeting to discuss the film.
*(brief)*

1. My nieghbor, Takara Asano, is a foriegn exchange student from Japan.

2. Two soloes by a famous opera singer will preceed tonight's concert.

3. I know she will easily succede as leader of the altoes.

4. I was disatisfied with the overipe fruit.

5. Suddenly the two children burst into an outragous arguement.

6. We bought plentyful supplyes before the storm.

7. Dentists usualy offer new teethbrush to their patients after yearly checkups.

8. The Sanchezs will spend a liesure weekend in Galveston.

9. The factories are shiping the stereoes in heavy boxes to avoid damage.

10. Our ponys wear colorful harnesses when pulling the slieghs.

11. The receeding floodwaters had ruined the crops in the feilds.

12. I admire my freind's openess.

13. Were you planing to make such a gracful entrance?

14. The spot on the carpet is realy noticable!

15. The store recieved ninty hatboxes today.

16. How many flys ball did you catch in the outfeild today?

17. After traceing the vase's outline, Melba easly added the color.

18. The men carriing the bags were my shipsmate.

19. The students wanted to meet all of thier facultys sponsor.

20. The flock of wild geeses flying above us was a beautyful sight.

## B.  Proofreading a Paragraph to Correct Spelling Errors

The paragraph below contains twenty spelling errors. Underline each misspelled word, and write the correct spelling above it.

EX.    [1] Diver Michael Grofik found a treasure in the *reefs* reeves off the
       Florida coast.

[1] Grofik is one of the memberes of a team sent to the Florida

waters by a company nameed Historical Research & Development,

Inc.  [2] He and his freinds and partners were diveing about one

hundred yards off the coast of Sebastian, Florida, in eight foots of

water.  [3] When the other mans and womans on the team took their

dayly break to eat their lunchs, Grofik did not.  [4] He decided that

continueing his searchs for treasure might be more rewarding than

stoping for lunch.  [5] That decision luckyly payed off; in fact, it

exceded even Grofik's bigest dreams and expectationes.   [6] He

found many peices of gold jewelry, which historyans beleive came

from a Spanish ship that sank off the Florida coast in 1715!

## C.   Identifying Correctly Spelled Words

For each of the following items, underline the correctly spelled word in parentheses.

EX.    1.  a (*brief*, *breif*) vacation

1.  a (*belief, beleif*) in children

2.  the (*weight, wieght*) of the package

3.  a painted (*ceiling, cieling*)

4.  a (*mispelled, misspelled*) word

5.  many (*skaters, skatters*)

6.  a silly (*argument, arguement*)

7.  an (*immpossible, impossible*) dream

8. (*skateing, skating*) on the pond

9. a (*changeable, changable*) nature

10. (*drying, driing*) the towels

11. an (*unatural, unnatural*) appearance

12. two new (*radioes, radios*)

13. serving mashed (*potatos, potatoes*)

14. living near the (*Kirkes, Kirks*)

15. washing the (*knives, knifes*)

16. (*trays, trayes*) for the salad

17. three (*sopranoes, sopranos*)

18. eight (*geese, gooses*)

19. several (*man-of-war, men-of-war*)

20. (*their, thier*) new home

## D. Writing a Language Workshop Lesson

You are a student intern who has been asked by the United Nations to travel to another country. Your assignment is to run a spelling workshop for students who are learning English as a second language. Select five spelling rules from this chapter to present in your first class. On the lines on the following page, write each rule. Then provide examples. Finally, for each rule, create five exercise items to give to the students to check their understanding of the rule. For each exercise, create a list of answers on a separate piece of paper.

EX. 1. RULE: To form plurals of nouns ending in s, x, z, ch, or sh, you must add *-es*.
EXAMPLES: glass, glasses; box, boxes; waltz, waltzes; beach, beaches; wish, wishes
EXERCISE ITEM: 1. fox     1. foxes

# COMMONLY MISSPELLED WORDS

The following list contains seventy-five words that are often misspelled. To find out which words give you difficulty, ask someone to read you the list in groups of twenty-five. Write down each word; then check your spelling. Make a list in your spelling notebook of any word you misspelled. Keep reviewing your list until you have mastered the correct spelling.

| 75 Commonly Misspelled Words | | |
| --- | --- | --- |
| ache | forty | speak |
| across | friend | speech |
| again | grammar | straight |
| all right | guess | sugar |
| almost | half | surely |
| always | having | tear |
| answer | heard | though |
| belief | hour | through |
| built | instead | tired |
| business | knew | together |
| busy | know | tomorrow |
| buy | laid | tonight |
| can't | likely | tough |
| color | making | trouble |
| coming | meant | truly |
| cough | minute | Tuesday |
| could | often | until |
| country | once | wear |
| doctor | ready | Wednesday |
| doesn't | really | where |
| don't | safety | which |
| eager | said | whole |
| easy | says | women |
| every | shoes | won't |
| February | since | write |

# SPELLING WORDS

Learn to spell the following words if you don't already know how. They're grouped so that you can study them ten at a time.

| 300 Spelling Words | |
|---|---|
| absence | authority |
| absolutely | available |
| acceptance | basically |
| accidentally | beginning |
| accommodate | believe |
| accompany | benefit |
| accomplish | benefited |
| accurate | boundary |
| accustomed | calendar |
| achievement | campaign |
| acquaintance | capital |
| actually | category |
| administration | certificate |
| affectionate | characteristic |
| agriculture | chief |
| amateur | circuit |
| ambassador | circumstance |
| analysis | civilization |
| analyze | column |
| announcement | commissioner |
| anticipate | committee |
| apology | comparison |
| apparent | competent |
| appearance | competition |
| approach | conceivable |
| approval | conception |
| arguing | confidential |
| argument | conscience |
| assurance | conscious |
| attendance | consistency |

| 300 Spelling Words (continued) | |
|---|---|
| constitution | embarrass |
| continuous | emergency |
| control | employee |
| cooperate | encouraging |
| corporation | environment |
| correspondence | equipped |
| criticism | essential |
| criticize | evidently |
| cylinder | exaggerate |
| debtor | exceedingly |
| decision | excellent |
| definite | excessive |
| definition | excitable |
| deny | exercise |
| description | existence |
| despise | expense |
| diameter | extraordinary |
| disappearance | fascinating |
| disappointment | fatal |
| discipline | favorably |
| disgusted | fictitious |
| distinction | financier |
| distinguished | flourish |
| dominant | fraternity |
| duplicate | frequent |
| economic | further |
| efficiency | glimpse |
| eighth | glorious |
| elaborate | grabbed |
| eligible | gracious |

## 300 Spelling Words (continued)

| | |
|---|---|
| graduating | knowledge |
| grammar | leisure |
| gross | lengthen |
| gymnasium | lieutenant |
| happiness | likelihood |
| hasten | liveliness |
| heavily | loneliness |
| hindrance | magazine |
| humorous | maneuver |
| hungrily | marriage |
| hypocrisy | marvelous |
| hypocrite | mechanical |
| icy | medieval |
| ignorance | merchandise |
| imagination | minimum |
| immediately | mortgage |
| immense | multitude |
| incidentally | muscle |
| indicate | mutual |
| indispensable | narrative |
| inevitable | naturally |
| innocence | necessary |
| inquiry | negligible |
| insurance | niece |
| intelligence | noticeable |
| interfere | obligation |
| interpretation | obstacle |
| interrupt | occasionally |
| investigation | occurrence |
| judgment | offense |

| 300 Spelling Words (continued) | |
|---|---|
| official | practically |
| omit | precede |
| operation | precisely |
| opportunity | preferred |
| oppose | prejudice |
| optimism | preparation |
| orchestra | pressure |
| organization | primitive |
| originally | privilege |
| paid | probably |
| paradise | procedure |
| parallel | proceed |
| particularly | professor |
| peasant | proportion |
| peculiar | psychology |
| percentage | publicity |
| performance | pursuit |
| personal | qualities |
| personality | quantities |
| perspiration | readily |
| persuade | reasonably |
| petition | receipt |
| philosopher | recognize |
| picnic | recommendation |
| planning | referring |
| pleasant | regretting |
| policies | reign |
| politician | relieve |
| possess | remembrance |
| possibility | removal |

| 300 Spelling Words (continued) | |
| --- | --- |
| renewal | sponsor |
| repetition | straighten |
| representative | substantial |
| requirement | substitute |
| residence | subtle |
| resistance | succeed |
| responsibility | successful |
| restaurant | sufficient |
| rhythm | summary |
| ridiculous | superior |
| sacrifice | suppress |
| satire | surprise |
| satisfied | survey |
| scarcely | suspense |
| scheme | suspicion |
| scholarship | temperament |
| scissors | tendency |
| senate | thorough |
| sensibility | transferring |
| separate | tremendous |
| sergeant | truly |
| several | unanimous |
| shepherd | unfortunately |
| sheriff | unnecessary |
| similar | urgent |
| skis | useful |
| solemn | using |
| sophomore | vacancies |
| source | vacuum |
| specific | varies |